IVA HELEN LEE

McLennan Community College

DOS/VSE
and VSE/POWER
Job Control Language
and Concepts

PRENTICE HALL, Englewood Cliffs, New Jersey 07632

Library of Congress Cataloging-in-Publication Data

Lee, Iva Helen
   DOS/VSE and VSE/POWER job control language and concepts / Iva
Helen Lee.
      p.   cm.
   Includes index.
   ISBN 0-13-218629-2
   1. DOS/VSE (Computer operating system)   2. POWER (Computer
program)   3. Job Control Language (Computer program language)
I. Title.
QA76.76.063L44   1990
005.4'46—dc20   89-33563
                    CIP

To
Dr. and Mrs. Joseph Morgan and my parents
who always encouraged me in my educational endeavors

Editorial/production supervision: *Edith Riker*
Cover design: *Photo Plus Art*
Manufacturing buyer: *Mary Noonan*

The author and publisher of this book have used their best efforts
in preparing this book. These efforts include the development,
research and testing of the theories and programs to determine
their effectiveness. The author and publisher make no warranty
of any kind, expressed or implied, with regard to these programs
or the documentation contained in this book. The author and
publisher shall not be liable in any event for incidental or con-
sequential damages in connection with, or arising out of, the fur-
nishing, performance, or use of these programs.

Printed in the United States of America

10 9 8 7 6 5 4 3

ISBN 0-13-218629-2

Prentice-Hall International (UK) Limited, *London*
Prentice-Hall of Australia Pty. Limited, *Sydney*
Prentice-Hall Canada Inc., *Toronto*
Prentice-Hall Hispanoamericana, S.A., *Mexico*
Prentice-Hall of India Private Limited, *New Delhi*
Prentice-Hall of Japan, Inc., *Tokyo*
Simon & Schuster Asia Pte. Ltd., *Singapore*
Editora Prentice-Hall do Brasil, Ltda., *Rio de Janeiro*

Contents

Preface

Recent developments have made it increasingly important that programmers be able to code their own job control statements. Many industries now require that the programmers not only code the necessary job control, but that they also include this job control in their program and operations documentation.

There are few textbooks available on IBM DOS/VSE job control. It appears that IBM plans to continue to support this DOS/VSE operating system since it has incorporated the year 2099 as a maximum year for the TLBL and DLBL job control statements in the latest versions of DOS/VSE.

Recent books that have been written are either too narrow in scope or do not have enough practical job control work that the student can do. The purpose of this book is to:

1. Cover the aspects of job control, including the most recent versions of DOS/VSE/SP, needed by the beginning programmer.
2. Provide typical coding exercises in job control for the student to do.
3. Provide research problems that will aid the student in learning how to use manufacturer manuals.

The book has 13 chapters, which can be summarized briefly as follows:

Chapter 1, "Operating Systems," discusses the roll and parts of an operating system and reviews sample hardware components.

Chapter 2, "Introduction to Job Control," introduces main storage organization concepts and DOS/VSE and POWER commands.

Chapter 3, "The Content of System Libraries and Directories," discusses the four system and private libraries of DOS/VSE, version 1.

Chapter 4, "POWER/VSE JECL," and Chapter 5, "DOS/VSE Job Control Language," introduce some beginning POWER and DOS/VSE commands.

Chapter 6, "ICCF, The Terminal Program," discusses portions of ICCF needed by the student when working on a terminal.

Chapter 7, "The Compilation and Execution of Jobs," introduces the job control necessary for simple jobs not concerned with disk or tape I/O.

Chapter 8, "Magnetic Tape Job Control," discusses the job control necessary for programs using tape I/O.

Chapter 9, "Magnetic Disk Job Control," discusses the job control necessary for programs using disk I/O. This chapter deals with native types of file organization (SAM, ISAM, and DAM).

Chapter 1∅, "Virtual Storage and VSAM," introduces virtual storage and VSAM concepts. It also covers the job control necessary for processing nonnative VSAM files (ESDS, KSDS, and RRDS).

Chapter 11, "Service Programs," covers the service programs: LNKEDT, AMS, and the LIBRARIAN. The LIBRARIAN dealt with in this chapter is the DOS/VSE version 1 LIBRARIAN.

Chapter 12, "DOS/VSE/SP (versions 2 and 3 of DOS/VSE) Additions and Changes," covers the job control changes and additions made in the new DOS/VSE/SP versions and the substantial changes made in the LIBRARIAN program.

Chapter 13, "Utility Programs," covers the utility programs: LVTOC, DITTO, sort/merge, and a few miscellaneous programs. These programs can be worked into earlier chapters (8 through 1∅) if the instructor so desires.

The appendices provide additional helpful information in summary form along with a list of the programs that may be used to allow students to test the job control they have coded for selected exercises in the text. These exercises can be used as lab problems.

A comprehensive glossary is provided at the end of the book.

To avoid confusion, zeros are slashed (∅) to distinguish them from the letter O.

An *Instructor's Guide* provides the following aids for teaching:

1. Answers to study guide questions in the text.
2. Answers to coding exercises and lab problems in the text.
3. Answers to research questions in the text.
4. Unit tests that can be photocopied and answers to test questions.
5. A list of helpful manuals and other materials.
6. Transparency originals.

ACKNOWLEDGMENTS

My thanks go to instructor Ron Williams and my students at McLennan Community College for their enthusiastic participation in improving my manuscript. Thanks also go to Daniel Rindfleisch of Fairfax Station, Virginia for his thorough review of the manuscript.

Finally, thanks go to the Prentice Hall personnel, especially Senior Managing Editor Marcia Horton, Supplements Editor Alice Dworkin, and Production Editor Edie Riker and her very efficient staff.

Iva Helen Lee
Waco, Texas

chapter 1

Operating Systems

THE ROLE OF THE OPERATING SYSTEM

As computer hardware (physical machinery) became more complex, a central controlling program for the computer was needed. This controlling program, called an operating system, has a role similar to that of a policeman.

One of the duties of a policeman is to direct the flow of traffic at street intersections. In a sense, this is the main purpose of an operating system. An *operating system* is a group of programs (software) that control the activities and equipment resources of a computer system.

An operating system provides some of the following services:

1. It keeps the computer system operating at or near full capacity. Very little processing time is wasted.
2. It controls resources such as:
   a. I/O devices: for example, terminals, printers, and card readers.
   b. *Secondary storage devices* such as magnetic disk drives and magnetic tape drives
   c. Main storage
   d. The processor
3. It handles unusual conditions automatically, thus reducing the need for operator intervention. For example, if a program requires division and the divisor is zero, this causes an abnormal ending (*ABEND*) because the result is undefined.† In the old days before operating systems existed, the computer would just stop when such an event occurred. The operator would look up a number code that was displayed on the console in a manual that was provided. Then the operator would follow the

---

† You will remember that a number divided by zero yields an infinitely large number which the computer is unable to process.

directions in the manual to cause the computer to skip the rest of the program and start on the next task. Now, an operating system handles this process automatically without operator intervention.

HARDWARE COMPONENT REVIEW

A computer system is made up of the central processing unit (CPU) and peripheral equipment. An example of such a system is shown in Figure 1.1.

You will recall that:

1. Memory or *main (core) storage* contains instructions (programs) and data to be manipulated.
2. The arithmetic/logic unit does arithmetic calculations and makes simple comparisons.
3. The control unit receives and interprets program instructions.
4. The input devices send data or instructions to main storage. Examples of such devices are card readers and terminals.
5. Output devices are used to display data or results. Examples of display devices are the printer and the terminal.
6. *Secondary storage devices,* or I/O devices, act as both input or output devices, but they also are used to store instructions or data for later use. This is done because large computers have *dynamic memory.*† That is, when the computer is turned off, instructions or data is lost. Therefore, if anything is to be saved, it is saved on secondary storage devices such as hard disk drives, floppy disk (diskette) drives, and magnetic tape drives. (Some large computers also use magnetic drum or mass storage systems.) Large mainframes, or computer systems, use mainly magnetic tape or disk as secondary storage devices. These devices are discussed in detail in later chapters.
7. I/O devices are connected to the CPU by *channels.* Channels carry or transmit data just as river channels carry water. However, these channels also act as a small computer which can execute I/O instructions called channel commands. On smaller models, *I/O adapters* are used instead of channels. There are two types of channels. A *selector channel* can have only one device attached to it, whereas a *multiplexor channel* can have more than one device attached. Of these, *byte multiplexor channels* usually have slow-speed devices attached, such as terminals and card readers. *Block multiplexor channels* have high-speed I/O devices attached, such as tape and disk drives.

IBM has many different models, called series. In this book we use as an example a 4300 series which uses an operating system called DOS/VSE (*d*isk *o*perating *s*ystem/*v*irtual *s*torage *e*xtended). The DOS/VSE operating system is also used on the IBM System/370, 3030, and 3080 series. Commands are given to this operating system by the use of JCL (*j*ob *c*ontrol *l*anguage).

Other operating systems exist for these models. For example, IBM has an operating system called MVS (*m*ultiple *v*irtual *s*torage), which is often used on the very large mainframes in the systems noted above. MVS grew out of an IBM operating system called OS/MVT.

---

† In contrast, some microcomputers use *static memory* for such things as the BASIC interpreter. With static memory, the information does not disappear when the computer power is turned off.

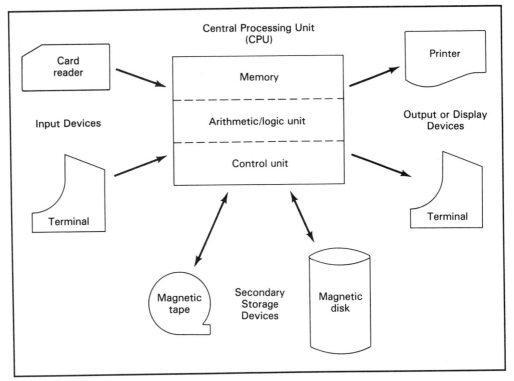

Figure 1.1 A computer system.

Other computers have different operating systems. Indeed, you may eventually work with some other operating system or computer. But by learning DOS/VSE JCL, you will have mastered many concepts that will be helpful in learning other operating systems and their associated job control language.

A SAMPLE SYSTEM

Each of the devices in the computer system shown in Figure 1.2 has a *device address*. This address is a three-digit hexadecimal (hex) number.† The first digit represents a channel number and the next two digits represent a unit number. For example, in Figure 1.2 the 88Ø9 tape drives have device addresses of 3ØØ and 3Ø1. This means that both drives have a channel number of 3 and the drives' unit numbers are ØØ and Ø1. In this case we could have up to six drives.

Notice that the 337Ø disk drives have addresses of 22Ø–227, meaning these drives are on channel 2. The diskette reader, printers, and card reader punch must be on channel Ø.

PARTS OF AN OPERATING SYSTEM

The operating system, *DOS/VSE*, is a collection of programs (software) written by IBM.‡ It is designed to make full use of the resources of the data processing

---

† Hex digits (base 16 number system) are Ø–9 and A–F.

‡ This system is composed of what IBM terms "VSE/advanced functions" and some source control programs (SCPs) necessary for multiprogramming.

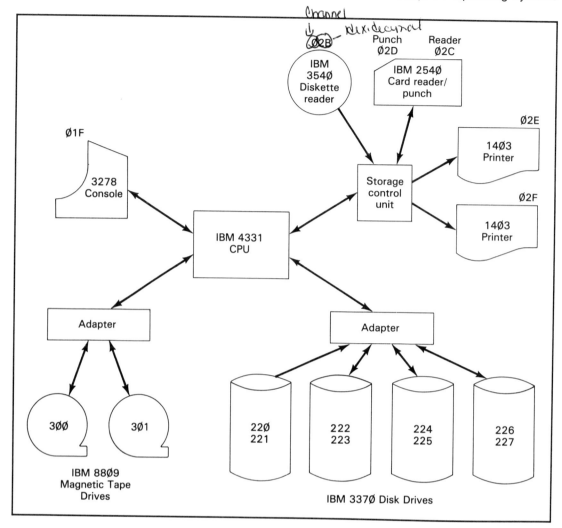

Figure 1.2 IBM 4331 computer system and device addresses.

system. DOS/VSE will allow more than one program to be executed at the same time (*multiprogramming*) in the CPU.

There are currently three versions of DOS/VSE. Version 1 is simply called DOS/VSE. Versions 2 and 3 are called DOS/VSE/SP. The differences found in versions 2 and 3 are discussed in Chapter 12.

When an operating system is received, it is tailored to meet the specific needs of the computer center. This process is called *system generation* (*SYS-GEN*). With the newer operating system versions, skeletons or patterns are sent which may be altered. In this case, complete system generation is often not necessary.

An example of the steps needed to generate a system would be as follows:

1. The entire operating system is sent to the computer center on tape or disk. It is written for all I/O devices that can exist for the system and allows certain operational options to be chosen. For example, if a program ends abnormally, is a memory dump to be printed or not? An option must be chosen.

2. The computer center manager knows what I/O devices the center has.

3. Following the directions in a systems generation manual, the manager or IBM systems rep (representative) creates a copy of the operating system sent, deleting unneeded programs for I/O devices not used in the center. Also during this process, options must be chosen for various situations listed in the manual. The final copy is the operating system used by the center.

4. A backup copy is also kept since these SYSGENs are very time consuming. (A *backup copy* is a duplicate copy kept in case the original is accidentally destroyed.)

5. If at a later date, new equipment comes in or different options are needed, the system is regenerated. That is, the manager does another SYSGEN.

This operating system is kept on-line on disk. The disk drive that contains the operating system is called the *system residence* pack (*SYSRES*).

The component programs of DOS/VSE are the control programs, the processing programs, and the data management programs.

1. The *control programs* control the execution of the IBM and user-supplied programs. They are:
   a. The *IPL* (*i*nitial *p*rogram *l*oader) program. When the computer is powered up at the beginning of the day, this program loads the *nucleus* of the operating system into lower memory from disk as shown in Figure 1.3. The nucleus of the operating system remains in lower memory at all times while the computer is in operation.

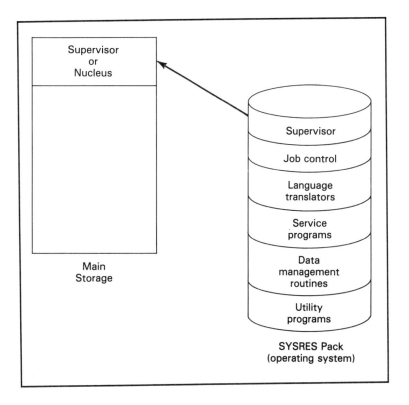

Figure 1.3 DOS/VSE operating system.

  b. The *supervisor*. IBM calls this second control program the "supervisor." The *supervisor* or *nucleus* is the part of the operating system that remains in lower memory at all times during operations. Other computer companies refer to this nucleus by different names, such as the *monitor*, the *executive*, or simply the *control program*.

    Part of the operating system is *not* needed at all times in main storage. It remains on disk until needed. This part of the operating system has the *transient routines*. You will recall that a transient person is one who does not stay in one place or location for a very long time. In this case, the programs are called transient because they stay in main storage only as long as needed. An example of a transient routine would be a tape read/write error recovery program.

  c. The *job control program* (*JCP*). This program is called in by the supervisor when needed. It reads and interprets the DOS/VSE job control statements or commands that we will learn to write in this book.

2. The *processing programs* are those programs whose execution is initiated (or begun) by the job control program mentioned above. The processing programs are composed of:

  a. The language *translators*, which translate the higher level or *source programs* (COBOL, FORTRAN, RPG, PL/1, etc.) into machine language instructions that the computer can execute. These translators are called *compilers*. (In the case of assembly language, the translator is called an *assembler*.) You should recognize the difference between compilers and the interpreters used on microcomputers. Compilers translate all of the source instructions at one time and then give error messages (*diagnostics*) and then attempt to create the *object* (or resulting machine language) *program*. *Interpreters*, on the other hand, translate one instruction and then attempt to execute it (giving an error message if appropriate). On micros, the BASIC language translator is usually an interpreter, whereas on large computers the BASIC translator is usually a compiler. One disadvantage of an interpreter is that it is much slower than a compiler.

  b. *Service programs* assist in the successful execution of problem programs without directly controlling the system or production results. Examples of service programs are:

    (1) The *linkage editor program*, which prepares the output of the language translators for execution

    (2) The *LIBRARIAN*, which is a set of programs that maintains, services, and organizes the system and private libraries

    (3) VSE/POWER, which is a spooling program

    These service programs and libraries are discussed in detail in later chapters.

  c. *Utility programs*, which perform day-to-day tasks. Examples that you may use in your center are DITTO and the sort/merge program.

  d. *Application programs*, which are user-written programs (or in some cases, programs written by IBM or software companies).

3. *Data management programs*, which are programs that assist in organizing, storing, and retrieving data. These programs are discussed later.

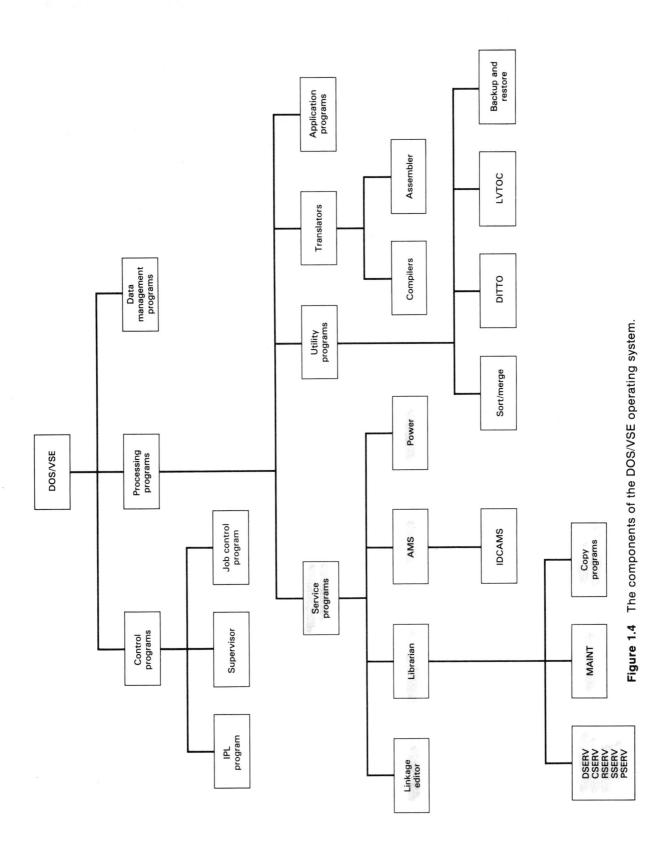

Figure 1.4 The components of the DOS/VSE operating system.

7

SUMMARY

An operating system is a collection of programs designed to make full use of the resources of the computer system. It is divided into two parts: the supervisor and transient routines. The supervisor stays in lower memory as long as the computer is in operation.

When an operating system is received on tape or disk, a systems generation (SYSGEN) takes place. The system is tailored at this time to the needs of the particular computer center. The disk pack that the operating system resides on is called the systems residence (SYSRES) pack.

Operating systems reduce the need for operator intervention, keep the computer operating at full capacity, and handle unusual conditions automatically.

I/O devices are connected to the CPU either by channels or by I/O adapters. Each I/O device has a three-digit device address.

The components of the DOS/VSE operating system are:

1. Control programs
2. Processing programs
3. Data management routines

    The IBM control programs are:

1. The IPL program
2. The supervisor
3. The job control program

    Examples of processing programs are:

1. Translators or compilers
2. Service programs
3. Utility programs
4. Application programs

    Figure 1.4 summarizes the components of the DOS/VSE operating system.

TERMS TO REMEMBER

ABEND	I/O adapter
Application program	IPL
Assembler	JCP
Backup copy	Main storage
Block multiplexor channel	Multiplexor channel
Byte multiplexor channel	Nucleus
Channel	Object program
Compiler	Operating system
Control program	Processing program
Data management program	Secondary storage
Device address	Selector channel
Diagnostics	Service program
DOS/VSE	Source program
Dynamic memory	Static memory
Interpreter	Storage control unit

Supervisor

System residence file

SYSGEN

Transient routine

SYSRES

Translator

System generation

Utility program

STUDY GUIDE

1. Draw a floor plan of your computer room and its computer equipment. Label each part of the equipment. Write the device address beside each I/O device. (These addresses must be memorized for future work in this book.)

2. Name at least two services that an operating system provides.

    (a) Keeps the computer system operating at or near full capacity

    (b) Controls Resources

3. Define the following terms.

    (a) Device address 3 digit number that identifies a particular I/O device

    (b) Channel Device than connects the cpu & I/O Devices

    (c) Supervisor Part of the operating system that stays in lower memory at all times during operation

    nucleus

    (d) System generation Process of tayloring an operating system for the specific needs of a particular computer center

    80% / 80% ~

    (e) Dynamic memory Memory for which Information dissapears or it is erased when the power is turned off.

    (f) Control program Controls the execution of IBM & user supplied programs

4. Give the words that the following abbreviations represent.

    (a) IPL Initial program load

    (b) JCP Job Control Program

    (c) SYSGEN System Generation

    (d) SYSRES System residence

    (e) ABEND Abnormal Ending

5. (a) Name the three IBM control programs.

(1) _IPL_

(2) _Supervisor_

(3) _JCP_

(b) Of these, the _Supervisor_ remains in lower memory as long as the power is on.

6. List four examples of processing programs in our operating system.

(a) _language translators_

(b) _Service programs_

(c) _Utility Programs_

(d) _Data Management Programs_

chapter 2

Introduction to Job Control

MAIN STORAGE ORGANIZATION

Multiprogramming is the processing of two or more programs in a CPU at the same time. This should not be confused with *multiprocessing*, which means using more than one processor or CPU in a computer system.

To do multiprogramming, main storage is divided into sections called *partitions*. For example, Figure 2.1 shows how this division of memory into partitions might appear. These partitions are referred to as follows:

1. Background   (BG)
2. Foreground 1 (F1)
3. Foreground 2 (F2)
4. Foreground 3 (F3)
5. Foreground 4 (F4)

6. Foreground 5 (F5)
7. Foreground 6 (F6)
8. Foreground 7 (F7)
9. Foreground 8 (F8)

Such an arrangement is called *fixed partition programming*. The size and number of partitions used are defined at systems generation time. However, the size of the partitions can be temporarily redefined by the computer operator. The minimum number of partitions is 2, and the maximum number is 12 (including background). This means that a maximum of 12 different programs can be executed at the same time in the CPU.

Each partition has a small GETVIS area in the highest storage area of the partition. The *GETVIS area* is used to allow programs to use additional storage as they execute. This process is referred to as allowing programs to "acquire storage dynamically." The entire system also has a GETVIS area.

The size of each partition and its GETVIS area can be obtained by the use of a central operator command, called the MAP command. The results of the use of this command are shown in Figure 2.2. The total size of the partition is the contents of the size column plus the GETVIS column.

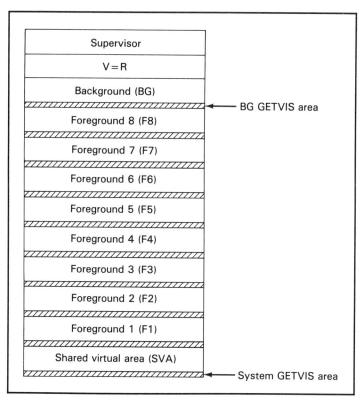

Figure 2.1 Main storage organization.

The *partition priority* is a rank determining that partition's precedence in receiving processing time. The default priorities (low to high) are BG, F8, F7, F6, F5, F4, F3, F2, and F1. This means that F1 gets first priority. (A *default* is that value assumed if none is specified.) If a different order is desired, this can be assigned at systems generation time.

When the system is generated, uses are determined for each partition. For example, the arrangement shown in Figure 2.3 might be for a college computer center. Then partition priorities of BG = F3 = F4 = F7, F6, F5, F4, F8, F2, F1 might be chosen at system generation time. This means that the partition containing VSE/POWER (F1) has top priority. The next-highest priority would be the F2 partition containing the IBM licensed terminal program, ICCF. Of the remaining partitions, administrative work in partitions F8 and F5 get highest priority, with

AREA		SIZE	GETVIS	REAL	UPPER-LIMIT	NAME
SP		198K		166K	317FF	$$A$SUPA
BG	A5V	2914K	48K	40K	315FFF	NO NAME
F8	A3V	2452K	48K	100K	586FFF	CICSEXEC
F7	A5V	352K	48K	40K	5EAFFF	NO NAME
F6	A5V	464K	48K	40K	66AFFF	NO NAME
F5	A4V	464K	48K	40K	6EAFFF	NO NAME
F4	A5V	464K	48K	40K	76AFFF	NO NAME
F3	A5V	464K	48K	40K	7EAFFF	NO NAME
F2	A2V	6096K	48K	128K	DEAFFF	ICCFEXEC
F1	A1V	-464K	48K	80K	F6AFFF	DTFPOWER
SVA	A	1240K	380K		FFFFFF	
PP				3254K		

Figure 2.2 A storage map produced by the map command.

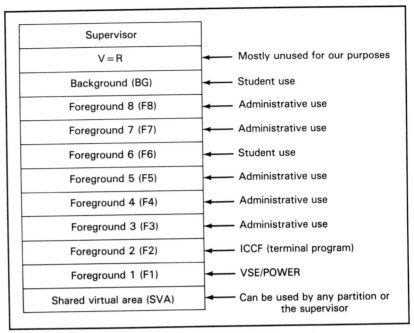

Figure 2.3 Main storage organization and uses.

the rest of the partitions having equal priorities on a "first come, first served" basis.

We will see later that due to VSE/POWER, each partition can also be assigned class priorities. The *class priority* determines which job (of several waiting for the *same* partition) will run first in that particular partition. Class priorities are assigned by the letters A–Z and the digits 0–9.

For example, class priorities might be as follows:

Partition	Possible Class Priorities (High to Low)
BG	J, R, S, 0
F1	1
F2	2
F3	3, A, B, C
F4	4
F5	5, D, E, F
F6	J, S, 6
F7	7
F8	8

This means that:

1. For a class priority of J, the job will run in either BG or F6, whichever is free first for a new job. (No other partition has the class priority of J.)
2. If a job has a priority of R, it will run only in BG, since no other partition has the class priority of R.
3. If one job has a priority of J and one has a priority of S and F6 is busy, the job with a J will run first in BG since J is higher than S. We will see later how these class priorities are assigned.

VSE/POWER

POWER (*p*riority *o*utput *w*riters' *e*xecution *p*rocessors and input *r*eaders) is an IBM-licensed program designed to improve the throughput of a computing system. It separates unit-record I/O (i.e., reading and punching cards, printing reports, and reading diskettes) from the application program operations.

POWER places all unit-record I/O out on disk in *queues*. This process is called *spooling* (*s*imultaneous *p*eripheral *o*perations *on-l*ine). The unit-record I/O operations are overlapped for all partitions, resulting in faster I/O time. Thus the CPU does not have to waste time waiting for the slow unit-record I/O operations.

POWER is not the only spooling program available. All modern operating systems have some method of spooling. *HASP* (*H*ouston *a*utomatic *s*pooling *p*riority system) is another spooling program that is often used on IBM systems. It was developed in Houston, Texas, by IBM and NASA (the space agency).

POWER supports *RJE* (*r*emote *j*ob *e*ntry) so that jobs may be submitted from remote terminals. POWER divides up the I/O jobs into three "waiting" queues† on disk. They are:

1. The *READER* (*RDR*) *queue*. This queue contains jobs waiting to be executed.
2. The *LIST* (*LST*) *queue*. This queue contains output jobs waiting to be displayed or printed.
3. The *PUNCH* (*PUN*) *queue*. This queue contains output to be punched in cards. The PUN queue is seldom used now, due to the disappearance of card I/O. However, as we will see later, this queue does have some special uses.

There are three sets of POWER commands:

1. The *JECL* (*j*ob *e*ntry *c*ontrol *l*anguage) commands
2. The central operator commands
3. The RJE terminal operator commands

These commands are summarized in the useful IBM booklet *VSE/POWER Reference Summary* (SH12-5435). Your instructor may ask you to buy and use this reference summary in class. Of the command types listed above, we will be using only the first set, the JECL commands. If you take a computer operations course, you will be using the second and possibly the third type of commands.

There are six JECL commands that we work with mainly in this book. They are:

1. The *JOB* statement. This statement describes the attributes (characteristics) of a job waiting in the READER queue.
2. The *LIST* (*LST*) statement. This statement describes the attributes of an output job waiting in the LIST queue.
3. The *PUNCH* (*PUN*) statement. This statement defines the attributes of an output job waiting in the PUNCH queue.
4. The *READER* (*RDR*) statement. This statement inserts a diskette file into the input job stream from the card reader.
5. The *SOURCE LIBRARY INPUT* (*SLI*) statement. This statement in-

---

† A synonym for a queue is a *line*. The British "queue up" in front of a ticket window.

serts data or source statements from the disk source library into the job stream. (The source library is discussed in Chapter 3.)

6. The *END OF JOB* (*EOJ*) statement. This statement indicates the end of a POWER job.

The general format for these POWER commands is

```
*b$$boperationboperands separated by commasbcomment
```
(handwritten: ID)

where b = a blank. An example of a POWER JOB command is

```
* $$ JOB JNM=LEE,CLASS=J        PAYROLL JOB
```

1. The first five positions (*b$$b) are sometimes referred to as the *identification field*.
2. The *operation field* specifies the JECL operation or op code. Examples of op codes are JOB, LST, SLI, EOJ, RDR, and PUN. In this case, the op code is JOB.
3. The *operand field* contains one or more positional or keyword operands (or parameters) separated by commas. The presence of one or more blanks terminate the operand field. There are two possible *formats* for the operands: *positional* or *keyword*. As will be seen, keyword format is easier to use because the operands can be linked in any order. In the example above, JNM = LEE and CLASS = J are operands.
4. The *comment field* may be used to give information. It is an optional field. In the example above, PAYROLL JOB is a comment.
5. Column 72 is a *continuation field*. It is seldom used. However, if it is used to continue operands, the operand field must end with a comma. Then any nonblank character can be used in column 72 to indicate the continuation. The continuation statement must also have the * $$ in the identification field, and the operands must start again in columns 6–16.
6. Columns 73–80 can be used as a *sequence field*, but are seldom used. If used, the sequence number must start in column 73. We practice writing JECL commands in a later chapter. Each command will be studied in detail.

DOS/VSE JOB CONTROL COMMANDS

Commands to POWER are called JECL, whereas commands to DOS/VSE are called *JCL* (*job control language*). Job control statements are often divided into four basic elements:

1. Job or systems statements, such as a beginning job statement
2. Step or task statements, such as an execute statement
3. Data description statements, such as assign, disk label, and extent statements, and tape label statements
4. Special statements, such as end of task, job, or procedure statements

IBM has three types of JCL statements:

1. *JCS or job control statements*. These statements are entered by the programmer as part of the input stream.

2. *JCC or job control commands.* These statements are issued between jobs either in a job control stream or at the console.
3. *AR or attention routine commands.* These statements can be issued at any time at the console.

In this book we will be concerned primarily with the first type, the JCS. These commands, along with others, are summarized in IBM's *VSE/Advanced Functions Reference Summary* booklet (GX33-9010). Your instructor may ask you to purchase this booklet to use in class.

The general format of all JCS statements is

```
//boperationboperands separated by commasbcomment
```

Operation	Function
ASSGN	Assigns a logical or symbolic device address to a physical device
DATE	Places a temporary date (different from the IPL date) in the communication region
DLBL	Gives disk header label information
EXEC	Indicates the end-of-job control information and the beginning of a job execution
EXTENT	Gives information for the location of data on a disk area
†GOTO	Causes job control to skip all the following statements (except JOB, /&, / +) up to the statement specified
ID	Specifies user information and password if using the access control facility
†IF	Causes skipping or execution of the following statement dependent on the specified condition
JOB	Indicates the beginning of a DOS/VSE job
LIBDEF	Used to define private libraries
LIBDROP	Used to drop private library assignments
LIBLIST	Used to list private library assignments
LISTIO	Used to list I/O assignments in each partition
MTC	Used to control magnetic operations
PAUSE	Causes a pause in processing after this statement
†ON	Causes the specified action to be done if the specified condition is true after any step in the following job stream
†PROC	Defines and initializes symbolic parameters in a procedure
RESET	Resets I/O assignments to standard assignments
†SETPARM	Assigns a character string or return code to the specified parameter
TLBL	Gives standard header tape label information
UPSI	Allows the user to set program switches
/*	End of file or job task
/&	End of DOS/VSE job
/ +	End of procedure
*	Indicates a job control comment
†/.	Label statement

† Does not exist in DOS/VSE version 1.

Figure 2.4 Job control statement operation codes.

where ♭ = a blank. There are five exceptions to this rule. They are the special statements

- /* (end of task or data)
- /& (end of a DOS/VSE job)
- /+ (end of a procedure)
- * (job control comment)
- /. (label statement; this statement does not exist in DOS/VSE version 1)

An example of the use of the general JCS format (which is always a positional format) is

```
// ASSGN SYS008,300      ASSIGN TAPE INPUT DEVICE
```

1. The identification field is positions 1–3, which contain //♭.
2. The operation field is the second field. We will be studying the possible *operation codes* (*op codes*) shown in Figure 2.4. In the example above, ASSGN is the op code.
3. Operands are separated by commas (no blanks). The operands in the example above are SYS008 and 300. One or more blanks terminates the operation field. There are a few statements, such as the PAUSE statement, that have no operand field.
4. The comment field may be used to give information and should not go past column 71. In the example above, the comment is ASSIGN TAPE INPUT DEVICE.
5. The JCS statement can be continued by entering a nonblank character in column 72. The continuation line must start in column 16. The continuation column 72 is seldom used. However, if it is used, it can be used only with the DLBL, EXEC, IF, LIBDEF, LIBDROP, LIBLIST, PROC, SETPARM, SETPRT, and TLBL statements, which will be studied in later chapters. There can be only two continuation statements in these cases.

SUMMARY

Multiprogramming is the processing of two or more programs in a CPU at the same time. Multiprocessing means using more than one processor or CPU in a computer system.

To do multiprogramming, memory is divided up into parts called partitions. It is possible to have a maximum of 12 partitions. These partitions can be assigned partition priority at system generation time. Each partition can also be assigned class priorities.

A default is the value assumed if none is specified.

The purpose of the spooling program POWER is to speed up I/O. It places tasks into three queues on disk. These queues are:

1. The READER (RDR) queue, which holds jobs waiting to be executed in the CPU.
2. The LIST (LST) queue, which holds jobs waiting to be displayed or printed.

3. The PUNCH (PUN) queue, which holds jobs waiting to be punched. This queue is not used a great deal.

Commands to POWER are called JECL, whereas commands to the operating system, DOS/VSE, are called JCL. Both commands have the same general format except for the contents of the identification field. It is

```
ID fieldboperationboperands separated by commasbcomment
```

For POWER or JECL the ID field is *ƀ$$ƀ, and for DOS/VSE or JCL it is //ƀ, where ƀ = a blank. Column 72 can be used for continuing a statement, but this use is very restricted in JCS.

JCS has five special statements. They are:

/*   End of task or file
/&   End of a DOS/VSE job
/+   End of procedure
*   Used to make a long JCS comment
/.   Label statement

There are six POWER commands that we will be using. They are:

1. The JOB statement
2. The LST statement
3. The PUN statement
4. The SLI statement
5. The RDR statement
6. The EOJ statement

TERMS TO REMEMBER

AR command
Class priority
Comment field
Continuation field
Default
EOJ
GETVIS area
HASP
Identification field
JCC
JCL
JCS
JECL
Keyword format
List queue
Multiprocessing

Multiprogramming
Operation (op) code
Operand field
Operation field
Partition
Partition priority
Positional format
POWER
Punch queue
Queue
Reader queue
RJE
Sequence field
SLI
Spooling program

STUDY GUIDE

1. Draw a picture of the partitions used in your computer center. Label each partition and the supervisor and state at the right what type of work is done in each partition. Then appoint a class member who is interning in operations or ask the computer center operator to use the central operator MAP command (a JCC or AR command) to produce a map of storage similar to that shown in Figure 2.2. Then label your drawing, showing the size of each partition.

2. State the partition priorities for your center.

   _____

3. State the class priorities for each of your partitions.

   _____   _____

   _____   _____

   _____   _____

   _____   _____

   _____   _____

4. Define.

   (a) Multiprocessing _Using more than one processor or cpu in a computer system_

   (b) Multiprogramming _more than one program is executed at the sametime or concurrently in one cpu_

   (c) Default _value assumed if none is specified._

   (d) Partition _A subdivision of memory_

   (e) Queue _line of tasks on disk waiting to be processed_

   (f) Identification field for JECL _first field in a command_

5. Give the terms represented by the following abbreviations.

   (a) RDR _Reader Queue_

   (b) LST _List Queue_

(c) JCL _Job Control Language_

(d) JECL _Job entry control Language_

(e) JCS _Job Control Statement_

(f) RJE _Remote Job entry_

6. Write the general format for JCS statements.

// b operation b operands Separated comma b comment

7. Write the five exceptions or special statements for Problem 6 and give the meaning of each.

(a) _/* End of task or file_

(b) _/& End of a DOS/VSE Job_

(c) _/+ End of procedure_

(d) _* used to make a long JCS comment_

(e) _. Label Statement Separated comma b comment_

8. Write the general format for all JECL statements.

ID field b operation b operands

9. What does the POWER JOB statement describe?

attributes of a Job waiting in the

reader Queue

* b $$ b operation b operand (separated by commas b comment

The Content of System Libraries and Directories

INTRODUCTION

As you know from your educational experiences, a library is a permanent collection of materials such as books, records, prints, and so on. The person who works with the materials and assists the user is called a librarian. Placing materials in the library is called cataloging, and a list of the materials in this library is in a directory called a card catalog. Each piece of material (i.e., book) in the library is identified by a unique catalog number. (The word *unique* means being "one of a kind.")

Similar concepts exist in regard to computer systems software (programs). In computer work, a *library* is defined as a collection of files or programs that are related by some common characteristic. Each element in the library has a *unique* name. The *system libraries* are kept on the DOS resident volume (SYSRES) or systems resident pack. The number of the disk drive varies according to the computer center, but this volume is often referred to as SYSRES.

When an element is placed in a library, it is said to be *cataloged*. The service program that allows us to catalog, delete, or update these programs is called the *LIBRARIAN* program. Actually, the LIBRARIAN is a *set* of programs. We will learn how to use these to catalog and maintain the entries in a library in a later chapter.

THE DOS/VSE VERSION 1 LIBRARIES

The four system libraries used in version 1 of DOS/VSE are:

1. *The core image library (CIL)*. This library contains edited programs in executable form. They are complete and contain all subprograms (subroutines and I/O macros) needed. Entries in this library are called

phases. (A phase is the smallest complete unit that can be referenced in the core image library.) Large programs may have several phases.

Among the CIL programs are compilers (RPG, PL/1, FORTRAN, and COBOL), the assembler, the supervisor, POWER, the job control program, utility programs such as DITTO, the LIBRARIAN, and user programs that have been cataloged. All of these programs have been processed by the LINKAGE EDITOR program and are in executable form.

2. *The relocatable library (RL)*. This library contains frequently used object modules which have not been link edited. (A *module* is a distinct, identifiable unit of a program.) Entries in this library are called *modules*. Examples include FORTRAN, COBOL, or PL/1 service and mathematical subprograms (subroutines) and I/O functions or routines.

   When the user references these modules, they are edited by the LINKAGE EDITOR program for inclusion in the core image program. (The LINKAGE EDITOR program combines or links separately produced object modules or programs into an executable form called a phase.)

3. *The source library (SL)*. This library has routines not yet compiled, such as source programs and assembler programs. It can contain parts of programs such as a DATA DIVISION in a COBOL program or assembly language DTFs. It can also contain data records. Each entry in this library is called a *book*.

4. *The procedure library (PL)*. This library has sets of job control and linkage editor statements in 8Ø-column format. These cataloged procedures can be included in a job control input stream. Entries in this library are called *procedures*.

DIRECTORIES

Each of these libraries has a *directory*. The directory includes such information as the name of the entry, the number of records necessary to contain it, the number of bytes in the last record, and the starting disk address. Entries are in the order cataloged.

The *DSERV* (directory service) program can be used to print the directory of each library. An option allows you to print the entries in alphabetical order. We will learn how to do this in a later chapter.

REASONS FOR SYSTEM LIBRARIES

The use of these libraries described above has originated for several reasons:

1. The core image library originated because once an applications program has been debugged and documented, it is a waste of time to compile it each time the program is used. Therefore, it is put out into the CIL in executable form, ready for use. This saves computer time. As we will see, entries in this library can be utilized by the use of the EXEC JCL statement.

2. The relocatable library (or subroutine and macro library) originated because there is no point "in reinventing the wheel." For example, programmers often need to convert a standard date in the form MM/DD/YY to a Julian date in the form YY/DDD, or they need to be able to calculate the square root of a number. Why should *everyone* write the same code to do this?

Therefore, the RL originated. This library contains *subroutines* or subprograms that perform a special task. It also contains commonly used I/O routines called *macros*.† These routines may be link edited with your program and thus be used without your writing the routines. Each programming language has a standard method of referencing these routines, and the linkage to your program occurs when we use the EXEC LNKEDT job control command. This command will be studied in a later chapter.

3. The source library originated in the card-oriented days, but it is still much used. In the "old" days, departments in industry were charged so much per card that was read in and so much per page that was printed. Source programs were often an entire card tray long, or about 4000 cards. A charge might be 1 cent per card read. Therefore, 4000 cards would cost $4000 \times 0.01 = \$40$. Let us say that during the first compile you made five errors. Then these must be corrected, the entire tray of cards read in again, and another charge of $40 occurs.

Therefore, when magnetic disk and drum were invented, it became possible to rent space in a source library on these devices. A method was devised for updating or making changes to these existing programs once they were read onto disk or drum. To change five incorrect cards would cost only 5 cents. Thus the source library originated.

The source library is now used for parts of COBOL programs that many people use, such as standard COBOL DATA DIVISIONs used in some industries. It is also used in universities and industry for standard test data that everyone may use.

If a center uses POWER, the method used to access material in the source library is by the use of the POWER SLI statement. We will see in Chapter 4 how this statement can be used. In COBOL, the BASIS option and COPY statement are sometimes used instead of the SLI statement.

4. The procedure library originated because standard sets of JCL are often needed for many jobs. Thus these sets of procedures are placed in the procedure library and may be called into any JCL setup by the use of the EXEC PROC job control statement that we will study in a later chapter.

THE PRIVATE LIBRARY

It is possible to have core image, relocatable, source, and procedure libraries in a *private library*. A private library is kept on another direct-access storage device separate and distinct from the system library. These libraries also have a directory and the contents may be listed by the use of the DSERV program.

There are two important reasons why private libraries are used:

1. There may be no more space left for programs in the system library on SYSRES. In this case more programs may be put in a private library on another drive.
2. The systems analyst may not want others cataloging in the systems library because of security problems. Thus other programmers are restricted to the use of a private library. This may be the case in your college or school.

Access to the private library is facilitated by the use of the LIBDEF job control statement, as we will see in a later chapter.

---

† *Macro* is a Greek word meaning to enlarge. A macro instruction generates several machine language instructions.

THE DOS/VSE/SP LIBRARIES

The latest versions (2 and 3) of DOS/VSE, called DOS/VSE/SP, combine all the libraries discussed in this chapter into one big library. This library is subdivided into *sublibraries*. The sublibraries are organized into units called *members*. This system of libraries is examined in Chapter 12. If you have DOS/VSE/SP, you should read the section on DOS/VSE/SP library organization in Chapter 12.

SUMMARY

There are four systems libraries:

1. The core image library (CIL), which contains programs in executable form. Entries in this library are called phases.
2. The relocatable library (RL), which contains object programs that may be link edited and used by main programs. Entries in this library are called modules. This library is sometimes called the subroutine or macro library.
3. The source library (SL), which contains whole or parts of source programs or data records. Entries in this library are called books.
4. The procedure library (PL), which contains streams of job control statements. Entries in this library are called procedures.

All of these libraries have a directory containing information on each program. This directory may be listed by the use of the DSERV program.

If more library space is needed or security demands it, a private library can be created on another direct-access storage device. This library can also contain a CIL, RL, SL, and PL, and it is separate and distinct from the systems library on SYSRES.

In DOS/VSE/SP the CIL, RL, SL, and PL are combined into one large library. DOS/VSE/SP is a later version of DOS/VSE.

TERMS TO REMEMBER

Book	Module
Catalog	Phase
Core image library	Private library
Directory	Procedure
DSERV program	Procedure library
LIBRARIAN program	Relocatable library
Library	Source library
Library member	Subroutine
Link edit	System library
Macro	Unique

STUDY GUIDE

1. Name the four possible system libraries, describe the contents of each, and state what the entries in each are called.

    (a) _Core image Library (CIL) - contains edited programs in executable form - phases._

    (b) _relocatable Library (RL) - contains frequently used object modules which have not been link edited - modules_

    (c) _Source Library (SL) - has routines not yet compiled, such as source programs & Assembler programs - Book_

    (d) _Procedure Library (PL) - sets of Job Control & linkage editor statements in 80-column format - procedures_

2. How are the directories of these libraries listed?

    D serv program

    order that cateraloged

3. Name two reasons why private libraries are used.

    (a) _There is no more space left for programs in the system Library on sysres._

    (b) _System analyst may not want others cataloging in the system Libraries because of security problems._

chapter 4

POWER/VSE JECL

INTRODUCTION

There are three types of POWER commands:

1. JECL commands used in programmer job streams
2. Central operator commands used by the console operator
3. RJE terminal operator commands used in some networks by the terminal operator

In this book we will be concerned with the first type of command, JECL commands. *JECL commands* allow the programmer to specify how a particular job will be handled. For example, by the use of JECL commands, the programmer may:

1. Hold jobs in one or more POWER queues
2. Direct printed or punched output to tape
3. Specify the partition in which a job will execute
4. Specify which device output will go to, such as a specific printer
5. Segment lengthy output
6. Specify passwords to prevent jobs from being processed by unauthorized operators
7. Direct output or messages to terminal users

This chapter covers the most frequently used JECL statements and their application. At the end of the chapter, there are exercises to help you learn how to write typical JECL commands that are needed by the programmer.

┼THE JOB STATEMENT

The POWER JOB command indicates the beginning of a VSE/POWER job and defines the *attributes* (characteristics) of the job waiting in the RDR queue. The formats are shown in Figure 4.1.

The advantages of using the keyword format rather than the positional format are as follows:

1. An operand may be omitted simply by not coding it, whereas in the positional format, two commas must be used to omit an operand.
2. Operands may be coded in any order in the keyword format since the operands are identified by the keyword used.
3. More operands are possible in the keyword format.

Study the following syntax rules carefully so that you will be able to understand the format notation.

1. Underlined items represent default values that VSE/POWER assumes if the option is omitted. In the example

   ```
   * $$ JOB JNM=LEE
   ```

   the job name (JNM) is LEE. If the JNM operand is omitted, the default or value assumed is AUTONAME since AUTONAME is underlined.

2. Brackets, [ ], which enclose an item, indicate that the operand can be included or omitted. In other words,

$$\left[JNM = \left\{ \begin{array}{l} \underline{AUTONAME} \\ jobname \end{array} \right\} \right]$$

   means that the entire contents between the brackets can be omitted or included. However, as stated above, if omitted, any default value indicated will be assumed.

3. However, if the operand is used, the contents between the braces, { }, must be used. The stacked option represents alternatives, one and only one of which may be chosen.

```
Positional format
* $$ JOB [AUTONAME],[D          ],[priority],[class]
         [jobname ] [disposition]

Keyword format
* $$ JOB [JNM={AUTONAME}][,DISP={D          }][,PRI=priority]
              {jobname }        {disposition}

         [,CLASS=class][,PWD=password][,USER=user-information]

         [,SYSID=n][,LDEST={nodied2        }][,NTFY={yes          }]
                          {(noeid2,userid2)}       {(noeid,userid)}

         [,PDEST={noeid3         }][,XDEST={nodeid1         }]
                {(nodeid3,userid3)}       {(nodeid1,userid1)}
```

Figure 4.1 The POWER JOB statement formats.

4. Uppercase letters and punctuation marks must be coded as shown (except for the braces and brackets).

5. Lowercase letters represent information that you, the user, supply. In the example in rule 1, LEE was a value supplied for the job name.

6. Commas have to be coded as indicated. Trailing commas should not be used.

These rules apply to all the JECL commands that we will study.

The JOB command keywords that we will concentrate on are as follows:

1. JOB NAME (JNM) This operand gives the POWER job a name. The name can be one to eight alphameric characters. This operand should always be used. Unless otherwise instructed by your teacher, we will always use the first eight letters (or fewer) of your last name. Example:

```
JNM=LEE          (LEE is the last name.)
JNM=STRICKLA     (STRICKLAND is the last name.)
```

2. DISPOSITION (DISP) *Disposition* specifies how POWER is to route and schedule the associated entry in a queue. Specifically, the JOB statement disposition operand indicates: (a) if the job is available for immediate execution and (b) if the job should be retained or deleted *after* execution. Possible disposition values are:

(1) D = Delete = immediate execution and delete from the RDR queue after execution

(2) K = Keep = immediate execution but leave in the RDR queue after processing (changes to L)

(3) H = Hold = must be released by the console operator to execute and is deleted from the RDR queue after processing

(4) L = Leave = must be released by the console operator to execute and is left in the RDR queue after processing

The default value is D.

3. PRIORITY (PRI) *Priority* is a rank assigned to each job within its class that determines its precedence in receiving system resources.

The priority operand is expressed as a number $\emptyset$–9, where 9 is the highest priority. The default depends on what value is chosen at systems generation time. We will assume for the purposes of this book that the default value for priority is 3 unless your instructor tells you otherwise.

For example, assume that two jobs are in the RDR queue waiting for execution in partition four. A job with a priority of 4 will run before a job with a priority of 3, providing that the CLASS is the same. (CLASS is analyzed before PRIORITY.) You will probably be asked to run on the default priority in your center and should always do so unless otherwise instructed by a center employee or your teacher. Do *not* confuse this priority with the partition priority discussed in Chapter 2.

4. CLASS *Class* is a means of grouping jobs that require the same set of resources for their execution. There are input and output classes, which differ in meaning.

The JOB class operand determines the partition that the job will run in *and* the priority within that partition. The class is expressed as a letter A–Z or a partition number. You or your instructor can determine the classes that your systems analyst has assigned to each partition by using the D A (display activity) central operator command at the console.

The default for the JOB class (input class) is:

a. That shown in the POWER CTL command, if any

b. That shown in the PSTART command, if given

c. To A

The CTL command is discussed later in this chapter. The PSTART command is a POWER central operator command which starts a partition or task. It specifies, among other things, the default class for specific devices. This is included in the *IPL* (powering-up) *routine* but can be changed during the day.

Unless your instructor tells you otherwise, we will assume for the purposes of this book that the default class assigned is X.

Examples of the use of the POWER JOB statement follow.

EXAMPLE 4.1

Write a POWER job command using the keyword format for a job named HURST. It is to run in partition 4, have the default priority, and should be held to be released later. It should be deleted from the queue after processing.

Answer in keyword format

```
* $$ JOB JNM=HURST,CLASS=4,DISP=H
```

Note that these operands can be coded in any order and that PRI is omitted.

Answer in positional format

```
* $$ JOB HURST,H,,4
```

In the positional case, the operands *must* be coded in the order above. *Two* commas indicate that the priority, or third operand, is omitted and a default of 3 (in our case) will be assumed.

Let us say further that the class priorities for the BG and F6 partitions are those given in Chapter 2:

BG   J, R, S, Ø

F6   J,S,6

Then a CLASS = J or S would cause the job to run in either BG or F6 since both have a class of J. A class of R or Ø would run in BG only, but the R class would run before a Ø class if each class existed for jobs in the RDR queue.

Look again at the keyword format for the JOB statement. There are other operands that have not been discussed. The keywords LDEST, NTFY, PDEST, and XDEST are used for installations that have a RJE setup. For these cases:

1. Nodeid and userid are node and user identifiers to show where POWER is to send notify messages. NTFY = YES is used for ICCF users.

2. Nodeid1 and userid1 are node and user identifiers indicating where the job is to be routed.

3. Nodeid2 and userid2 are node and user identifiers indicating where list output is to be routed.

4. Nodeid3 and userid3 are node and user ientifiers indicating where punched output is to be routed.

You will recall that a *node* is any terminal, station, or communications computer in a computer network.

We will not be using these keywords or the three remaining keywords: PWD, SYSID, and USER. The PWD operand is often used in industry for security purposes. SYSID is used only in shared spooling cases. (*Shared spooling* occurs when two or more VSE systems running under POWER share a single set of POWER spool files.) USER allows up to 16 bytes of user information that can be printed on SYSLOG (the console) when execution of the job begins.

THE LST STATEMENT

The POWER LST statement defines the attributes or characteristics of a job waiting in the list queue. The formats are shown in Figure 4.2.

As you can see, the LST statement in keyword format has 25 possible operands. Of these, the keyword operands BURST, CHARS, COPYG, DEFLT, FLASH, and MODIFY apply to the IBM 3800 printer only (a nonimpact laser printing subsystem). The operand DEST and REMOTE are used in RJE operations. The operands RBM and RBS are used in segmenting output. (Sometimes it is helpful to start printing long reports before the program has finished processing all records. In these cases the output is segmented or divided up so that the first part can start printing before the last part has been finished.) The PSW and USER keywords can be used for security purposes.

The LST operands that we will be using are as follows:

1. CLASS For a print task, this operand usually specifies the output device. If the positional format is used, the disposition must also be specified. The default is that class indicated in the PSTART command. If none is specified in the PSTART command, the default is A.

For the purposes of this book we will assume that a CLASS of:

- B directs output to an administrative printer, 02E
- Z directs output to a student printer, 02F
- Q holds output in the LST queue for viewing on a terminal before printing

2. DISPOSITION (DISP) The disposition operand indicates the disposition of the printed output *after* the job is executed. Possible values are:

• D = Delete	=	immediate printing and delete from the LST queue after printing. This is the default.
• K = Keep	=	immediate printing and leave in the LST queue after printing (changes to a L).
• H = Hold	=	must be released by the console operator to print and is deleted from the queue after printing.
• L = Leave	=	must be released by the console operator to print and is left in the LST queue after printing.
• N = Not Spooled	=	output is *not* spooled to disk. It is printed immediately.
• T = Tape	=	printed output should be spooled to tape for storage and perhaps printed later or put on microfilm.

```
Positional format:

* $$ LST ⎡D                  ⎤ ,[forms-number],
         ⎣disposition[class] ⎦

         ⎡1               ⎤
         ⎢number-of-copies⎥ ,[norbm1][,linetab]
         ⎣tapeaddr        ⎦


Keyword format:

* $$ LST [BURST= ⎰Y⎱ ][,CHARS=(tablename[,tablename...])]
                 ⎱N⎰

         [,CLASS=class][,CMPACT= ⎰name⎱ ][,COPY= ⎰1               ⎱ ]
                                 ⎱NO  ⎰        ⎱number-of-copies⎰

         [,COPYG=(groupvalue[,groupvalue...])][,DEST= ⎰nodied          ⎱
                                                      ⎱(nodeid,userid)⎰

         [,DFLT= ⎰Y⎱ ][,DISP= ⎰D          ⎱ ][,FCB=phasename]
                 ⎱N⎰          ⎱disposition⎰

         [,FLASH=([overlayname][,count])][,FNO= ⎰4 blanks      ⎱ ]
                                                ⎱forms-number⎰

         [,JSEP= (sep[,option])][,LST=1staddr][,LTAB=linetab]

         [,MODIFY=(copymodname)[,tablename]][,PRI=priority]

         [,PWD=password][,RBM=(norbm1,norbm2)][,RBS=norbs]

         [REMOTE=remid][,SYSID= ⎰sysid⎱ ][,TADDR=tapeaddr]
                                ⎱N    ⎰

         [,UCS=(phasename[,option])][,USER=user-information]
```

Figure 4.2 The POWER LST statement formats.

3. **PRIORITY (PRI)** The PRIORITY operand is expressed as a number 0–9, where 9 is the highest. As in the JOB statement, the default depends on what is chosen at SYSGEN time. We will assume for the purposes of this book that the default is 3 unless your instructor tells you otherwise.

4. **COPY** The COPY operand specifies the number of copies of printed output desired for this job. The default is 1.

5. **FORMS CONTROL BUFFER (FCB)** The old 1403 printers used carriage control tapes to control vertical formatting or spacing. Now, most printers use a program stored in the core image library to control formatting. These programs indicate how long the form is from top to bottom. This corresponds to the channel 1 and channel 12 concepts on carriage tapes. The program also controls any intermediate skipping.

At SYSGEN time, the standard form skipping is specified through the LTAB operand. This LTAB value is the default value. If a special form is used, the FCB operand is utilized. This operand gives the phasename of the vertical formatting program needed from the CIL. The phasename can be one to eight alphameric characters.

6. **FORMS NUMBER (FNO)** The FNO operand can be used to specify the number of any special forms to be mounted. It causes a PAUSE condition on the console so that the operator can check to see if the proper forms have been mounted. (The operator must use the central operator PGO command to continue.)

The forms number can be from one to four alphameric characters. As can be seen in Figure 4.2, the default is four blanks.

This operand can also be used on the 1403 printers to allow a pause to mount special carriage control tapes.

7. JOB SEPARATOR (JSEP)   The JSEP operand specifies the number of job separation pages desired between job printouts. The value, sep, must be a single number, Ø–9. The default for this operand is Ø.

An option, either Y or N, may follow after this number if a comma is used. If used:

- Y = produce separator pages also between multiple copies of this job
- N = suppress separator pages on multiple-copy output

When this operand is used, the separator page will contain the POWER jobname and other information taken from the * $$ JOB statement. It also will have the date and time.

8. TAPE ADDRESS (TADDR)   This operand can be used to give the hex tape unit address if printed output is to be spooled to tape (DISP=T).

Examples of the use of the POWER LST statement follow.

EXAMPLE 4.2

Assume that two printers exist. Printer Ø2E has a class of B, and printer Ø2F has a class of Z. If output is to be held in the LST queue for viewing, a Q class should be used.

Write the POWER LST statements for the following conditions:

(a)   Output is to be on printer Ø2E. It is to be printed immediately (according to class and priority) and is to be left in the LST queue after printing. Print three copies of the job with one separator page.

Answer

```
* $$ LST CLASS=B,DISP=K,COPY=3,JSEP=1
```

(Operands can be in any order since this is keyword format.)

(b)   Output is to be spooled to a tape mounted on drive 3ØØ.

Answer

```
* $$ LST DISP=T,TADDR=3ØØ
```

(c)   Output is to be held in the LST queue for *viewing* on the terminal. There will be a forms number, SX12. The output should be held for release but will be deleted after processing.

Answer

```
* $$ LST CLASS=Q,DISP=H,FNO=SX12
```

Other operands exist, but will not be used except as research problems at the end of the chapter.

THE PUN STATEMENT

The PUN statement defines the attributes of jobs in the punch queue. This statement is not used much nowdays except in specialized cases such as cataloging in the relocatable library. Such a case will be discussed in a later chapter. The PUN statement formats are shown in Figure 4.3.

```
Positional format
* $$ PUN ⎡D          ⎤[class],[forms-number],
        ⎣disposition⎦

        ⎡1                          ⎤
        ⎢number-of-copies ,[norbml] ⎥
        ⎣tapeaddr                   ⎦


Keyword format
* $$ PUN [CLASS=class][,COPY=⎧1               ⎫]
                           ⎩number-of-copies⎭

        [,DEST=⎧nodied          ⎫][,DISP=⎧D          ⎫]
               ⎩(nodeid,userid)⎭        ⎩disposition⎭

        [,FNO=forms-number][,JSEP=(sep[,option])]

        [,PRI=priority][,PUN=punaddr][PWD=password]

        [,RBM=(norbml,norbm2)][,RBS=norbs][,REMOTE=remid]

        [,SYSID=⎧sysid⎫][,TADDR=tapeaddr][,USER=user-information]
                ⎩N    ⎭
```

Figure 4.3 The POWER PUN statement formats.

The operands CLASS, COPY, DISP, FNO, JSEP, PRI, and TADDR have much the same use as in the POWER LST statement. The DISP operand does have one additional disposition, DISP = I. In some situations it is useful to return the punched output directly to the input queue. This is the purpose of the I disposition.

EXAMPLE 4.3

Write the POWER PUN statement for the following: Two copies of output are to be punched with two separator cards. The output is to be held in the punch queue but deleted after processing.

Answer

```
* $$ PUN COPY=2,JSEP=2,DISP=H
```

THE RDR STATEMENT

The RDR statement is used to insert a diskette file into an input stream. The statement formats are shown in Figure 4.4. The RDR operands are:

1. DEVICE ADDRESS (DEV) This operand specifies the hex diskette device address.
2. FEED This operand specifies if the diskette is to be ejected when an end-of-file (EOF) is read. If two files are to be read from the same diskette, the option NO would be used. Note in Figure 4.4 that NO is the default value since NO is underlined. If only one file is to read, FEED = YES should be used.
3. FILE IDENTIFICATION (FID) This operand can have one to eight alphameric characters enclosed in quotes. This should be the desired

```
Positional format

* $$ RDR [diskette-addr],['file-id'],⎡1                  ⎤,[S]
                                     ⎣number-of-diskettes⎦


Keyword format

* $$ RDR [DEV=diskette-addr][,FEED=⎰NO ⎱][,FID='file-id']
                                   ⎱YES⎰

        [,NOD=1                  ][,VER=⎰NO ⎱][,VSC=⎰NO ⎱]
              number-of-diskettes       ⎱YES⎰       ⎱YES⎰
```

Figure 4.4 The POWER RDR statement formats.

filename in the diskette header label. (Each file on a diskette has a header label, and one entry is the filename.) An example would be

FID='INVENTRY'.

If this entry is not specified, the first nonsecured file is read.

4. **NUMBER OF DISKETTES (NOD)**   The NOD operand specifies the maximum number of diskettes to be read. Values used can be 1 to 255. The default value is 1.

5. **FILE VERIFICATION (VER)**   VER = YES specifies that a check is to be made to see if the file has been verified. (Verified files have a code in the header label.) If a file has been *verified*, it means that it has been rekeyed to detect any errors. (Some industries that still use diskettes have a verifier operator.)

6. **VOLUME SEQUENCE CHECKING (VSC—keyword format; S—positional format)**   VSC = YES in the keyword format causes volume sequence number checking. (The diskettes have a volume number in the volume label.) The default is NO. When an S is used in the positional format, the volume sequence number is checked for sequencing.

EXAMPLE 4.4

Two files are to be read from diskette device number Ø2B. The first file has a filename of JANPAY87 and the second FEBPAY87. The files should have been verified.

Answer   First file:

```
     * $$ RDR DEV=Ø2B,FID='JANPAY87'      (NO is the default
                                          for the FEED operand.)
```

Second file:

```
     * $$ RDR DEV=Ø2B,FID='FEBPAY87',FEED=YES
```

THE SLI STATEMENT (DOS/VSE, VERSION 1)

If you have DOS/VSE, versions 2 or 3, refer to the discussion of the SLI statement in Chapter 12.

The SLI statement inserts an entry or book from the source library into the job stream. POWER searches the source library for the bookname. The SLI statement format is shown in Figure 4.5.

Example

```
* $$ SLI P.PAYROLL
```

Here P. is the sublibrary name. This name can be A–Z or $\emptyset$–9, $, #, or @ followed by a period. The bookname can be one to eight of the alphameric characters above, the first of which must be a letter.

```
* $$ SLI [sublib.]bookname
```

Figure 4.5 The POWER SLI statement format for DOS/VSE, version 1.

THE EOJ STATEMENT

This statement indicates the end of a POWER job. Its format is shown in Figure 4.6.

```
* $$ EOJ
```

Figure 4.6 The POWER EOJ statement format.

THE CTL STATEMENT

The CTL statement can be used to assign another default input class for the RDR queue. It remains in effect until another CTL statement is encountered. The CTL statement format is shown in Figure 4.7.

$$* \$\$ \text{ CTL } \left[\text{CLASS} = \left\{ \begin{matrix} \text{A} \\ \text{class} \end{matrix} \right\} \right]$$

Figure 4.7 The POWER CTL statement format.

The default class is A unless another default was established in the PSTART statement at IPL time. In summary, the CLASS defaults for the POWER *JOB* statement are:

1. To the CTL value, if any
2. To the PSTART class, if given
3. To A

As stated previously, the console POWER PSTART command (S) can start a partition, a reader task, a writer task, or a RJE task. The first three have a CLASS operand which overrides the A defaults above.

The CLASS defaults for the *LST* and *PUN* statements are:

1. To the PSTART class, if given
2. To A

SUMMARY

The functions of the seven POWER JECL commands studied in this chapter are as follows:

1. The JOB statement announces the beginning of a POWER job and defines the attributes of a job waiting in the RDR queue.
2. The LST statement defines the attributes of a job waiting in the LST queue.
3. The PUN statement defines the attributes of a job waiting in the PUN queue.
4. The RDR statement inserts records from a diskette file into the input stream.
5. The SLI statement inserts an entry or book from the source library into the input stream.
6. The EOJ statement indicates the end of a POWER job.
7. The CTL statement assigns a new default *input* class.

The general format for all of these POWER statements is

```
*b$$bop code/boperands separated by commasbcomment
```

There are two possible formats: positional and keyword. Keyword format is the best format to use because:

1. An operand may be omitted by not coding it.
2. The order the operands are coded in does not matter.
3. There are more operand options available in this format.

The CLASS of the JOB statement determines the partition in which the job will execute, whereas the CLASS of the LST statement determines the output device used. The JOB CLASS can be changed by the use of a CTL statement.

Four important dispositions (DISP) are:

1. *D,* which means that the job does not need to be released and will be deleted from the queue after processing. D is the default.
2. K, which means that the job does not need to be released, and it will be kept in the queue after processing.
3. H, which means that the job must be released to process, and it will be deleted from the queue after processing.
4. L, which means that the job must be released to process, and it will be kept in the queue after processing.

Know

TERMS TO REMEMBER

Attribute
Class
Disposition
IPL routine
JECL commands

Node
Priority
PSTART command
Verified file

STUDY GUIDE

1. Write the general format of POWER JECL commands.

   K5 $D00 code/ Doperands separated by comas5 comma

2. Name three advantages of the keyword format over the positional format.

   (a) An operand may be omitted Simply by not coding it where as in positional 2 commas must be used to omitted it.

   (b) Operands may be coded in any order

   (c) More operands are possible

3. State the general purpose of the following POWER commands.

   (a) JOB indicates the beginning of a USE/power Job + defines the attributes of a Job waiting in the RDR Queue

   (b) LST defines the attributes or characteristics of a Job waiting in the list Queue

   (c) RDR used to insert a diskette file into an input stream

   (d) CTL used to assign another default input class for the RDR Queue

   (e) SLI Inserts an entry or book from the Source Library into the Job stream

   (f) PUN defines the attributes of Job in the punch Queue

   (g) EOJ indicates the end of a power Job

4. Name two things that the D, K, H, and L dispositions describe in both the RDR and LST queues. Which of these values is the default?

   (a) _If job is available_

   (b) _If job should be given_

   The default is _D_

5. (a) What is the meaning of the T disposition in the LST statement?

   Printed output spooler to tape

   (b) What other keyword is used in conjunction with the T disposition?

   TAPE   DISP=H

6. (a) Distinguish between the meaning of the CLASS keyword for the JOB and LST statements.

   (1) JOB class _determines   the partition_
   that will execute
   (2) LST class _output device_

   (b) What do you think would happen if the CLASS keyword were omitted?

   Abend

7. Write down the possible JOB statement classes for each partition in your center. List each partition beginning with BG and F1.

Partition	Classes	Partition	Classes
BG	3 4	F4	8
F1	2	F5	9
F2	6		
F3	7		

8. Write down the possible classes for the LST statement in your center and give the meaning of each.

Class	Meaning
4	
5	
6	
9	

9. Write down the defaults in your center for the following operands.

   (a) JOB class _____ 45 _____

   (b) LST class _____ 5 _____

   (c) PRI _____ 7 _____

   (d) JSEP (LST) _____ 3 _____

   (e) COPY (LST) _____ 2 _____

   (f) FNO (LST) _____ 8 _____

10. Give the purpose of the following LST operands.

   (a) JSEP _Specifies the number of Job separating pages desired between Job printouts._

   (b) COPY _Specifies the # of copies of printed output desired for the Job (default is 1)_

   (c) TADDR _Used to give the hex tape unit address if printed output is to be spooled to tape._

   (d) FNO _Specify the # of any special forms to be mounted_

   (e) FCB _indicate how long the form is from top to bottom_

11. State the purpose of the following RDR statement operands.

   (a) FID _file identification_

   (b) FEED _Specifies if the diskette is to be ejected when an end of file is read_

   (c) NOD _Specifies the maximum number of diskettes to be read_

Due

CODING EXERCISES _Will be on Test_

Code the following POWER statements on a coding sheet. Use the conventions in the book or in your center if different. Assume the printer classes below (unless instructed otherwise).

- B = administrative printer
- Z = student printer
- Q = hold in LST queue for viewing

1. Code a JOB statement for you, the programmer, running in F4. The program is to be released, but deleted from the queue after processing.

2. Code a JOB statement for you, running in BG only. The program will run immediately but be kept in the RDR queue after execution. Priority is the highest possible.

3. Code a LST statement to hold the printout but delete from the queue after the printing. Twenty-five copies are needed with a separation page. Use the student printer.

4. Code a LST statement to hold the printout in the queue and keep it in the queue after processing. There will be a forms number of PAYR. Use the administrative printer.

5. Code a PUN statement to punch three copies, punch one separator card, and use a forms number of your three initials.

6. Code a statement to bring in data from the source library. The data are named P.RPG12.

7. Code a statement to bring in data from a diskette. The file identification name is PAYROLL, and there is only one file.

8. Code a statement to end a POWER job.

9. Code a statement to change the input class to Y.

RESEARCH PROBLEMS

Using a POWER manual available in your center or one on file in your library, answer the following problems in essay style.

1. State the effect of the LTAB operand (in the system generation POWER macro) on the POWER LST statement FCB operand. Explain how the LTAB operand is coded. Then code the LTAB operand for a form that is 66 lines long and has nine lines between the preceding page and channel 1 of the new page. Channel 1 is the same as the first line of the printed page. Channel 2 is used and is eight lines from the channel 1 line. The other channels are not used.

2. What is the purpose of the POWER DATA statement that we have not discussed? How do you think this could be used?

3. How would the PRELEASE central operator command be used in conjunction with the POWER JECL JOB and LST statements? How would the PGO command be used in conjunction with the POWER LST and PUN statements?

chapter 5

DOS/VSE Job Control Language

There are three types of job control language statements. They are:

1. *Job control statements* (JCS). Job control statements are written by the programmer. They are part of the input stream through *SYSRDR* or the system reader. The *system reader* is the device that reads the job control statements.

2. *Job control commands* (JCC). These commands are issued *between* jobs through SYSRDR or SYSLOG, the console device. *SYSLOG* is the communication device between the system and the operator and is used for logging job control statements. This device is usually a visual display unit (the display operator console), but it can be a printer. The term *log* means a record of transactions. A *hard copy* of these transactions may be obtained by means of the PRINTLOG program. The console display copy is referred to as a *soft copy* of the log.

3. *Attention routine* (AR). The AR commands are issued through the console keyboard by the console operator at whatever time needed. These commands are used in a multiprogramming environment.

In this book we will be concerned primarily with job control statements (JCS), although we discuss a few job control commands (JCC). In Chapter 2 we saw that the general format of all JCS, with five exceptions, is

```
//bop codeboperands separated by commasbcomment
```

Coding should not go past column 71. A few commands can be continued by using a nonblank character in column 72.

Job control commands (JCC) differ in format from JCS in that there is no //b at the beginning of the statement. A JCC may begin in column 1.

Unlike POWER commands, job control statements must be written in positional format *even though some operands have possible keywords*. Syntax rules are much the same as POWER command syntax rules. The rules are:

1. [ ] represents an option that can be omitted or included.

2. Stacked options may be written two ways: [A|B] or $\begin{bmatrix} A \\ B \end{bmatrix}$. A and B represent alternatives, one of which may be chosen.

3. Defaults are written in bold (dark) print, but in this book defaults are underlined.

4. Uppercase letters and punctuation marks must be coded exactly as shown. Lowercase letters represent information to be supplied by the programmer. Numeric characters to be supplied are shown by an n or m, and alphameric characters are shown by an x or y.

5. { } means that this entry must be used.

6. An *ellipsis* (...) indicates that a variable number of items may be included.

7. Parentheses must be coded as shown.

8. Frequent abbreviations used are:
    a. cuu = a hex device number indicating channel and unit number. X'cuu' is no longer required but is accepted. cuu is all that is necessary.
    b. volser = the six-character (A–Z, ∅–9, @, #, or $) volume or serial number for a tape or DASD.

Most of the job control statements that we will study were shown in Figure 2.4. Job control statements can be classified as follows:

Type	OP Codes
1. Job identification	JOB and the /& statement
2. User identification	ID
3. File definition	DLBL, EXTENT, TLBL, and the /* and /+ statements
4. Library definitions	LIBDEF, LIBDROP, LIBLST
5. Pass information to the program	DATE, OPTION, OVEND, UPSI
6. Job stream control and operator communication	PAUSE, ZONE, and the * statement
7. I/O system	ASSGN, CLOSE, LISTIO, MTC, PWD, RESET, SETPRT
8. Program execution	EXEC, RSTRT

It might be noted here that the /*, /&, and /+ statements are often referred to as *delimiter* statements. A delimiter statement, in job control, marks the end of data, a job, or a task.

A discussion of some of these job control statements follows. Tape- and disk-oriented commands will be deferred until later chapters.

```
// JOB jobname [accounting information]                        (JCS)
```

Figure 5.1   The JOB statement format.

THE JOB STATEMENT

A DOS/VSE job is a unit of work, the beginning of which is indicated by the JOB statement. The JOB statement format is shown in Figure 5.1.

The jobname can be one to eight alphameric characters (A–Z, Ø–9, @, #, $) or a /, -, or a period. In this book we use the first eight letters or less of your last name as we did in the POWER job statement. The optional accounting information operand will not be used unless you are instructed otherwise.

The JOB statement is the first DOS job statement coded in a job stream after the POWER JOB and LST statements (and PUN statement if used). An example of a JOB statement would be

```
        // JOB LEE        PAYROLL JOB
```

Here JOB is the op code, LEE is the jobname, and PAYROLL JOB is a comment.

THE END-OF-JOB STATEMENT

A /& in columns 1 and 2 indicate the end of a DOS job. It resets all options and symbolic device numbers back to those chosen at SYSGEN time. (See the ASSGN and OPTION statement discussion below.)

THE OPTION STATEMENT

The OPTION statement allows a change in certain *system* options that were chosen at SYSGEN time. These changes apply only to the current job. After the job

```
// OPTION option[,option]...                                  (JCS)

where option = ACANCEL|NOACANCEL
               ALIGN|NOALIGN
               CATAL
               DECK|NODECK
               DUMP|PARTDUMP|NODUMP
               EDECK|NOEDECK
               ERRS|NOERRS
            *  JCANCEL|NOJCANCEL
               LINK|NOLINK
               LIST|NOLIST
               LISTX|NOLISTX
               LOG|NOLOG
            *  LOGSRC|NOLOGSRC
               NOFASTTR
               ONLINE|NOONLINE
               PARSTD={ADD|DELETE|Fn}
               RLD|NORLD
               STDLABEL={ADD|DELETE}
               STDLABEL|USRLABEL|PARSTD
               SUBLIB={DF|AE}
               SYM|NOSYM
               SYSDMP|NOSYSDMP
               SYSPARM='string'
               TERM|NOTERM
               XREF|SXREF|NOXREF
               48C|60C

    * Not supported in DOS/VSE version 1.
```

Figure 5.2   The OPTION statement format.

is finished (when a /& is read), these changes revert back to the original options chosen at SYSGEN time.

The format for the OPTION statement is shown in Figure 5.2. The possible options and meanings are listed below. You or your instructor need to find out from your center what your system default is for each option. You should underline each default in the following list.

Option	Purpose
ACANCEL/NOACANCEL	Indicates that the job will or will not be canceled automatically if an attempt to assign a device is unsuccessful.
ALIGN/NOALIGN	The assembler will align constants and data areas on the proper boundaries and check for proper alignment in instructions.
CATAL	Indicates that a phase or program is to be permanently cataloged in the library after it has been link-edited. (CATAL implies the LINK option.)
DECK/NODECK	Indicates that the language translator should or should not put out an object module on SYSPCH. (*SYSPCH* is the device on which the system produces punched output.)
DUMP/PARTDUMP/NODUMP	If a job aborts, DUMP dumps the entire partition, registers, and so on. PARTDUMP dumps only the part of the partition used for the program and certain selected areas. NODUMP will not dump at all. PARTDUMP is usually the best choice. (A *dump* is a printout of the contents of memory and certain areas, such as the contents of registers. On most IBM computers a dump is in hex.)
EDECK/NOEDECK	Indicates that source macros are or are not to be punched on SYSPCH.
ERRS/NOERRS	Indicates that the FORTRAN, COBOL, and PL/1 compilers will or will not print *diagnostics* (compilation error messages) on SYSLST. (*SYSLST* is the device used for the printed output of the system.)
JCANCEL/NOJCANCEL	If a job control error occurs, JCANCEL causes the system to skip to the EOJ instead of waiting for operator intervention.

Option	Purpose
	NOJCANCEL is underlined because it is the system default. This option does not exist in DOS/VSE version 1.
LINK/NOLINK	Indicates that a link-edit is or is not to take place. If the EXEC LNKEDT command is to be used, this option must be used. (The CATAL option implies LINK.)
LIST/NOLIST	The language translators will or will not print the source program.
LISTX/NOLISTX	The COBOL compiler will or will not produce a *PROCEDURE DIVISION map* on SYSLST. This map shows addresses and the machine language program generated. This option, when used for the FORTRAN and PL/1 compilers, produces object modules on SYSLST.
LOG/NOLOG	Prints or does not print job control statements on SYSLST.
LOGSRC/NOLOGSRC	This option deals with symbolic parameters and gives an option as to how they are printed. We will not use this option. The system default is NOLOGSRC. This option does not exist in DOS/VSE version 1.
ONLINE/NOONLINE	Causes the system to fetch all programs for execution from the system CIL, although a private library may have been assigned.
PARSTD/PARSTD = ADD/ PARSTD = DELETE/ PARSTD = Fn	These options concern DASD and tape labels and are highly technical. We will not be concerned with these options at this time.
RLD/NORLD	The assembler will or will not write a relocation dictionary on SYSLST. Assembler programmers sometimes use this information, which is produced for the linkage editor.
STDLABEL/STDLABEL = ADD/ STDLABEL = DELETE	These options have to do with where disk labels are written for the system. Standard labels can be stored permanently in a label information area (LIA) on SYSRES. We will not be using these options at this time.

Option	Purpose
SUBLIB = DF/SUBLIB = AE SYM/NOSYM	We will not be concerned with this option. The COBOL compiler produces a DATA DIVISION map on SYSLST. A *DATA DIVISION map* shows the offset location of symbolic names used in the program. The PL/1 compiler can also produce this list.
SYSDUMP/NOSYSDUMP (for version 1, SYSDMP/NOSYSDMP)	SYSDUMP (or *SYSDMP*) indicates that dumps are to be written in an area called a *system dump file* defined on disk. NOSYDUMP (or NOSYSDMP) indicates that dumps are to be written on SYSLST.
SYSPARM = 'string'	We will not be concerned with this option.
TERM/NOTERM	Error messages will or will not be written on SYSLOG for compilers that support this function. (SYSLOG is the operator console device.)
USRLABEL	We will not be using this option since we are not using user labels.
XREF/SXREF/NOXREF	The assembler does or does not write a *cross-reference dictionary*. This is a list of all symbolic terms used in a program and the program statement numbers where the name is used. This list is often helpful in debugging.
NOFASTTR	This is a systems generation option only, so we will not be using it.
48C/60C	Specifies the character set to be used on SYSIPT for the PL/1 compiler. (*SYSIPT* is the system input device that is used as the input unit for programs.)

An example of an option statement is

```
// OPTION LINK,LOG,PARTDUMP,LISTX
```

This statement specifies that the linkage editor is to be used; job control statements are to be printed; if the job aborts, a dump of the part of the partition used is to be printed; and a COBOL PROCEDURE DIVISION map is to be produced. (In FORTRAN or PL/1, this LISTX option would cause an object module to be printed in hex.)

The option statement usually follows the JOB statement.

THE EXEC STATEMENT

As seen in Figure 5.3, the EXEC command has two formats. The EXEC statement indicates:

1. That the control information for a job is complete and that the job name (program name) indicated in the EXEC statement is to be fetched from the CIL and is to be executed, *or*

2. That a procedure (specified by the procname) is to be fetched from the procedure library and inserted in the job stream

```
First format:                                        (JCS,JCC)

[//] EXEC [[PGM=]progname][,REAL][,SIZE=size][,GO][,PARM='value']

Second format:                                       (JCS,JCC)

[//] EXEC PROC=procname,[,OV]
```

Figure 5.3 The EXEC statement formats.

First Format

The operands shown in this format must be coded in the order shown even though some have keywords.

The Program Name Operand.   The following examples show how the first operand, the program name, is coded.

Examples

1. // EXEC FCOBOL   This command loads the COBOL compiler from the CIL into memory and executes a COBOL compilation.

2. // EXEC PAYROLL or // EXEC PGM=PAYROLL   Either method is correct, but most programmers omit the keyword PGM=, which is optional. This statement loads a program named PAYROLL from the CIL into memory and executes it.

3. // EXEC LNKEDT   This command loads the linkage editor program from the CIL into memory and link-edits an object program with the routines needed for program execution.

4. // EXEC   If no name follows the EXEC op code, this indicates that the object program has just been produced by a compilation and link edit and is *not* in the CIL. The object program is in a *temporary* area on disk, and it is to be found there rather than in the CIL.

The REAL Operand.   The REAL operand of the EXEC statement is discussed later in the section on virtual storage. It is not used a great deal.

The SIZE Operand.   Figure 2.1 illustrated that each partition has a GETVIS area. Figure 2.2 illustrated that each partition has 48K of GETVIS area. VSE allows this amount of storage as a default. Some programs that use VSAM files need more GETVIS storage as they execute. (VSAM is a type of file organization that is discussed in a later chapter.) The SIZE operand provides a method of obtaining a larger GETVIS area.

Examples

```
// EXEC FCOBOL,SIZE=100K
// EXEC LNKEDT,SIZE=64K
```

It is standard procedure to use SIZE = AUTO on the EXEC statement for programs using VSAM data. This allows the system to calculate the space needed from information in the CIL. However, SIZE = AUTO should never be used for programs such as the linkage editor, compilers, or the LIBRARIAN programs (i.e., programs that dynamically allocate storage).

Definition. *Dynamic storage allocation* is a technique in which storage is assigned to computer programs and data while the program is executing.

SIZE = AUTO Example

```
// EXEC PAYROLL,SIZE=AUTO
```

or

```
// EXEC ,SIZE=AUTO
```

In the first case above, the program is in the CIL. In the second case above, the comma is used because the program has just been compiled (it is not in the CIL), and thus the program name operand is omitted.

The GO Operand. The GO operand is used in program development job streams. If used, the EXEC LNKEDT statement is not necessary. The program will be link-edited and executed automatically.

Example

```
// EXEC ,SIZE=AUTO,GO
```

The PARM Operand. This operand can be used if information from the job stream is needed by a application program. The value can be up to 100 characters and is enclosed in apostrophes. If an apostrophe is needed within the value, two apostrophes must be used. This method of passing information takes up less time than entering it on the console.

Second Format

The second format shown in Figure 5.3 allows a procedure, specified by the procname, to be retrieved from the procedure library and inserted into the job stream.

Example

```
// EXEC PROC=PAYJCL
```

Here the procname (procedure name) is PAYJCL. The procedure name can be one to eight alphameric characters. It cannot be ALL or begin with $$.

The operand OV is used if certain statements in the procedure being referenced are to be changed. (OV stands for override.) In Chapter 11 we will see how this is done in a research problem.

THE DATE STATEMENT

The DATE statement format is shown in Figure 5.4. The DATE statement is used if it is desired to override temporarily the date in the communications region for a particular job. This feature would be used if a job needed to be rerun with an old date. The format is month, day, and year (mm/dd/yy) unless specified differently in the STDOPT job control statement.

```
//DATE[mm/dd/yy|dd/mm/yy]                                    (JCS)
```

Figure 5.4 The DATE statement format.

THE LISTIO STATEMENT

The LISTIO statement can be used to obtain a list of the I/O assignments for any partition. Its format is shown in Figure 5.5.

```
[//] LISTIO {ALL|ASSGN|BG|cuu|DOWN|Fn|PROG|SYS|       (JCS,JCC)
            SYSxxx|UA|UNITS}
```

Figure 5.5 The LISTIO statement format.

Example

```
// LISTIO BG
```

The output produced from the statement above is shown in Figure 5.6. The system device numbers (the SYS names shown at the left), or *logical units*, are used in computer programs. If a SYS number is referenced in a program, it refers to the hex device number (the channel and unit number), or *physical unit*, shown on the right. For example, SYSRDR refers to device number Ø2C, which is the card reader in the system configuration in Chapter 1.

The letters UA under channel and unit number mean *unassigned*.

Rule. If a system device number is used in a program that is (1) unassigned or (2) refers to a different physical device number than is desired, *then* an ASSGN statement must be used in the job stream to specify the desired device number.

Possible operands for the LISTIO statement are shown below. However, only one operand can be used for the *listtype* in the format shown.

ALL	Lists the device numbers (physical units) assigned to all system devices (logical units) for *all* partitions.
ASSGN	Lists all assignments for the partition from which the command is issued. Does not list the unassigned units.
BG	Lists the device numbers for logical units in background only.
cuu	Lists the logical units assigned to cuu. [For example, if cuu is 3ØØ, it will list all logical units (SYS numbers) assigned to 3ØØ.]
DOWN	Lists all physical units that are down (inoperative).
Fn	Lists the device numbers for logical units in foreground n (where n is a number).

```
              *** BACKGROUND ***

       (LOGICAL)              (PHYSICAL)
       I/O UNIT ASSGMNT       CHNL   UNIT    MODE

          SYSRDR   PER          0      2C
          SYSIPT   PER          0      2C
          SYSPCH   PER          0      2D
          SYSLST   PER          0      2E
          SYSLOG   PER          0      1F
          SYSLNK   PER          2      23
          SYSRES   PER          2      23
          SYSSLB                *  UA  *
          SYSRLB                *  UA  *
          SYSUSE                *  UA  *
          SYSREC   PER          2      23
          SYSCLB                *  UA  *
          SYSDMP   PER          2      22
          SYSCAT   PER          2      23
          SYSTEM  FILES
          SYS000                *  UA  *
          SYS001   PER          2      22
          SYS002   PER          2      22
          SYS003   PER          2      22
          SYS004   PER          2      22
          SYS005   PER          0      2C
          SYS006   PER          0      2D
          SYS007   PER          0      2E
          SYS008                *  UA  *
          UP TO
          SYS019                *  UA  *
          SYS020   TEM          2      21
          SYS020   PER          *  UA  *
          SYS021   TEM          2      20
          SYS021   PER          *  UA  *
          SYS022   TEM          2      22
          SYS022   PER          *  UA  *
          SYS023   TEM          2      23
          SYS023   PER          *  UA  *
          SYS024                *  UA  *
          UP TO
          SYS099                *  UA  *
```

Figure 5.6 Output produced by the LISTIO statement format.

PROG	Lists the device numbers assigned to all programmer logical units of the partition from which the command is issued.
SYS	Lists the device numbers assigned to all system logical units of the partition from which the command is issued.
SYSxxx	Lists the device numbers assigned to the specified logical unit of the partition from which the command is issued.
UA	Lists all device numbers not currently assigned to a logical unit.
UNITS	Lists the logical units assigned to all physical units.

THE ASSGN STATEMENT

In Figure 5.6 we saw that the device assignments for each partition can be listed. These system device numbers (logical units) are frequently used in computer programs.

The ASSGN statement must be used in a job stream if:

1. The current assignment shown in the LISTIO printout is *not* that intended by the computer program, *or*

2. The system device number (SYSxxx) is currently unassigned (UA).

The format for the ASSGN statement is shown in Figure 5.7. There are three types of ASSGN statements: the *specific assignment*, the *generic assignment*, and the *address-list assignment*.

1. The Specific Assignment

This command assigns a system device number to a *specific* device.

Example

```
// ASSGN SYS005,300
```

Assuming that device number 300 is a magnetic tape device as shown in the Chapter 1 configuration, this statement assigns system device 005, used in a computer program, to tape unit 300. The 300 corresponds to the cuu in the format shown in Figure 5.7.

The disadvantage of the specific assignment is that the tape to be used *must be* mounted on tape drive 300 and no other.

Another Example

```
// ASSGN SYS005,UA
```

This command would unassign SYS005 from its current physical unit. If any operation is now attempted on this device, the job will be canceled.

2. The Generic Assignment

The word *generic* means of a particular class or type but *not* a specific kind. When a doctor writes a generic prescription, it means that the prescription states no specific medication. It merely gives a class of medication which may be one of several brands.

```
For disk devices:                                    (JCS,JCC)
[//] ASSGN SYSxxx,devaddr[,TEMP|,PERM][,VOL=number][,SHR]

For diskette devices:                                (JCS,JCC)
[//] ASSGN SYSxxx,devaddr[,TEMP|,PERM][,VOL=number]

For magnetic tape devices:                           (JCS,JCC)
[//] ASSGN SYSxxx,devaddr[,mode|ALT][,TEMP|,PERM][VOL=number]

For any other device:                                (JCS,JCC)
[//] ASSGN SYSxxx,devaddr[,TEMP|PERM]


where devaddr can be: cuu
                      address-list
                      UA
                      IGN
                      SYSyyy
                      device-class (see figure 5.8)
                      device-type  (see figure 5.8)
```

Figure 5.7 The ASSGN statement formats.

The advantage of using generic assignments in computer work is that it is not necessary to be concerned about the particular device on which the storage medium is mounted. If a generic assignment is given and there are several tape units, the system searches for the volume serial number specified in the generic assignment. When it finds it, it assigns the device it is on.

Definition. A *volume* is that portion of a storage medium accessible to one read-write arm. In most cases a volume can simply be considered a magnetic tape or a disk pack (or module).

There are two types of generic assignments, device-class and device-type. Possible device classes and types are shown in Figure 5.8.

Examples of Class Assignments

```
// ASSGN SYS008,READER   (This assigns SYS008 to any
                           card reader.)
// ASSGN SYS008,TAPE,VOL=PAYROL  (This assigns SYS008
                           to any tape device
                           with a tape having a
                           volume number of
                           PAYROL.)
```

Tape and disk generic assignments must have a volume number specified with the keyword entry VOL. The class entry for tape and disk causes a search of all devices of that class regardless of type number. In other words, the last assignment above would search all IBM 2400 *and* 8809 tape drives, if both exist, for the proper volume.

Examples of Type Assignments

```
// ASSGN SYS009,3800   (This assigns SYS009 to a 3800
                           laser printer.)
// ASSGN SYS010,8809,VOL=PAYROL  (This assigns SYS010
                           to an 8809 tape drive
                           with a tape that has
                           a volume number of
                           PAYROL.)
```

The class and type assignments provide a more flexible operational environment and should be used if possible. However, a generic assignment cannot be used if the tape or disk storage medium does not have a volume serial number.

3. The Address-List Assignment

The *address-list assignment* is really a combination of the specific and generic assignments. Up to seven hex device addresses may be listed.

Example

```
// ASSGN SYS008,(300,301,302,303,304,305,306)
```

If devices 300, 301, and 302 are in use, then 303 will be assigned to SYS008. If none are in use, 300 is assigned.

The JCC ASSGN Statement. If the //b is omitted from the command, the command becomes a *permanent assignment* that is in effect after an end-of-job statement is read. The JCC ASSGN command can begin in column 1 or after.

- **READER**
  1442N1, 2501, 2520B1, 2540R, 2560, 2596, 3504†, 3505, 3525RP, 5425
- **PRINTER**
  PRT1, 1403, 1403U, 1443, 3200, 3203†, 3211†, 3800, 3800B, 3800C, 3800BC,
  4248‡, 5203†, 5203U†
- **PUNCH**
  1442N1, 1442N2, 2520B1, 2520B2, 2520B3, 2540P, 2560, 2596, 3525P,
  3525RP, 5425
- **TAPE**
  2400T7†, 2400T9, 8809†, 3410T7†, 3410T9, 3420T7†, 3420T9, 3430
- **DISK**
  2311, 2314, 3330, 3330B, 3340, 3340R, 3350, FBA, 3375, 3380‡
- **CKD**
  2311, 2314, 3330, 3330B, 3340, 3340B, 3350, 3375, 3380‡
- **FBA**
- **DISKETTE**
  3540

† Supported in DOS/VSE version 1 only.

‡ Not supported in DOS/VSE version 1.

Figure 5.8 Device-class/Device-type codes.

Example

```
ASSGN SYS008,300
```

The TEMP/PERM Operand. This operand provides another way of making
an assignment permanent or temporary. The // ASSGN SYS008,300,PERM job
control statement has the same effect as the ASSGN SYS008,300 job control
command.

The SHR Operand. This operand can be used only for generic and address-
list *disk* assignments. Its use permits two different programs to use the same disk
drive assignments at the same time. Unless a private device is required for some
reason, this operand should be used in most cases involving generic and address-
list disk assignments.

THE RESET STATEMENT

The RESET statement resets any temporary assignments (made with the ASSGN
statement) back to the values chosen at SYSGEN time. This statement is sometimes used when several jobs are in the same POWER job and a /& statement
therefore does not exist to reset the assignments. The format for this statement
is shown in Figure 5.9. The function of the operands are as follows:

```
[//] RESET {SYS|PROG|ALL|SYSxxx}                          (JCS,JCC)
```

Figure 5.9 The RESET statement format.

SYS Resets all system logical unit assignments and library search chain definitions (see the LIBDEF statement below) to the permanent values.

PROG Resets all programmer logical units to their permanent values.

ALL Resets all system logical unit assignments and library chain definitions to their permanent values.

SYSxxx Resets the specified logical unit to its permanent assignment. (SYSIN and SYSOUT, described in Appendix A, cannot be specified.)

THE LIBDEF STATEMENT (DOS/VSE, VERSION 1)†

If a // EXEC PAYROLL,SIZE = AUTO statement were to appear, the operating system will look for the program in the system CIL on SYSRES. We learned in Chapter 3 that we can also have programs in a private CIL that is not on SYSRES. To search one or more private CIL libraries, we must use the LIBDEF statement. It sets up a chain (or concatenation) of libraries to be searched.

```
[//] LIBDEF {CL|RL|SL|PL}[,PERM|,TEMP]          (JCS,JCC)
            [,SEARCH=(name,name,...)]
            [,FROM=name][,TO=name][,NEW=name]
```

Figure 5.10 The LIBDEF statement format for DOS/VSE, version 1.

Definition. To *concatenate* is to link together into a series or chain.

The format for the LIBDEF statement is shown in Figure 5.10. Operands are as follows:

CL|RL|SL|PL This operand tells which library type is to be searched. Only one choice can be made.

SEARCH = Gives the library names to be chained. These libraries are to be searched for a program or programs. Each name can be one to seven characters and a maximum of 15 libraries can be chained. (These libraries are originally defined using a DLBL job control statement, and the library name must be what existed in that statement.)

FROM = Gives the name of the input library to be used by a service program.

TO = Used to give the name of an output library in cataloging or maintenance activities.

NEW = Used in creating a new volume of libraries.

PERM|TEMP Has the same meaning as in the ASSGN statement.

We will be using the first two operands, that is, the library choice and the SEARCH operand.

Example

```
// LIBDEF CL,SEARCH=(USRCL1,USRCL2)
```

† See Chapter 12 for details of the DOS/VSE/SP form of the LIBDEF statement.

DELIMITER STATEMENTS

The delimiter statements that we will be using frequently are:

- /* which means end of file or task
- /& which means end of a DOS/VSE job

COMMENTS

There are two methods of making informational comments in job control streams. They are:

1. Leave one or more spaces after the last operand. Example:

```
// JOB LEE     MARCH PAYROLL
```

2. Code an *, a blank, and then the comment. Example:

```
* BEGINNING OF PAYROLL JOB
```

It is important that you document job control statements just as you have been taught to document programs to make program maintenance easier. Documenting job control statements makes changes easier.

SUMMARY

There are three types of job control language statements. They are job control statements (JCS), job control commands (JCC), and attention routine commands (AR).

The general format for job control statements is

```
//bop codeboperands separated by commasbcomment
```

The job control commands have the same format except that they do not have the //b at the beginning.

Of the job control statements:

1. The JOB statement announces the beginning of a DOS/VSE job. It also gives the job a job name. The /& statement signifies the end of a DOS job.
2. The OPTION statement allows a change in certain system options that were chosen at SYSGEN time. The changes specified apply only to the current job. The most frequently used options are CATAL, LINK, PARTDUMP, LOG, LISTX, SYM, AND SXREF or XREF.
3. The EXEC statement is used to indicate:
   a. That a job is to be fetched from the CIL and executed, *or*
   b. That a procedure from the PL is to be inserted in the job stream.
4. The DATE statement is used to change temporarily the date in the communications region for a particular job.

5. The LISTIO statement can be used to determine what the current physical assignments are for each logical unit in each partition.

6. The ASSGN statement is used to assign a symbolic device unit used in a program to a physical I/O device. There are two types of assignment statements: a specific assignment and a generic assignment. The generic assignment can be by class or type. Generic assignments only specify a general class or type of I/O device. If the devices being assigned are tape or disk, a volume serial number must also be specified.

7. The RESET statement can be used to return any temporary assignment of I/O devices to the assignments specified at SYSGEN time.

8. The LIBDEF statement is used to name private libraries that are to be searched in addition to the system libraries. These libraries can be concatenated or chained together.

9. The /* statement means end of task or file.

10. Comments may be made by the use of an *b̸ statement as well as by leaving at least one blank after the last operand on job control statements.

TERMS TO REMEMBER

Address-list assignment   Log
AR command   Logical unit
Concatenate   Permanent assignment
Cross reference dictionary   Physical unit
DATA DIVISION map   PROCEDURE DIVISION map
Delimiter statement   Soft copy
Diagnostics   Specific assignment
Dump   SYSDMP
Dynamic storage allocation   SYSIPT
Ellipsis   SYSLST
Generic   SYSLOG
Generic assignment   SYSPCH
Hard copy   SYSRDR
JCC   System dump file
JCS   Volume

STUDY GUIDE

Answer the following questions in the space provided.

1. What is the general format for all DOS/VSE JCL statements (with five exceptions)?

    // b̸ op code b̸ operands Separated by commas b̸ comment

2. Give the meaning of the following job control statements.

(a) /* File Definitions (End of task)

(b) /& Job identification (End of Dos/use job)

(c) /+ File Definitions (End of Procedure)

3. State two ways that comments may be made in job control work.

(a) * b

(b) Leaving at least 1 blank after the last operand on job control statement.

4. Give the purpose or function of each of the following job control statements.

(a) JOB annouces the beginning of a Dos/use Job

(b) ASSGN assign a symbolic device unit used in a program to physical I/o device.

(c) DATE used to change temporarily the date in the communications region for a particular job

(d) OPTION Allows a change in certain system options that where chosen at sysgen

(e) EXEC used to indicate job is to be fetched from CIL & executed or a procedure from the PL is to be inserted

(f) LIBDEF name private libraries that are to search in addition to the system libraries

(g) RESET Return any temporary assignment of I/o devices to the assignments specified in sysgen

(h) LISTIO To determine what the current physical assignments are for each logical units in each partition

5. What do the following mean in JCL statements?

(a) cuu List the logical units assigned to cuu

(b) SYSxxx List the device #'s assigned to the specified logical unit of the partition from which command is issued

(c) SYSnnn
  ↳ List device #'s assigned to au system logical units of the partition from which the command is issued

6. How long will the following assignments be in effect?

   (a) ASSGN SYS009,301

   _____

   (b) // ASSGN SYS10,220

   _____

7. What is the advantage of using generic assignments rather than specific ASSGN statements?

not necessary to be concerned about the particular device on which the storage medium is mounted

8. List the defaults in your center for the operands in the OPTION job control statement.

Link

Dump

9. If the /& command resets all device assignments to the original assignments, why would the RESET command be used?

used when several jobs are in the same power job & /& does not exist

10. **(a)** Does your center have any restrictions on SYS numbers (symbolic device numbers) that are to be used for data files in a program? If so, what are the restrictions?

no

   (b) Are there standard SYS numbers for the card reader, printer, and punch in your center? If so, what are they? What is the advantage of having standard SYS numbers for these devices?

yes

CODING EXERCISES

Code the following DOS/VSE job control statements on a coding sheet. Assume OPTION defaults of NOACANCEL, ALIGN, NODECK, NODUMP, NO-DECK, ERRS, NOLINK, LIST, NOLISTX, LOG, ONLINE, NORLD, STDLA-BEL, NOSYM, NOSYSDMP, NOXREF, and 6ØC.

1. Code a generic CLASS assignment and then a TYPE assignment for the following devices. Assume a logical unit of SYSØ15 and a volume serial number of 666666 where appropriate. Use the devices indicated in Figure 1.2 unless instructed otherwise.
   (a) A card reader
   (b) A printer
   (c) A card punch
   (d) A diskette reader
   (e) A magnetic tape drive
   (f) A disk drive

2. Code a JOB statement for a job for you and use a comment to indicate that this is an inventory program for the month of December 1988.

3. Code a DATE statement for a date of November 1, 1988.

4. Code an OPTION statement to cause the job control statements not to be logged and to prepare for a link-edit process.

5. Code an ASSGN statement to indicate that the system residence is on disk drive 223.

6. Code an ASSGN statement to indicate that the system list device is the printer.

7. Code an ASSGN statement to indicate that SYSØ16 is assigned to tape drive 3Ø1.

8. Code a statement to list the I/O assignments in all partitions.

9. Code a statement to reset SYSØ2Ø to the value given at SYSGEN time.

10. Code a statement to unassign SYSØØ7.

11. Code an EXEC statement (including the SIZE operand) to:
    (a) Execute a program named ABCDE in the CIL.
    (b) Execute a program just compiled and link edited.
    (c) Execute a COBOL compilation (128K).
    (d) Execute an RPGII compilation (1ØØK).
    (e) Perform a link edit (64K).

RESEARCH PROBLEMS

Use a DOS/VSE Control and Services (Systems Control Statements) manual to answer the following problems in essay style.

1. Look up the CANCEL command.
   (a) Explain the meaning of the {BG|Fn} operand in the third format. What does the

   ```
   [DUMP|,PARTDUMP|,NODUMP]
   ```

   operand mean?
   (b) What does the AR in parentheses mean?

2. What is the purpose of the ID job control statement? When is it used?

3. When can the accounting information format operand be used in the DOS/VSE JOB statement?

4. Look up control statement conventions at the beginning of the manual. Considering these rules if a volume serial number of PAY2 is specified for a six-byte volser number, what is passed to the system for a volume serial number? What would be passed for 'PAY2'?

5. The IGN, MODE, and ALT operands for the ASSGN statement were not discussed in this chapter. State how you think:
   (a) IGN might be used.
   (b) MODE might be used for 8809 magnetic tape units.
   (c) ALT might be used.

chapter 6

ICCF, the Terminal Program

INTRODUCTION

Computer systems now use terminals rather than card readers to enter programs, data, and job control statements. IBM provides a general-purpose data base/data communications control program called CICS to allow the use of terminals. *CICS* is an abbreviation for *Customer Information Control System*. CICS allows transactions to be entered and processed at remote terminals.

Another IBM product, *ICCF*, allows an installation to submit jobs on an interactive basis as well as a batch basis. The terminal keyboard and display screen replace the card reader and printer I/O. ICCF is an abbreviation for *Interactive Computing and Control Facility*.

ICCF works in close conjunction with CICS. Other interactive terminal products exist, such as SPM (*Source Program Maintenance*), but ICCF is very popular in industry.

ICCF allows the terminal user to:

1. Build job streams and prepare input data and programs for immediate or later processing
2. Store job streams, programs, and/or data in a library
3. Change or edit previously stored material
4. Submit job streams to POWER for execution and determine the status of the job, canceling it if necessary
5. Direct output to be viewed on the terminal or to be printed, if desired

THE ICCF PARTITION

In the main storage organization shown in Figure 2.3, ICCF resides in the F2 partition. This partition is itself further subdivided as shown in Figure 6.1. Al-

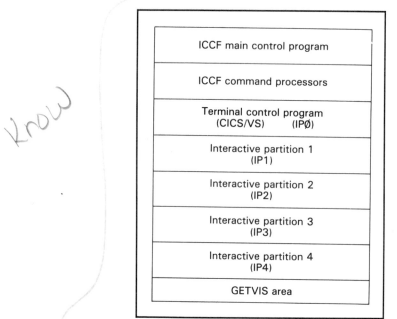

Figure 6.1 Organization of the ICCF foreground partition.

though Figure 6.1 shows only four interactive partitions, ICCF supports up to 35 interactive partitions. Of the ICCF partitions shown:

1. The main control program supervises all ICCF activities. It acts for the F2 partition as the supervisor in Figure 2.3 acts for *all* of memory.

2. The command processors interpret and handle all ICCF commands that are issued at the terminal. It acts much like the DOS/VSE job control

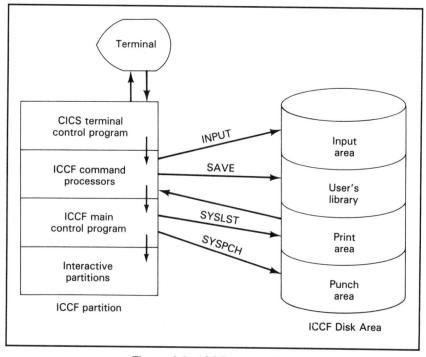

Figure 6.2 ICCF processing.

program that reads and interprets job control statements. This partition carries out requested functions, such as saving members in libraries and handling print requests.

3. The interactive partitions (IP1–IP35) are concerned with the compilation and execution of user programs.

4. The terminal control facility handles terminal activities. These functions are shown in Figure 6.2. (See page 62.)

ICCF LIBRARIES

ICCF has a library file that is processed *only by ICCF*. The file is different from the VSE libraries discussed in Chapter 3. This *ICCF library file* is on disk and is actually divided into several sublibraries.

The ICCF libraries can be private, public, or common libraries.

1. An ICCF *private library* can be owned by one or more users. As a student, you will probably be the only student owner of your private library.

2. A *public library* is accessible to all users on a read/write basis.

3. A *common library* is available to all users on a read-only basis.

Each user is assigned a *primary library*. Programs, data, or job control statements may be stored there. When an item is stored, it is said to be stored in a *library member*. Each of these items is stored under a member name.

Access to these ICCF libraries is controlled by an ICCF administrator. Usually, the *ICCF administrator* is a systems programmer who controls access to ICCF and ensures that it is working at a maximum level. This person also builds a user profile on the user.

A user profile is a record that contains information as to what ICCF libraries the user may access, user passwords, and how the user is allowed to interact with ICCF.

Definition. A *user profile* is a record that contains information necessary to inform the system about each user's requirements and security level.

Information in library members of the private library can be edited or changed. The definition of *edit*, as used in this book, is to enter, modify, or delete information. There are two editors available in ICCF: the full screen editor and the context editor. The full screen editor is the easiest to use.

Figure 6.2 shows the four disk areas involved in ICCF processing. The *input area* is a temporary area into which information can be keyed, modified, or edited. The *print area* is an intermediate storage area used to hold printed output for display on the terminal if desired. The *punch area* can hold punched output for later use by other programs. The *user library* is a place where information can be stored for later use.

ICCF COMMANDS

There are several types of ICCF commands: system commands, context editor commands, full screen editor commands, job entry statements, dump commands, and procedural and macro commands. Since ICCF is such a complex system, in this chapter we consider only the commands most helpful to students.

System Commands

The format for ICCF *system commands* is

```
/op codeboperands separated by blanks, commas, or parentheses
```

Blanks are usually used to separate operands. The syntax conventions are similar to those we have observed with POWER and DOS/VSE.

1. [ ] indicates optional operands.
2. {A|B} means that the operand is required. The | indicates that a choice is to be made.
3. Defaults are underlined.
4. Lowercase letters in operands indicate that the user is to supply a value.

Commonly used system commands are:

1.	/LOGON userid	Allows the user to log on.
2.	/LOGOF	Allows the user to log off.
3.	/LIBrary Full	Displays the names of library entries or members. (Lowercase letters indicate that LIB is all that is necessary.)
4.	/DQ [ALL] [queue] [jobname] [jobnumber]	Displays the contents of all queues; one queue; or one queue with the specified job-name.
5.	/LP jobname	Displays printed output in the list area for a particular job.
6.	/PP jobname (LD) is omac	Purges the jobname from the list area.
7.	/PURge name	Purges or erases the library member specified from the private library.
8.	/RENAMe oldname newname	Used to rename a library member.
9.	/RENUM program name $\begin{bmatrix} inc \\ \underline{100} \end{bmatrix}\begin{bmatrix} beg. \\ col. \\ \underline{73} \end{bmatrix}\begin{bmatrix} beg. \\ seq. no. \\ \underline{8} \end{bmatrix}$	Used to renumber or resequence program statements.
10.	/RP queue jobname [jobnumber] [printer class]	Takes the printout being held in the LST queue (CLASS = Q on the POWER 1ST statement) and prints it. Although the

printer class is an optional last operand, it is usually used to specify which printer the output is to be directed to.

11. /SW library number

Used to switch to another library number.

12. /TABset nl . . . nm|language|OFF

Used to make tab settings.

> where OFF clears the tab setting
> ASsembler sets (columns) 1Ø,16,36,72,73
> BASic sets 1Ø,2Ø,3Ø,4Ø,5Ø,6Ø
> COBol sets 8,12,16,2Ø,24,28,32,36,4Ø,44,73
> FORTran sets 7,73
> PL1 sets 5,1Ø,15,2Ø,25,3Ø,35,4Ø,45,5Ø
> RPG sets 6,2Ø,3Ø,4Ø,5Ø,6Ø

To use these commands, one must be in command mode.

Modes. When ICCF is brought up, a scale similar to that in Figure 6.3 appears at the top of the screen. The two letters at the far right indicate what mode you are in. Modes that you should be aware of are:

1. CM = command mode. You must be in this mode to enter a system command (a command beginning with a slash).
2. FS = full screen mode. This mode appears when you are in the edit mode, entering or changing information.
3. LS = list screen. This mode is used while a display to the screen is in progress. That is, you are viewing the printout of the contents of a LST queue entry. The class on the POWER LST statement must be Q for this feature to be possible.

Terminal Use. If you have used ICCF before, you know that to work on the terminal:

1. You sign on to CICS as instructed by your teacher.
2. You key in ICCF and press the ENTER key.
3. You key in /LOGONb _____ (and press ENTER) where the blank represents the user ID.
4. You key in your ICCF password given to you by the instructor and press the ENTER key.
   The following scale appears: *Note the mode:* ⌐

```
...+...1...+...2...+...3...+...4...+...5...+...6...7...+.CM
```

The CM indicates command mode. Command mode can be obtained anytime by pressing the equivalent of the PA2 key on the IBM 3278 terminal.

After bringing up ICCF, the edit mode can be obtained by keying in the ICCF macro, @ED, or @ED name. To begin a new keying job, only @ED is used. To view or change information that has been saved, the second form is used. When you have done this, the screen shown in Figure 6.3 appears. The FS at the right of the scale indicates full screen edit mode.

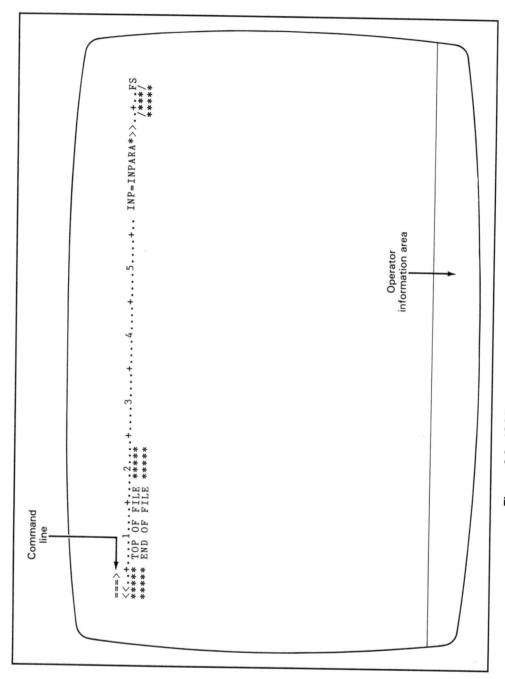

Figure 6.3 ICCF edit mode screen with empty member.

Command
line

Operator
information area

===>
<<.+...1....+...2....+...3....+...4....+...5....+... INP=INPARA*>>..+..FS
***** TOP OF FILE *****   /*****
***** END OF FILE *****   *****

To edit or key in new information, you need to remember only what are called type I, type II, and type III commands. To get to the command I and II entry area, the ENTER key should be pressed. To get to the command III area, the 3278 equivalent of the field advance (tab) key should be pressed.

Know

Full Screen Editor Type I and II Commands

Type I commands are those commands that are unique to the full screen editor, whereas *type II commands* exist for the context editor and for the full screen editor. In general, these commands are used to control the editing session. Some commands require further operands to define the function to be performed and some do not require any operands. Both type I and II commands are entered at the top of the screen in the command I and command II area. This area is identified at the top in Figure 6.4.

The type I and II commands that you should know are:

1. DELete [n|*|1|/string/]   This deletes the number of lines specified. DEL * will delete garbage that is sometimes left in an empty library member.

2. GETFILE member [first[number]]   This command is used to copy all
   name
   or part of a library member into a new member. The operand "first" represents the beginning line to be copied. The operand "number" represents the number of lines to be copied. If "first" and "number" are omitted, the entire file is copied.

3. INPUT   The INPUT command puts the terminal in input mode so that information can be entered. This command must be used after the @ED macro. INPUT is used to start keying a new library member. It causes an INPUT screen to appear. It has no operands.

4. SAVE name   The SAVE command saves what has been keyed under the name specified. It should be used after the first few lines have been keyed. Afterward, any information keyed is automatically added to the library member when the ENTER key is pressed.

5. QUIT   This command terminates editing and returns the screen to command mode. The command has no operands.

6. Scroll commands for the screen:
   BAckwards [nn|1]   where nn = number of screens back. (UP command does the same thing.)
   BOttom   (of the file)
   DOWN [n|1]   where n = number of lines down (or forward).
   (NEXT command does the same thing.)
   FOrward [nn|1]   where nn = number of screens forward.
   LEft [nn|1]   where nn = number of columns the screen is to be shifted to the left.
   RIght [nn|1]   where nn = number of columns the screen is to right.
   TOP   (of the file)
   UP [n|1]   where n = number of lines up (or back).
   ZONE [n1|1[n2|72|80]]   This restricts the effect of commands beginning with column n1 and ending with column n2. This command usually precedes a left or right shift of the screen.

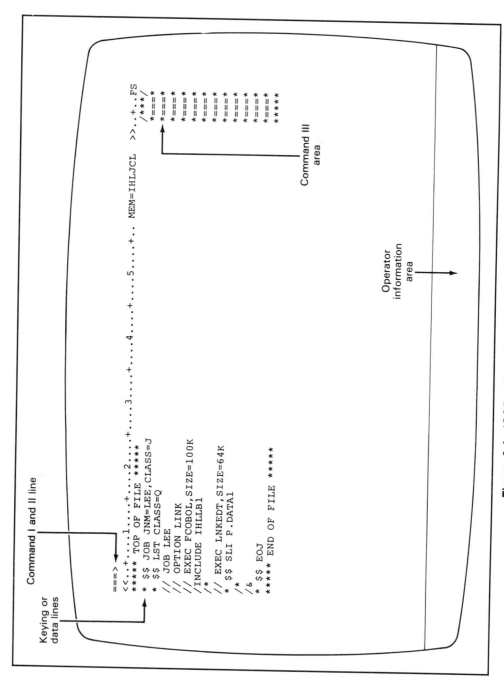

Figure 6.4 ICCF edit mode screen with JCL keyed.

Command I and II line

Keying or
data lines

```
===>
<<..+....1....+....2....+....3....+....4....+....5....+..  MEM=IHLJCL  >>..+..FS
***** TOP OF FILE *****                                                   /***/
* $$ JOB JNM=LEE,CLASS=J                                                  *====*
* $$ LST CLASS=Q                                                          *====*
// JOB LEE                                                                *====*
/// OPTION LINK                                                           *====*
// EXEC FCOBOL,SIZE=100K                                                  *====*
/INCLUDE IHLLB1                                                           *====*
/*                                                                        *====*
// EXEC LNKEDT,SIZE=64K                                                   *====*
* $$ SLI P.DATA1                                                          *====*
/*                                                                        *====*
/&                                                                        *====*
* $$ EOJ                                                                  *====*
***** END OF FILE *****                                                   *****
```

Command III
area

Operator
information
area

Know

Full Screen Editor Type III Commands

Type III commands carry out editing functions for one or more lines on the screen. They are unique to the full screen editor and are entered in the command III area at the right of the screen shown in Figure 6.4.

Some type III commands are:

1. A[nn]   where nn = number of blank lines to be *inserted*.

2. C[nn]   where nn = number of lines to be *copied*.

3. D[nn]   where nn = number of lines to be *deleted*.

4. I   indicates a point where lines are to be *inserted* with a move or copy type III command.

5. K[nn]   This is used to *keep* and stack lines from several screens to be inserted elsewhere. C is used for the first screen, and K is used for the remainder of the screens.

6. M[nn]   where nn = number of lines to be *moved*.

7. "[nn]   where nn = number of lines to be *duplicated* of the current line.

Know

Procedural and Macro Commands

One macro command has already been mentioned, @ED. *Procedures* and *macros* are ICCF library members which contain a sequence of ICCF statements that perform frequently used functions such as compilation, loading, and execution of programs, storing object programs, and sorting library members.

One difference between procedures and macros is that procedures can be used only in command mode, whereas macros can be used in edit mode. Also, macros begin with an @ sign.

Procedures and macros that you should be familiar with are:

DMAC (/ED)

1. @ED [name]   This macro places the screen in edit mode.

2. $DA   This procedure displays the current status of the VSE partitions. The activity in each partition is shown on the screen as a snapshot. To obtain continued views, the ENTER key must be pressed.

3. SORT name1 [XYYZZ] [punch name]
                 print *
     This command is used to sort *information* in a library member. One of your research problems at the end of this chapter is to determine how this command may be used.

4. SDSERV name   This command can be used to request a *sorted* directory directory display of your private library. It is often helpful in locating a name if the directory is lengthy.

5. SUBMIT name   This command submits a job stream for execution under VSE/POWER in one of the *POWER* partitions.

Job Entry Statements

Job entry statements look much like ICCF system commands in that they begin with a slash (/) followed by an op code. The difference between the two is that system commands have an immediate effect, whereas job entry statements do not take effect until a job is run.

The job entry statement that will be used in this book is the /INCLUDE name statement. This statement is used to insert library members into a job stream. The /INCLUDE statement will be used in Chapter 7.

SUMMARY

CICS is an IBM program product that allows transactions to be entered and processed at remote terminals. ICCF allows an installation to submit jobs on an interactive basis as well as a batch basis.

The ICCF partition is subdivided into partitions containing the ICCF main control program (the ICCF supervisor), the command processors (that interpret ICCF commands), the interactive partitions (IP1–IP35), and the terminal control facility program (CICS).

There are three ICCF libraries: private, public, and common libraries. Access to these libraries is controlled by an ICCF administrator. The administrator builds a user profile for each user.

Each user has a private library in which programs, data, or job control streams can be stored in library members. Members can be edited or changed by use of the full screen editor.

Three of the most frequently used ICCF modes are command mode (CM), full screen edit mode (FS), and list screen mode (LS).

System commands must be entered in command mode. These commands begin with one slash. Some of the most important are LOGON, LOGOFF, LIB, DQ, LP, PP, PUR, RENAME, RENUM, RP, SW, and TAB.

Full screen commands consist of type I, II, and III commands. Some of the most important I and II commands are DEL, GETFILE, INPUT, SAVE, QUIT, and the scroll commands. Some of the important type III commands are A, C, D, I, K, M, and ".

ICCF also has procedural and macro commands. Some of the most important are @ED, $DA, SORT, and SUBMIT. ICCF job entry statements, such as the /INCLUDE statement, begin with a slash and op code. They do not take effect until a job is run.

TERMS TO REMEMBER

CICS	Private library (ICCF)
Common library (ICCF)	Procedural command (ICCF)
Edit	Public library (ICCF)
ICCF	System command (ICCF)
ICCF administrator	Type I ICCF command
ICCF library file	Type II ICCF command
Job entry statement (ICCF)	Type III ICCF command
Macro command (ICCF)	User profile
Primary library	

STUDY GUIDE

Use ICCF manuals and class instructions provided by your instructor to answer the following questions in the space provided.

1. Write the steps necessary to sign on at a terminal in your computer center. (Assume that the terminal has been turned on.)

   /Logon user ID
   Password

2. Write the steps necessary for *you* to bring up ICCF.

   ① Logon to the network, ② Type A, ③ Enter ④ /logon userID ⑤ password

3. Write the system command necessary to display the names of the members in your private library.

   /LIB

4. Write the steps necessary to get into edit mode and obtain an INPUT screen for a new job.

   /Ed
   enter

5. (a) Assume that you have keyed a few lines in Problem 4 and wish to save these lines under the name LAB1. Write the steps necessary to do this.

   Save LAB1
   Enter

   (b) How can you look at the screen and see that this member has been saved under the name LAB1?   (/Lib full)
   It tells you what your filename is

   (c) What steps must be taken to continue keying information in this member?

   Type Information in then
   hit enter

   (d) What steps must be taken to stop working on this member and sign off?

   ① Save, ② Quit ③ /logoff

6. Assuming that you have signed on and ICCF has been brought up, write the steps necessary to bring up a library member named LAB1.

/Ec LAB1

7. Now that LAB1 is on the screen, write the commands necessary to do the following:

(a) Delete the fifth line of information on the screen.

GOTO TO Line 5 and type D in the Command III Area

(b) Move forward to the second screen.

FO1

(c) Add two lines after the fifth line on the screen.

GOTO Line 5 and type A2 on the Command III Area

(d) Copy the two lines in part (c) and insert them after the fifth line of the third screen.

GOTO to Line wanted copied in the Command II Area put C2, then goto Where you want them put

(e) Zone and shift the screen 2Ø columns to the left so that you can key information into columns 73–8Ø of a record.

Zone 02, L 7380

(f) Shift the screen back to the normal position.

Out

(g) Shift the screen forward 1Ø lines.

fo1Ø

(h) Shift the screen back 1Ø lines.

Ba1Ø

8. **(a)** Code the command to execute a job stream named CBLJCL in a VSE partition.

Submit CBJel

(b) Write the steps necessary to then display the POWER LST queue to see if the program is in the queue.

/DQ LST CBLJCL

RESEARCH PROBLEMS

1. Look up the SDSERV command in the ICCF manual and give a full explanation of its format and how it can be used. Specifically, how could it be used to sort your ICCF library member names that you see when you use the /LIB command. Write the answer in essay style on a sheet of paper.

2. Look up the TABSET command in the ICCF manual. Describe in essay style on a sheet of paper how one might set keying up for an RPGII program. Use a question mark for the tab character. Do the same for an assembler program and use a colon for the tab character.

3. Look up the ''LOCATE string'' command in the ICCF manual and give a full explanation of how it could be used when correcting or editing a COBOL or RPG program.

chapter 7

The Compilation and Execution of Jobs

INTRODUCTION

The purpose of this chapter is to:

1. Learn to code the job control necessary to compile and execute one or more source programs
2. Learn to code the job control necessary to execute a program cataloged in the core image library

Figure 7.1 shows in systems flowchart form the process necessary to compile and execute a COBOL program. The example consists of one DOS/VSE job in a POWER job. However, this DOS/VSE job is made up of the *three* job steps shown in Figure 7.1.

A *job step* or *task* is defined as the execution of a single processing program. It always begins with a // EXEC command. For FORTRAN, PL/1, or RPGII compile and execute programs, the steps would be exactly the same. These compilers, including the COBOL compiler, are on SYSRES in the core image library.

JOB CONTROL FOR COMPILING AND EXECUTING A COBOL PROGRAM

Know

Let us assume that a COBOL program has been written. In the FILE CONTROL paragraph of the ENVIRONMENT DIVISION we have

```
SELECT INV-FILE-IN
    ASSIGN TO SYS009-UR-2540R-S.
SELECT INV-FILE-OUT
    ASSIGN TO SYS010-UR-1403-S.
```

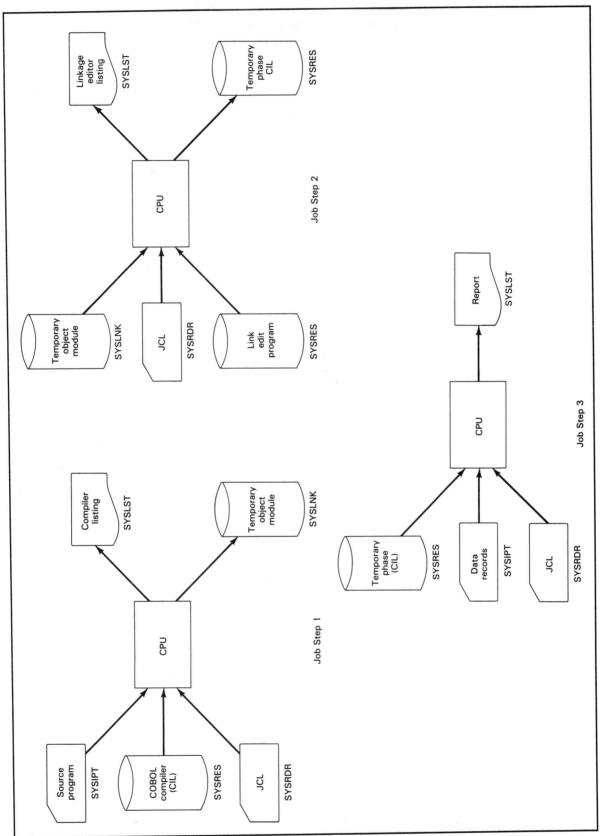

Figure 7.1 Compile and execute job.

Then Figure 7.2 shows the general plan for one COBOL compile and execute job. No tape or disk job control statements (TLBL, MTC, DLBL, EXTENT) are necessary since tape and disk are not being used. Let's examine each statement in Figure 7.2:

1. * $$ JOB JNM = LEE,CLASS = S   This statement announces the beginning of a POWER job named LEE which, according to the conventions of Chapter 2, will execute in the BG or F6 partition. (S was a class for BG and F6.)

This program has a default priority of 3, will execute without being released, and will be deleted from the RDR queue after execution.

2. * $$ LST CLASS = Q   This POWER LST statement says that the output will be held in the LST queue for viewing on the terminal. If printing without viewing were desired, a CLASS for a printer would be used (e.g., CLASS = Z).

3. // JOB LEE   This job statement announces the beginning of a DOS/ VSE job named LEE.

4. // OPTION LINK   This command temporarily overrides the system default, NOLINK, and indicates that a link-edit job step follows later in the job stream.

5. // EXEC FCOBOL,SIZE = 1ØØK   This EXEC command loads the COBOL compiler (in executable form) into main storage from the system CIL for a COBOL compilation. It indicates the beginning of the compilation and in this case, the beginning of job step 1.

If this were an RPGII program, the statement would be

```
// EXEC RPGII,SIZE=1ØØK
```

Each compiler has a unique name that is used in the // EXEC statement.

The compiler (be it COBOL, RPG, FORTRAN, PL/1, etc.) takes each source instruction and translates it into a machine language instruction. Each machine language instruction is in a number form with which the digital computer can work. The machine language instructions produced by the compiler make up an object program or object module. This object module is later processed by the linkage editor (see step 9 below).

6. CBL APOST,SXREF,STATE   This statement is unique to COBOL. It allows the programmer to alter certain options that were built into the COBOL compiler when it was written. (See Appendix B for a detailed explanation of this statement.) It says that single apostrophes should be accepted from the program rather than quotes (''); that a cross-reference listing is to be printed; and in case of an ABEND, the number of the last statement processed is to be printed.

If this were an RPGII program, the H control statement would be used in this step to alter any RPG compiler options desired. Most higher-level languages have some method of altering options built into the compiler when it was written.

Note that column 1 must be left blank before the CBL op code.

7. /INCLUDE library member name for program or * $$ SLI C.source library name.   Assume that the COBOL program has been saved in your ICCF library under the name LAB1. Then a /INCLUDE LAB1 statement would insert the program into the job stream at this point.

If the program were stored in the system source library under C.LAB1, the * $$ SLI C.LAB1 POWER statement would insert the program into the job stream at this point.

Of course, the entire COBOL source program could be keyed into the job stream at this point. But there is an advantage in *not* doing this. The advantage is that this job stream could be used again, with minor alterations, for other jobs.

8. The /* command indicates the end of the compilation task. In this case, it also signifies the end of job step 1.

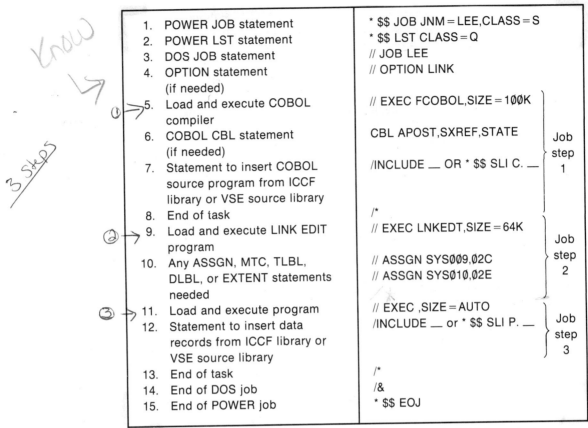

Figure 7.2   General order of COMPILE and EXECUTE job control statements.

9. // EXEC LNKEDT,SIZE = 64K   This EXEC command loads the link-edit program into main storage from the system CIL and begins the link-edit process. This fetches any I/O routines or subroutines needed by the main program from the relocatable library (RL). It then links them to the main program object module to form an executable object program. This object program is written in a temporary area on SYSRES.

10. // ASSGN SYS009,02C and // ASSGN SYS010,02E   These two assignments are necessary in this example because the COBOL program has the reader assigned to SYS009 in the COBOL SELECT statement, and it has SYS010 assigned to the printer. Note that the printer assignment is made to 02E regardless of what printer is used. POWER decides from the class in the POWER LST statement what printer to use.

It would also be possible to use generic assignments such as

```
// ASSGN SYS009,READER   or  // ASSGN SYS009,2540R
// ASSGN SYS010,PRINTER       // ASSGN SYS010,1403
```

Refer to Figure 5.6. If the COBOL SELECT statement had used SYS005 for the reader and SYS007 for the printer, these ASSGN statements would not be needed at all. Therefore, there is an advantage in knowing what the standard assignments are in your center.

11. // EXEC ,SIZE = AUTO   The EXEC statement indicates the beginning of job step 3. It loads the executable object program from a *temporary* area in the system CIL. This program is *not* cataloged in the CIL since there is no program name stated in this EXEC statement. The program execution begins. The program will read the data in step 12.

12. /INCLUDE ____ or * $$ SLI P.____   Assume that the data for this lab was saved under DATA1 in your ICCF library. Then /INCLUDE DATA1 would bring the data records from your library member into the job stream at this point.

If the data had been stored in the system source library (SL) under the name P.DATA1, the POWER command * $$ SLI P.DATA1 could be used instead of the /INCLUDE ICCF statement.

Again, it would be possible to key the data records into the job stream at this point, but such a practice limits the flexibility of your job stream use.

13. The /* command indicates that the end of file (data) and is the end of job step 3.

14. The /& command indicates the end of the *DOS/VSE* job named LEE.

15. The * $$ EOJ command indicates the end of the *POWER* job named LEE.

JOB CONTROL FOR MULTIPLE PROBLEM PROGRAMS IN A DOS/VSE JOB

The job control shown in Figure 7.2 shows three job tasks in one DOS/VSE job. It is important to note the distinction between a job and a job task. A *DOS/VSE job* is a specified group of job tasks. This may consist of several problem programs that are related. The job control example shown in Figure 7.3 would be the arrangement used if one job is dependent on another. In this case if the first program fails (aborts), the second program would not be executed. This would be the desired result if the input for the second program is dependent on the first.

A DOS/VSE job has only one JOB statement and one /& statement in the job stream. An example of two problem programs in one DOS/VSE job is shown in Figure 7.3. Note that in this example there is only one // JOB statement and one /& statement.

Let's analyze these commands in Figure 7.3:

1. * $$ JOB JNM = SMITH,CLASS = R,DISP = H   This is the beginning of a POWER job named SMITH which will run in the BG partition. The job must be released from the RDR queue to run. All other operands are defaults. That is, the priority is 3, and the job will be deleted from the RDR queue after execution.

2. * $$ LST CLASS = Z,COPY = 2   This statement assigns a class of Z to the printer (printer $02F$ in our book), and two copies are to be printed.

3. // JOB SMITH   This command announces the beginning of a DOS/VSE job named SMITH.

4. // OPTION LINK,PARTDUMP   This OPTION command is really the beginning of problem program command. There will be a link-edit; and in case of an ABEND, a part dump is desired.

5–13. These statements have the same functions as steps 5–13 in Figure 7.2. The program and data are stored in ICCF library members since the /INCLUDE statements are used. However, note step 10. Since there is only one generic ASSGN statement for the reader, this must mean that the printer has our standard assignment of SYS007 in this particular program. Note also that this program must use quotes ('') because there is no APOST operand in step 16.

```
(1)          * $$ JOB JNM=SMITH,CLASS=R,DISP=H        (Beginning of Power Job)
(2)          * $$ LST CLASS=Z,COPY=2
(3)          // JOB SMITH                BEGINNING OF A DOS/VSE JOB
(4)          // OPTION LINK,PARTDUMP      BEGINNING OF FIRST PROBLEM
(5)          // EXEC FCOBOL,SIZE=100K           PROGRAM  (compiles)
(6)          CBL STATE,SXREF
(7)          /INCLUDE INVRP1      (use loof Library)
(8)          /*         (End TASL)
(9)          // EXEC LNKEDT,SIZE=64K
(10)         // ASSGN SYS011,READER        /*
(11)         // EXEC ,SIZE=AUTO
(12)         /INCLUDE DATA1
(13)         /*                     END OF FIRST PROBLEM PROGRAM
(14)         // OPTION LINK         BEGINNING OF SECOND PROBLEM PROGRAM
(15)         // EXEC FCOBOL,SIZE=100K
(16)         CBL STATE,SXREF
(17)         * $$ SLI C.INVRP2
(18)         /*
(19)         // EXEC LNKEDT,SIZE=64K
(20)         // ASSGN SYS020,PRINTER
(21)         // EXEC ,SIZE=AUTO
(22)         * $$ SLI P.DATA2
(23)         /*                     END OF SECOND PROBLEM PROGRAM
(24)         /&                     END OF DOS/VSE JOB
(25)         * $$ EOJ                END OF POWER JOB
```

Figure 7.3   JCL for multiple problem programs in a DOS/VSE job.

14. A second OPTION statement is necessary for the second problem program. This is because any previous LINK or CATAL options are canceled after each occurrence of an EXEC statement with a *blank* operand.

15–23. Again, these statements have the same functions as steps 5–13 of Figure 7.2. However, this time the program and data must be stored in the system SL since the POWER SLI statement is used.

Note step 2∅. In the case of this second program, the reader must have the standard SYS∅∅5 assignment. The printer did not have the standard assignment, and therefore has an ASSGN statement.

JOB CONTROL FOR MULTIPLE DOS/VSE JOBS IN A POWER JOB   Option

If the two problem programs in Figure 7.3 were *independent* of each other, the coding would be as shown in Figure 7.4. In this case if the first program cancels, the second will still be processed. This implies that the programs are independent of each other.

```
(1)        * $$ JOB JNM=SMITH,CLASS=R    BEGINNING OF A POWER JOB
(2)        * $$ LST CLASS=Z,COPY=2
(3)      ⌠ // JOB SMITH1                 BEGINNING OF FIRST DOS/VSE JOB
(4)      | // OPTION LINK,PARTDUMP        BEGINNING OF FIRST PROBLEM
(5)      | // EXEC FCOBOL,SIZE=100K               PROGRAM
(6)      |   CBL STATE,SXREF
(7)      | /INCLUDE INVRP1
(8)      ⟨ /*
(9)      | // EXEC LNKEDT,SIZE=64K
(10)     | // ASSGN SYS011,READER
(11)     | // EXEC ,SIZE=AUTO
(12)     | /INCLUDE DATA1
(13)     | /*                            END OF FIRST PROBLEM PROGRAM
(14)     ⌊ /&                            END OF FIRST DOS/VSE JOB
(15)     ⌠ // JOB SMITH2                  BEGINNING OF SECOND DOS/VSE JOB
(16)     | // OPTION LINK                 BEGINNING OF SECOND PROBLEM
(17)     | // EXEC FCOBOL,SIZE=100K               PROGRAM
(18)     |   CBL STATE,SXREF
(19)     | * $$ SLI C.INVRP2
(20)     ⟨ /*
(21)     | // EXEC LNKEDT,SIZE=64K
(22)     | // ASSGN SYS020,PRINTER
(23)     | // EXEC ,SIZE=AUTO
(24)     | * $$ SLI P.DATA2
(25)     | /*                            END OF SECOND PROBLEM PROGRAM
(26)     ⌊ /&                            END OF SECOND DOS/VSE JOB
(27)       * $$ EOJ                       END OF POWER JOB
```

Figure 7.4   JCL for two DOS/VSE jobs in one POWER job.

Note that the only difference between the job streams in Figures 7.3 and 7.4 is that there are two sets of // JOB and /& statements. (See statements 3 and 14, and statements 15 and 26.) Note also that the two DOS/VSE jobs have different names SMITH1 and SMITH2. They could have the same names, but different names make it easier for you and the computer operator to monitor execution conditions.

JOB CONTROL FOR EXECUTION OF TWO DOS/VSE JOBS IN ONE POWER JOB

No compilations or link-editing is involved in this example. The programs have been cataloged in a core image library. Figure 7.5 shows the job control for executing the same two programs shown in Figure 7.4. The difference is that now the two programs are stored in a core image library.

1. * $$ JOB JNM = SMITH,CLASS = 4 This statement announces the beginning of a POWER job named SMITH which will execute in the F4 partition.

2. * $$ LST CLASS = Z,COPY = 2,JSEP = 1,DISP = H This POWER LST statement specifies that the printed output will be on the printer assigned a class of Z; two copies with one separation page will be printed; and the output will be held in the LST queue until released.

3. // JOB SMITH1 This statement announces the beginning of the first DOS/VSE job named SMITH1.

4. // OPTION PARTDUMP Note that there is *no* LINK operand in this statement. This is because the program is in executable form and no compile and/or link-edit is taking place. If no PARTDUMP were needed, the OPTION statement could be omitted entirely.

5–9. Note that there is no // EXEC FCOBOL or // EXEC LNKEDT statement in these steps. This is because no compilation and link edit functions are needed. Step 9 is the end of the first job.

10. // JOB SMITH2 This statement indicates the beginning of the second DOS/VSE job named SMITH2.

11. // LIBDEF CL,SEARCH = STUCIL The LIBDEF statement indicates that the second program INVRP2 is not in the *system* CIL as the INVRP1 program was. INVRP2 is in a DOS private CIL named STUCIL. Thus we must use the LIBDEF statement to tell the system to look in the private library, STUCIL, if it cannot find a program needed in the system CIL.

Since no LIBDEF statement was encountered when the // EXEC INVRP1 statement occurred, the program INVRP1 *must* be in the *system* CIL. The system CIL is always searched first.

```
(1)      * $$ JOB JNM=SMITH,CLASS=4
(2)      * $$ LST CLASS=Z,COPY=2,JSEP=1,DISP=H
(3)      // JOB SMITH1           BEGINNING OF FIRST DOS/VSE JOB
(4)      // OPTION PARTDUMP       BEGINNING OF FIRST PROBLEM
(5)      // ASSGN SYS011,READER        PROGRAM
(6)      // EXEC INVRP1,SIZE=AUTO
(7)      /INCLUDE DATA1
(8)      /*                      END OF FIRST PROBLEM PROGRAM
(9)      /&                      END OF FIRST DOS/VSE JOB
(10)     // JOB SMITH2           BEGINNING OF SECOND DOS/VSE JOB
(11)     // LIBDEF CL,SEARCH=STUCIL
(12)     // ASSGN SYS020,PRINTER  BEGINNING OF SECOND PROBLEM
(13)     // EXEC INVRP2,SIZE=AUTO        PROGRAM
(14)     * $$ SLI P.DATA2
(15)     /*                      END OF SECOND PROBLEM PROGRAM
(16)     /&                      END OF SECOND DOS/VSE JOB
(17)     * $$ EOJ                END OF POWER JOB
```

Figure 7.5 JCL for executing two DOS/VSE jobs in one POWER job.

Then the private library or libraries are searched in the order shown on the LIBDEF statement.

12–16.   The program INVRP2 is loaded from the private library STUCIL and is executed with data (DATA2) brought in from the source library. Step 16 is the end of the second DOS job.

17.   End of the POWER job.

SUMMARY

A DOS/VSE job is a specified group of job tasks. It begins with a // JOB statement and ends with a /& statement.

A job step or task is defined as the execution of a single processing program. It always begins with a // EXEC statement.

It is possible to have several DOS/VSE jobs in one POWER job. Such a job stream implies that each DOS job is independent of the other. Each DOS job within the POWER job begins with a // JOB statement and ends with a /& statement.

It is also possible to have several problem programs within one DOS/VSE job. This implies that each program is dependent on the other. If a preceding program is canceled, all the programs will be canceled.

TERMS TO REMEMBER

Job (DOS/VSE)   Job task

Job step

CODING EXERCISES

Assume printer assignments of Ø2F for a class of Z and Ø2E for a class of B. Assume the following partition class priorities:

BG—J, R, S, Ø   F5—5, D, E, F

F1—1   F6—J, S, 6

F2—2   F7—7

F3—3, A, B, C   F8—8

F4—4

Code the following job streams (both POWER and DOS/VSE statements) on coding sheets.

1.   Given an input device assignment of Ø2C and the following COBOL SELECT sentences:

```
SELECT INPUT-FILE, ASSIGN TO SYSØØ4-UR-254ØR-S.
SELECT OUTPUT-FILE, ASSIGN TO SYSØØ6-UR-14Ø3-S.
```

Write the job control stream to compile under the following conditions:

(a)   The job should run in either BG or F6; use printer Ø2F.

(b) It is a COBOL compilation only (no link-edit). The job control statements should not be printed. The program uses single apostrophes. Use the cross-reference listing in the CBL statement.

(c) The program is stored in an ICCF library under the name PAYROL.

2. Write exercise 1 for a compile and execute. The data is stored in an ICCF library under the name PDATA. For the CBL statement, use the options to (1) print the statement number last executed if there is an ABEND, and (2) print a cross-reference listing. Write specific assignments using printer Ø2F for the output device and Ø2C for the input device.

3. Given the following COBOL SELECT statements:

```
SELECT INV-INPUT-FILE, ASSIGN TO SYSØ13-UR-254ØR-S.
SELECT INV-OUTPUT-FILE, ASSIGN TO SYSØ14-UR-14Ø3-S.
```

Write the job stream to do a compile and execute under the following conditions:

(a) The job is to run in F5 and is to be held until released from the RDR queue.

(b) A system option of PARTDUMP is desired. Compiler options of a cross-reference listing and the last statement executed are desired. The program uses quotes ('').

(c) Printer Ø2E is to be used. Print three copies with one separator page. The input device is Ø2C.

(d) Use generic type assignments.

(e) The program and data are stored in the system SL. The program is under the name C.INVTRY and the data is under the name P.INVDAT.

4. Two COBOL programs are to be compiled and executed as two separate DOS/VSE jobs in one POWER job. The job is to be run in F8. It does not need to be released but should be kept in the RDR queue after execution. One copy of the output is desired. Printer Ø2F is to be used. The input device is Ø2C.

(a) *First program*

(1) Given the following COBOL SELECT statements:

```
SELECT COLLEGE-INPUT-FILE, ASSIGN TO SYSØ2Ø-UR-25Ø1-S.
SELECT COLLEGE-OUTPUT-FILE, ASSIGN TO SYSØ21-UR-32Ø3-S.
```

(25Ø1 is a card reader, and 32Ø3 is a printer.)

(2) The program is in an ICCF library under the name TJCTA. The program has been written using quotes (''). The data is in an ICCF library under the name JCDATA.

(3) Use generic *class* assignments.

(b) *Second program*

(1) Given the following COBOL SELECT statements:

```
SELECT EQUIPMENT-INPUT-FILE, ASSIGN TO SYSØ18-UR-25Ø1-S.
SELECT EQUIPMENT-OUTPUT-FILE, ASSIGN TO SYSØ19-UR-32Ø3-S.
```

(2) The program is in the system source library under the name C.EQLIST. The program has been written with apostrophes. The data is in the system source library under the name P.EQUIP.

(3) Use generic *type* assignments.

5. There are three parts to this exercise, which is to be keyed and run. Your instructor will give you instructions as to the partition and equipment to be used and where and under what names the program and data are stored.

   Use a comment statement after the DOS job statement giving your full name, lab number, and lab part (i.e., a, b, or c).

   Write and key the job stream to:
   (a) Compile the program in Appendix D for Chapter 7.
   (b) Compile, link edit, and execute this program using the data in Appendix D. (Make two copies of the output for this part.)
   (c) Execute this program assuming that it has been stored in the system CIL. Your instructor will give you the name it has been stored under. (There will be *no* compile and link edit.)
   Run these parts and write a report in essay style reporting:
   (a) Any problems that you had.
   (b) Why a compile was unnecessary in part (c).
   (c) Why a link edit was unneeded in parts (a) and (c).
   Turn these runs and the report in to your instructor. Keep a copy of part (b) for yourself.

RESEARCH PROBLEMS

Use a Control and Service (Systems Control Statements) manual to do the following:

1. Code, key, and *run* the *job stream* necessary to list your system's I/O assignments for *all* your partitions (see the LISTIO command). File the results in your notebook for future reference.

2. Look up the linkage editor section in the manual. Answer the following questions.
   (a) The linkage edit program itself will accept four link edit control statements. Name them and briefly describe the function of each.
   (b) What is the linkage editor control statement format?
   (c) Where should the ACTION control statement be placed and of what use might the NOMAP operand be?
   (d) Run Coding Exercise 5(b) with this statement. Compare it to the copy of Coding Exercise 5(b) that you kept and report on the differences.
   (e) If the PHASE control statement is used:
       (1) Where is it placed in the job stream, and of what use is it?
       (2) What are the restrictions on the name operand?

chapter 8

Magnetic Tape
Job Control

INTRODUCTION

When a magnetic tape reel is received in a computer center, it is assigned a unique *reel* or *volume number*. This volume number is written on a label and is affixed externally to the reel. If a tape has what is called a standard internal volume label, this volume number is also a part of an 8∅-*byte volume label* which is written at the beginning of the tape.

External labels on a reel often contain information such as how many and what types of files are on the tape, the creation date, the expiration date, and so on. Such information can also be written on internal tape labels called *header* and *trailer labels*.

TYPES OF INTERNAL TAPE LABELS

There are four possible conditions when dealing with internal tape labels. The tape may have been written with standard labels, user standard labels, nonstandard labels, or with no labels.

1. *Standard labels*. There are three types of standard labels. These are shown in Figure 8.1.
   a. The first is the 8∅-byte volume label. A *volume label* uniquely identifies a magnetic tape reel. It can be placed on a tape by the use of a tape initialization program.
   b. The second label is an 8∅-byte file or header label that precedes each file of data. Information for this label is supplied primarily by the tape label (TLBL) job control statement. Some important fields in this label are the file name, a file ID, a creation date, and an expiration date.

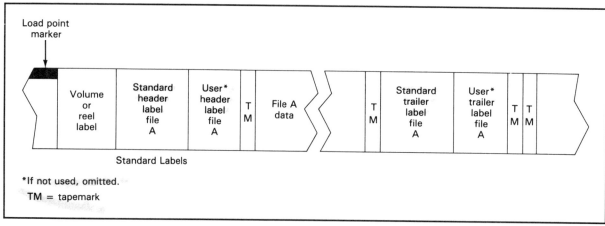

Figure 8.1   Standard tape labels.

c. The third label is an 8Ø-byte trailer label at the end of the file of
data. It is similar to the header label and is needed because tape
drives often read files as the tape moves backward.

2. *User standard labels.* It is also possible to have 8Ø-byte standard header
and trailer labels as shown in Figure 8.1. These are *file labels.* The user
must write his or her own label-checking subroutine which is called by
the main program. User labels are sometimes used for security purposes.
Since these are used in special-purpose situations, we will not use these
labels.

3. *Nonstandard labels.* These labels have no fixed format and can be any
length. Their use arises mainly when tapes must be read that have been
written on non-IBM equipment. The use and handling of these labels
are the responsibility of the user.

4. *No labels.* Unlabeled files have no labels. The beginning and end of the
file is defined by tape marks. A *tape mark* is a special character written
on a magnetic tape to indicate the beginning or end of an associated
group of records. These records may be data or label records. Magnetic
tape (MTC) job control commands must be used to write these tape
marks and position the tape for reading and writing. In the ''old days''
this was the only way of processing tape files. Figure 8.2 shows an
example of an unlabeled tape.

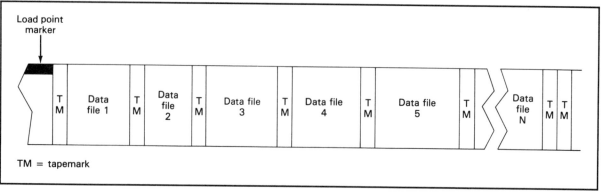

Figure 8.2   An unlabeled tape.

✳ *THE MTC STATEMENT*

The magnetic tape control command is sometimes used in standard label tape processing as well as unlabeled tape processing. It is usually used for spacing a tape backward or forward a certain number of files or records, for rewinding and/or unloading a tape, or for writing tape marks.

The format of the MTC command is shown in Figure 8.3. The meanings and possible values of the operands are as follows:

1. Op code meanings are as follows:
   BSF   Backspace one file.
   BSR   Backspace one record.
   DSE   Data security erase. This code is used only on the IBM 34ØØ series tape drives. It can be used to erase data from the current point to the end-of-tape (EOT) marker. (An *EOT* or end-of-reel (*EOR*) *marker* is a silver reflector 12 feet from the end of the tape.) If the current point is at the beginning of the tape, it will erase the beginning tape mark or volume label.
   ERG   Erase gap.
   FSF   Forward space one file.
   FSR   Forward space one record.
   REW   Rewind the tape to the load point marker. (A *load point marker* is a silver reflector 12 feet from the beginning of the tape. It indicates the beginning of the recording area.)
   RUN   Rewind and unload the tape.
   WTM   Write a tape mark.

2. cuu or SYSnnn operand. As mentioned earlier, cuu is the channel and unit number (hex address) for the device being used. SYSnnn is the symbolic device number. Either can be used to specify the tape drive.

3. nn. This represents a number from Ø1 to 99. It indicates the number of times the operation is to be performed. The default is 1.

Examples

1. Rewind a tape on drive 3ØØ.

   ```
   // MTC REW,300
   ```

2. Rewind and unload a tape on SYSØ15.

   ```
   // MTC RUN,SYS015
   ```

3. Space a tape on drive 3Ø1 forward one file; three files.

   ```
   // MTC FSF,301
   // MTC FSF,301,3
   ```

```
[//] MTC opcode,{cuu|SYSxxx}{,nn}                      (JCC,JCS)

   where opcode can be BSF,BSR,DSE,ERG,FSR,RUN,REW, or WTM
```

Figure 8.3 The MTC statement format.

4. Backspace a tape on SYSØ16, two records.

```
// MTC BSR,SYSØ16,2
```

5. Write a tapemark on a tape on SYSØ16.

```
// MTC WTM,SYSØ16
```

STANDARD LABEL TAPE PROCESSING

Standard labels are valuable for two reasons:

1. On a multifile volume (tape), data can be located automatically, thus eliminating the need of any special handling such as positioning the tape. (A *multifile volume* is a tape or disk pack that contains more than one data file.)
2. Standard labels provide file protection. If a volume number or file name in the label does not agree with the information the user supplies on the tape label (TLBL) statement, the operator is notified. This prevents accidental destruction of information.

THE VOLUME LABEL

The contents of a volume label are shown in Figure 8.4. The circled numbers at the top of the figure represent field numbers. The numbers at the bottom of the figure represent column numbers. The label is 8Ø bytes long and the contents of the fields are as follows:

Fields	Contents
1 and 2	The contents are always VOL1.
3	A six-character ID that is given to the tape when it

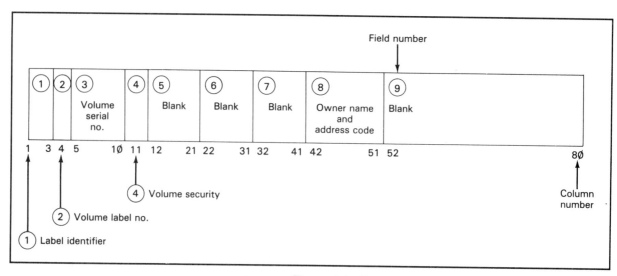

Figure 8.4 The volume label.

	is initialized. It can be composed of any letter or number or the @, $, or # signs.
4	This field is not used by DOS/VSE. Some other IBM operating systems, such as OS, use it for security protection. $\emptyset$ = no security; 1 = security protection.
5	This field is used by DASD only.
6 and 7	Not used.
8	A 10-character name can be written here when the tape is initialized. The use of this field is optional.
9	Not used.

TAPE INITIALIZATION

An IBM utility program named INTTP is provided to enable the user write a volume label (*initialize*) one or more tapes. A *utility program* is a program that performs day-to-day tasks. They usually deal with manipulating data files. These programs are provided by the computer manufacturer or software companies.

To use this program, the first tape to be initialized must be mounted on SYS$\emptyset\emptyset\emptyset$. Any additional tapes to be initialized should be assigned to SYS$\emptyset\emptyset$1–SYS$\emptyset$15.

The order of the DOS job control statements is as follows:

1. The JOB statements.
2. Any informational statements needed on mounting tapes.
3. The ASSGN statements beginning with SYS$\emptyset\emptyset\emptyset$.
4. A // EXEC INTTP,SIZE = 1$\emptyset$K statement.
5. The following utility control statement:

```
// INTT CARD,REWIND
```

This statement says that the volume label follows in an 8$\emptyset$-byte (card) image and the tape is to be rewound after the label is written.

6. The 8$\emptyset$-byte card image. Example:

```
VOL1XXXXXX
```

where XXXXXX is the volume serial number that you wish to assign.

7. The // END statement used to indicate the end of any series of utility control statements. If two or more tapes are to be initialized at the same time, a // END would follow each VOL1 card image.
8. End-of-task statement.
9. End-of-job statement. This /& statement *resets* all symbolic device assignments back to the standard assignments. If there are several problem programs in this DOS job, the /& statement cannot be used. In this case the RESET job control statement must be used to reset the device assignments.

An example of the JCL needed to initialize a tape is shown in Figure 8.5. Further options for this program are discussed in your center's utility program manual.

```
* $$ JOB JNM=LEE,CLASS=J
* $$ LST CLASS=Q
// JOB LEE
*          INITIALIZE TAPE ON DRIVE 300
// PAUSE    LEE, MOUNT TAPE ON DRIVE 300
// ASSGN SYS000,300
// EXEC INTTP,SIZE=10K
// INTT CARD,REWIND
VOL1IHL251
// END
/*
/&
* $$ EOJ
```

Figure 8.5   Initialize tape JCL.

THE PAUSE STATEMENT

Notice the fourth and fifth statements, the comment and // PAUSE statements, shown in Figure 8.5. The comment statement is one of the two ways for giving information that we have discussed previously. It simply says that this job task is initializing a tape.

The fifth statement is a PAUSE statement. The format for the PAUSE statement is shown in Figure 8.6.

For a JCS *statement*, the PAUSE statement causes a pause immediately after processing the statement. For a JCC statement, the PAUSE *command* causes a pause at the end of the current job step.

In the case shown in Figure 8.5, there is a pause for the operator to determine if a tape has been mounted on drive 3ØØ. If it has not, the operator is given a chance to mount the tape and press the ENTER key on the console. Or if desired, the operator could cancel the run. Of course, to save time, the operator should already have the tape mounted. But if a mistake has been made, the use of the PAUSE statement gives the operator a chance to correct the error.

In summary, the PAUSE statement provides information and gives the operator a chance to take some action if necessary.

FILE LABELS

The plan shown in Figure 8.7 is for a standard header or trailer label. The circled numbers at the top of the figure represent field numbers. The numbers at the bottom of the figure represent column numbers. The contents of the fields are listed below.

Field number	Contents
1	HDR for header label; EOF for trailer label; EOV for end-of-volume label.
2	Always 1.

```
[//] PAUSE [any user comment]                    (JCS,JCC)
```

Figure 8.6   The PAUSE statement format.

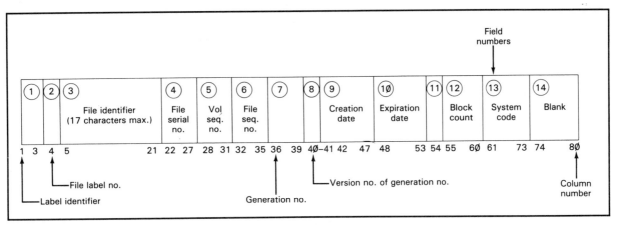

Figure 8.7 A file label.

3	A 17-character or less file identifier, which has nothing to do with the program file names.
4	A file serial number. This is the *volume serial number* given to the tape when it is initialized.
5	A four-byte volume sequence number, usually 1. In multivolume files, the number is increased by 1. A *multivolume file* is a file that requires more than one tape or disk. The number in this field would prevent an operator from mounting the second volume before the first.
6	A four-byte file sequence number. This number increases by one on a multifile volume.
7	A four-byte file generation or edition number. If used, this number could indicate an update number (grandfather, father, son concept). Another example would be using it for a month number during a payroll year.
8	A two-byte file version number. This number could identify a file within a generation. For example, it could represent a week number within a month.
9	A creation date. When the file is created, the system extracts the date from the communications region and writes it in this field in *Julian date* form. (YY/DDD)
1Ø	An expiration date. A Julian date that indicates when the file is inactive and may be deleted by overwriting. Before the expiration date, the operating system notifies the operator that an attempt is being made to overwrite an unexpired file, allowing cancellation if a mistake has been made.
11	File security code. This one-byte field is not used by DOS/VSE. It is used in some other operating systems, such as OS. For other systems if the content is 1, it indicates security protection. Other information must then be supplied before the file can be processed.

12	Block count. This six-byte field is used only for trailer labels. It gives the total number of (logical) records in a file. It can be used as a hash total to be sure that all records have been read. In header labels, this field is all zeros.
13	System code. This 13-byte field indicates the programming system in use when the label was written. This code might be helpful in an installation where several programming systems are in use.
14	Not used.

✗ THE TAPE LABEL (TLBL) COMMAND

The TLBL statement gives file information for checking and writing file (header and trailer) labels. The label information given in this statement is read and stored in an area, usually on SYSRES, called the *label information area*. The format is shown in Figure 8.8.

Items of information given by the operands in this statement are placed in the header and trailer labels for the file. The operands are:

1. *A filename.* This name can be one to seven alphameric characters, the first of which must be alphabetic. In RPGII, this filename is given on the file description specification form. In assembly language, the filename is given in the name field of the DTF (define the file) statement.

   In COBOL there are two filename possibilities. They are shown in the following examples. In the first,

   ```
   SELECT PAYROLL-INPUT-FILE,
        ASSIGN TO SYS008-UT-3430-S-PAYROLL.
              ↳(tape drive)        ↳(file name)
   ```

   the first operand on the TLBL statement should be PAYROLL.
   In the second,

   ```
      SELECT PAYROLL-INPUT-FILE, ASSIGN TO SYS008-UT-3430-S
   ```

   the filename has been omitted in the ASSIGN clause. For *COBOL only*, the filename then defaults to the symbolic device number. In this case it defaults to SYS008 and SYS008 is used as the filename.

2. *'File-ID'*. This operand can be 1 to 17 alphameric characters enclosed in apostrophes. If this operand is omitted for output files, the default is the filename used in the first operand.

3. *Date.* For output files this may be:
   a. A retention period in days in the form DDDD, where DDDD may range from 0 to 9999, *or*

```
                                                              (JCS)

// TLBL filename,['file-ID'],[date],[file-serial-number],
        [volume-sequence-number],[file-sequence-number],
        [generation-number],[version-number][,DISP={NEW|OLD|MOD}]
```

Figure 8.8 The TLBL statement format for EBCDIC files.

b. An absolute Julian expiration date in the form YY/DDD, where YY is the last two digits of the year (19∅∅–1999) and DDD ranges from ∅–366 (366 in the case of leap year). DOS/VSE versions 2 and 3 now allow an absolute expiration date of 19YY/DDD or 2∅YY/DDD. YY/DDD defaults to 19YY/DDD. 2∅YY/DDD is not accepted for diskette files. *If this operand is omitted on an output file, it defaults to ∅ days.*

For input files, the date is of the form above. However, this operand on input checks the *creation* date, which was taken from the communications region and written on the tape header label when the file was created. If this date does not match the tape label creation date, processing is interrupted and a message is issued.

If the date is omitted on an input file, no checking takes place.

4. *File-serial-number.* Despite a different name, this is the volume serial number given to the tape when it was initialized. If it is omitted for an input file, no label checking is done.

These four operands are often all that is coded. Notice in the TLBL format in Figure 8.8 that the filename is really the only operand that is required. Coding only the first operand is sometimes done for *input files*. In this case, no label checking takes place for this file.

The remaining operands, volume-sequence-number, file-sequence-number, generation-number, and version-number, were discussed in the file label section. The default is 1 in all cases.

A new operand, DISP = *NEW*|OLD|MOD, has been added with the advanced functions addition to DOS/VSE. This operand applies only to assembler programs written under the VSE/Advanced Functions release. This is a very specialized operand. For example, the file cannot have a header or trailer label, and it must be the only file in the volume. We will not be using this operand.

TLBL CODING EXAMPLES

EXAMPLE 8.1

Given the following COBOL tape SELECT statement for an output file:

```
SELECT STUDENT-OUTPUT-FILE, ASSIGN TO SYS∅1∅-UT-24∅∅-S-
                    STROLL.
```

The file ID is SPRING 88 ROLL. The volume serial number is 163824. The file should expire on March 23, 1989. Use default values for the volume-sequence-number, the file-sequence-number, the generation number, and the version number.

Answer

```
// TLBL STROLL,'SPRING 88 ROLL',89/∅82,163824
```

EXAMPLE 8.2

Given the following COBOL tape SELECT statement for an input file:

```
SELECT PAYROLL-INPUT-FILE, ASSIGN TO SYS∅∅8-UT-24∅∅-S.
```

The volume serial number is PAY001, and the expiration date is 125 days after the file is created. The generation number is 2. The file ID is Jan 88 PAYROLL. Take the default on all other operands.

Answer

```
// TLBL SYS008,'JAN 88 PAYROLL',125,PAY001,,,2
```

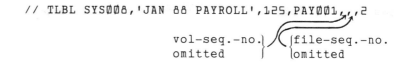

```
                    vol-seq.-no.    file-seq.-no.
                    omitted         omitted
```

EXAMPLE 8.3

Write a complete job stream to initialize a tape to 000001. Then in the same DOS/VSE job, compile and execute a COBOL program named CDTP, which is in an ICCF library. Data records are in an ICCF library under the name CTDATA. The program reads card image records and writes them on a magnetic tape with a volume serial number of 000001. The program SELECT statements are

```
SELECT INPUT-FILE, ASSIGN TO SYS008-UR-2540R-S.
SELECT OUTPUT-FILE, ASSIGN TO SYS020-UT-8809-S.
```

The expiration date should be December 31, 1989. The file ID should be 89 INVENTORY. The output file is version 2 of generation 5. The input device is 02C.

Answer

```
* $$ JOB JNM=LEE,CLASS=J
* $$ LST CLASS=Z
// JOB LEE
// PAUSE                      JOB LEE, MOUNT NEW TAPE ON
                              DRIVE 301
// ASSGN SYS000,301
// EXEC INTTP,SIZE=10K        INITIALIZE TAPE JOB TASK
// INTT CARD,REWIND
VOL1000001
// END
// RESET SYS000
// OPTION LINK
// EXEC FCOBOL,SIZE=100K       COMPILE CDTP TASK
 CBL APOST,STATE
/INCLUDE CDTP
/*
// EXEC LNKEDT,SIZE=64K
// ASSGN SYS008,02C (or // ASSGN SYS008,2540R)  INPUT DATA
// ASSGN SYS020,301 (or // ASSGN SYS020,8809,VOL=000001)
                                                 OUTPUT TAPE
// TLBL SYS020,'89 INVENTORY',89/365,000001,,,5,2
// EXEC ,SIZE=AUTO           EXECUTE PROGRAM
/INCLUDE CTDATA
/*
// MTC RUN,SYS020            REWIND AND UNLOAD OUTPUT TAPE
/&
* $$ EOJ
```

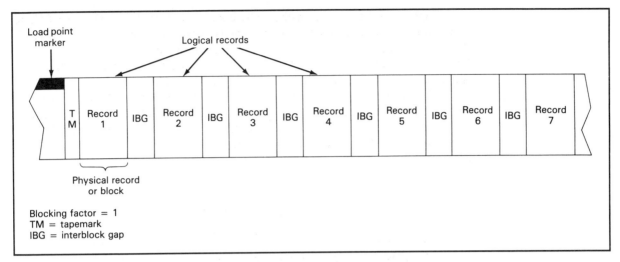

Figure 8.9 An unblocked tape.

⭐LOGICAL AND PHYSICAL RECORD REVIEW

Logical records are composed of fields of related data. If for each program write command, a logical record is written on tape, the records appear as shown in Figure 8.9. Each logical record forms a *block* that is separated by what is called an *interrecord gap* or *interblock gap*.

If more than one logical record is written per program write command, the tape is said to be blocked. A blocked tape is shown in Figure 8.1∅. This tape has a *blocking factor* of 4 because there are four logical records per block. A synonym for a block is a *physical record*. Tape drives read and write blocks or physical records. If a tape is unblocked, there is only one logical record per block.

Records on tapes are blocked:

1. To get more data on a tape reel. (There are fewer interblock gaps.)
2. To speed up I/O. (With just one read command, more data can be read in for processing.)

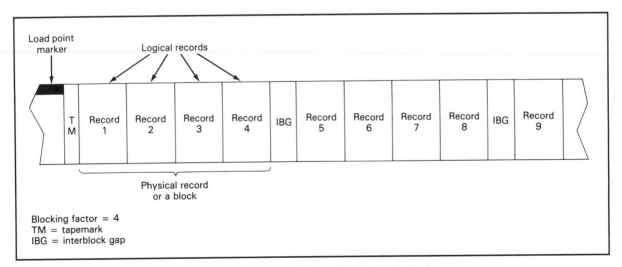

Figure 8.10 A blocked tape.

Tapes may be written in the BCD code (seven-track tapes), the EBCDIC code (nine- or 18-track tapes), or the ASCII code. The tapes may be written in different *densities* or *bytes per inch* (*bpi*). Present-day common densities are 16ØØ and 625Ø bpi. However, the IBM 348Ø tape drive writes in 38,ØØØ bpi. The higher the density, the more data that can be written on the tape.

The BCD code is a six-bit code. These six bits plus a *check* or *parity bit* form a character—thus the *seven-track tape*. *The EBCDIC code* is an eight-bit code. These eight bits plus a check or parity bit form a character—thus the *nine-track tape*. The IBM 348Ø tape drive writes an 18-track tape (two EBCDIC characters).

SUMMARY

The most common way of processing tapes is either with standard labels or no labels. If tapes are processed with no labels, the MTC command must be used to write tape marks and position the tape for reading and writing.

The three types of standard labels are:

1. *The volume label.* This 8Ø-byte label is at the beginning of the tape. It begins with VOL1 and has a unique volume serial number as the second field. A tape can be initialized by the INTTP (initialize tape) program.
2. *The header label.* This label is at the beginning of each file of data. Information for this label is given by a TLBL job control statement.
3. *The trailer label.* This label repeats much of the information in the header label. It has a block count field giving the number records in the file.

Important fields in the header and trailer labels are a filename, a file-ID, an expiration date, and an volume serial number. Volume sequence, file sequence, generation, and version numbers can also be specified.

The PAUSE job control statement can be used to give information and allow the operator to take some action.

The MTC statement is used primarily to position tapes and write tapemarks. Important abbreviations and meanings to remember are WTM, FSF, FSR, BSF, BSR, REW, and RUN.

The TLBL job control statement is used to give information for file header and trailer labels.

A logical record is a collection of fields of data. If a tape is blocked, it has more than one logical record per block or physical record. The blocking factor is the number of logical records per block. Blocking speeds up I/O and saves space on tape due to fewer IBGs. IRGs or IBGs separate blocks of data.

TERMS TO REMEMBER

BCD code	EOT marker
Block	File label
Blocking factor	Header label
BPI	Initialize
Byte	Interblock gap
Density	Interrecord gap
EBCDIC code	Julian date
EOR marker	Label information area

Load point marker
Logical record
Multifile volume
Multivolume file
Nine-track tape
Parity bit
Physical record

Seven-track tape
Standard labels
Tape mark
Trailer label
Volume label
Volume serial number

STUDY GUIDE

Answer the following questions in the space provided.

1. State two advantages of using standard internal tape labels.

   (a) _data can be located automatically_

   (b) _provide file protection_

2. Name the three standard labels and tell where each is located.

	Label	Location
(a)	Volume	first on a tape tape
(b)	Header	next to 80 bytes following record
(c)	Trailer	next 80 bytes following record

3. Give the purpose of the following job control statements.

   (a) ASSGN _Assigns a system #_

   (b) TLBL _Information for checking + writing file label_

   (c) MTC _Spacing a tape backward or forward a certain # of records or files_

   (d) PAUSE _Causes a pause immediately after processing this statement_

   (e) RESET _Reset the device assignments_

4. Given the following TLBL statement:

   ```
   // TLBL INVFILE,'MAR 89 INVENTORY',,,INV001,,,,0002,03
   ```

   In this statement:

   (a) The file name is _INVFILE_ (what).

   (b) The expiration date is _mar 89_ (when).

   (c) INV001 is the _Serial number_ (what).

   (d) The file sequence number is _001_ (what).

   (e) 0002 represents _Generation Version_ (what).

5. Give the meaning of the following magnetic tape op code operands.

   (a) BSF _Back Space one file_

   (b) WTM _Write a tape mark_

   (c) RUN _Rewind & unload Tape_

   (d) FSR _Forward one file record_

6. Given the following command:

   ```
   // MTC FSF,300,3
   ```

   Fill in the blanks about the statement above.

   (a) FSF means _any forward space file_ (what).

   (b) 300 represents _Sys # (iw)_ (what).

   (c) 3 represents _How many Records_ (what).

7. Explain what initializing a tape does.

   writes a volume label

8. What is the name of the tape initialization program that we used in this chapter? _INTP_

9. List below the following information for equipment in *your* computer center:

Tape drive name and number	Density (BPI)	Number of tracks (7, 9, or 18)	How tape is mounted (horizontal, vertical, or cartridge)

CODING EXERCISES

Code the following job control on coding sheets. Code commands to do the following:

1. Rewind a tape on drive 301.
2. Rewind and unload a tape on drive 300.
3. Write a tapemark on a tape on symbolic device number 8.
4. Forward space a tape to the beginning of the fourth file. The tape is on symbolic drive number 12.
5. Backspace a tape on drive 300 one record.
6. Return symbolic device number 1 to its standard assignment.
7. Cause a pause with a comment to mount payroll tape for March 87 on drive 300.

8. Code an assign and tape label statement given the following information:

```
SELECT LIFE-INS-OUTPUT-FILE, ASSIGN TO SYS016-UT-8809-S-
                       LIFEINS.
```

The file ID is SP 87 LIFE INS, and the volume serial number is 001987. The expiration data is 365 days after the date it is created. The generation number is 1 and the version number is 2. Defaults should be used for the volume and file sequence numbers.

9. Code the assign and tape label statements given the following information:

```
SELECT CE-FILE-OUT, ASSIGN TO SYS008-UT-3420-S.
```

The file is to expire on February 10, 1989. The volume serial number is CE8901. Use defaults for all other operands.

10. Code the job control stream to initialize two tapes mounted on drives 300 and 301 with volume serial numbers of PAY001 and PAY002, respectively. Use partition 6 and a printer with a class of Z. Use a PAUSE statement for operator instructions.

11. Code the job control stream given the following information:

```
SELECT CARD-INPUT-FILE, ASSIGN TO SYS011-UR-2540R-S.
SELECT TAPE-INPUT-MASTER-FILE, ASSIGN TO SYS009-UT-8809-S.
SELECT TAPE-OUTPUT-MASTER-FILE, ASSIGN TO SYS010-UT-8809-S.
```

The old master file can be on any drive and has an expiration date of July 30, 1989, a volume serial number of PAY001, a file ID of PAY MASTER, a generation number of 7, and a version number of 1.

The new master file can be on any drive and should have an expiration date of August 31, 1989, a volume serial number of PAY002, a file ID of PAY MASTER, a generation number of 7, and a version number of 2.

The COBOL program is stored in the CIL under the name PAYROLL. Use a pause statement and message. The card image data is in the SL under the name P.AUG89. Use the same partition and printer as in Exercise 10.

12. This exercise is to be keyed and actually run. Your instructor will give you directions as to the partition and equipment to be used and where and under what names the programs and data are stored. You will need to mount a tape before running this job. Use a comment statement after the DOS/VSE job statement giving your full name and chapter and problem number.

The three jobs below are to be done in *one* POWER job and *one* DOS job.

(a) *First job*. Set up the job control to initialize a tape. The volume serial number should be III001, where III represents your initials. Use a PAUSE statement giving instructions on mounting the tape. Remember to reset to standard assignments at the end of this job task.

(b) *Second job*. Compile and link edit the card image-to-tape program in Appendix D and use the data in Appendix D.

(c) *Third job*. Compile and link edit the tape-to-printer program in Appendix D. Write a report in essay style, including the following items:
   (1) Any problems that you had.
   (2) An explanation of why no data records were brought in from the source library in the third job.
   (3) An explanation of why these jobs should all be in *one* DOS/VSE job rather than *three* separate DOS/VSE jobs in a POWER job.

RESEARCH PROBLEMS

Use a Control and Service (Systems Control Statements) manual to answer the following questions. Use an essay style.

1. Look up the PAUSE statement and explain the AR form of it.
2. Look up the MTC statement. Explain precautions that should be taken if the MTC DSE command is used at the load point. Why might the MTC ERG command be needed?
3. Given the job control *command:*

$$\text{ASSGN SYS010,300}$$

   (a) Look up the ASSGN statement and explain from your reading how long the assignment above is in effect.
   (b) Explain the TEMP|PERM operand. Give an example of its use in making the command above temporary.
4. Look up the CLOSE job control statement.
   (a) What is the purpose of this statement?
   (b) Copy the format of the JCS statement.
   (c) What is actually written on tape when this command is used?

Use a utility or System Management Guide manual. Look up the initialize tape program and answer the following questions.

5. What are the two options possible to create standard tape labels? Which option would you use for a volume serial number of INV001?
6. Must SYSIPT and SYSLOG be assigned? Did you assign them in Coding Exercise 12? Why or why not?
7. On the INTT utility control statement:
   (a) Must the parameters be specified in the order stated?
   (b) What is the definition of a parameter? Look it up if you do not know.
   (c) How are optional parameters handled if you wish to omit one?
   (d) What does the A parameter indicate? What happens if it is omitted?
   (e) Why did we not use the parameter SERIAL?
   (f) How many tapes can be initialized in one job at your computer center? (*Hint:* How many tape drives do you have?)

chapter 9

Magnetic Disk Job Control

INTRODUCTION

Four main types of direct-access storage are used on mainframe computers: floppy disks or diskettes, magnetic (hard) disk, magnetic drum, and mass storage systems. It has already been shown how diskette I/O is handled with the use of the POWER RDR statement. IBM does not use magnetic drum, although some computer companies still do.

In this chapter we deal with magnetic disk job control.

⭐ FILE ORGANIZATION AND PROCESSING REVIEW

File organization is the method used for arranging data records when the file is originally built or loaded on a storage device.

There are three types of *native file organization*. By native, we mean original to the first DOS release. The following are the native types of file organization:

1. *Sequential organization.* A *sequentially organized file* is established by arranging records on a storage media in the physical sequence that they will be processed. Sometimes, but not always, the records are in sequential order by a key.

Card, printer, and tape files are always organized sequentially; and DASD files may be so organized. The disadvantage of this type of organization is that to reach the one-hundredth record the preceding 99 records must be processed to reach it. However, it is a very effective type of file organization for *highly active, volatile files*.

2. *Indexed organization.* An *indexed sequential file* is established by loading the records in the file sequentially by a *key* and establishing at least two indices as the file is loaded. The location of a record in the file can be determined from the indices.

This method is good for low-activity files where information is needed immediately.

3. *Direct file organization.* A *direct file* is established by a nonsequential organization method in which each record is located by (a) an algorithm or (b) a relative record number.

An *algorithm* is a finite set of rules (a formula) for the solution of a problem.

A *relative record number* (*RRN*) is a number that indicates the location of a logical record, expressed as a difference with respect to a base address.

The direct method is also good for low-activity files where information is needed immediately. It is used for files whose characteristics do not permit sequential organization. The disadvantage of this method is that the user is primarily responsible for the program logic necessary to locate a record.

An *access method* is the technique used for moving data from an I/O device to storage, and vice versa. Sequential, indexed sequential, and direct files are frequently referred to as *SAM* (sequential access method), *ISAM* (indexed sequential access method), and *DAM* (direct-access method) files.

The term file processing means the act of retrieving, updating, and adding records to a file.

1. A *record addition* takes place when a new record is added to an already established master file.
2. A *record deletion* takes place when a record is physically removed or marked for deletion from an established master file.
3. A *record update* takes place when a change is made for some or all of the information in a record.

The two types of *file processing* are:

1. *Sequential processing.* Sequential processing occurs when each record is examined and processed in the order in which it was loaded.
2. *Random processing.* Random processing occurs when the user supplies the program with a key or disk address to locate the specified record to be retrieved.

DISK DRIVE CLASSIFICATION

Disk drives are classified in several ways. One way that is of importance in job control work is the classification as a CKD or FBA device.

A *count key data* (*CKD*) *device* is one in which data is accessed by a cylinder and track number. (A *cylinder* is that portion of a disk pack accessible by one movement of the read/write arm. A *track* is that portion of a disk pack accessible to one read/write head.) An example of a CKD device and its cylinders and tracks is shown in Figure 9.1.

A *fixed block architecture* (*FBA*) *device* is one in which data is accessed by a block number.

DISK LABELS

DASD files require standard labels, unlike magnetic tape files. As with standard magnetic tape labels, disk has a volume label; and each file has file labels.

The standard file labels for all files on a volume are stored together in a specific area on the disk pack. This area is called a *VTOC* (*Volume Table of Contents*); it is a directory.

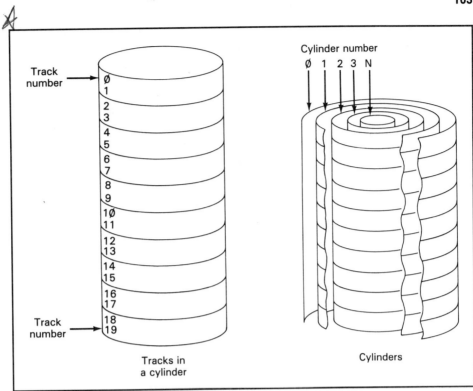

Track number → Ø 1 2 3 4 5 6 7 8 9 1Ø 11 12 13 14 15 16 17 18 19 ← Track number

Tracks in a cylinder

Cylinder number
Ø 1 2 3 N

Cylinders

Figure 9.1 Disk cylinders and tracks.

On CKD devices it is located within one cylinder of the device. On many models, the VTOC is on the first cylinder (cylinder Ø) of the device, although it can be elsewhere. On FBA devices it is within a specific number of blocks.

On disk there are four types of file labels: format 1, 2, 3, and 4 labels. These types will be discussed in the applicable section. Briefly, they are:

1. *Format 1 label*. The format 1 label is the primary label for a file and is similar to the tape header label. It describes where the data is located on the disk pack. This label is discussed in the sequential file label section.

2. *Format 2 label*. The format 2 label is used for ISAM files to describe the location of the cylinder index. This index is discussed in the ISAM file review section.

3. *Format 3 label*. The format 3 label is used if a file occupies more than three separate disk areas.

4. *Format 4 label*. The format 4 label is used to define the VTOC area. It is used when the disk is initialized or given a volume serial number.

The areas occupied on disk are called extents. An *extent* is a continuous area on disk defined by an upper and a lower limit. This limit may be described by a cylinder and track number for a CKD device or by a block number for a FBA device.

The Volume Label

Figure 9.2 shows the contents of a disk volume label. The circled numbers at the top of the figure indicate the field number. The numbers at the bottom of the

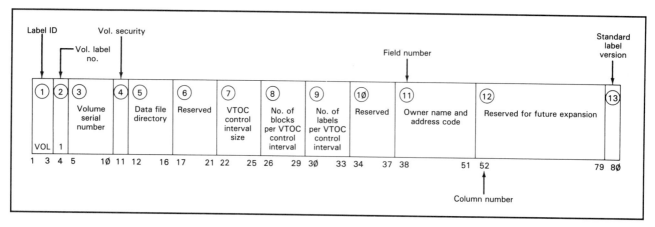

Figure 9.2 The standard disk volume label.

figure indicate the column numbers for each field. An explanation of the fields follows:

Field Number	Contents
1	VOL
2	1
3	Volume serial number given to the disk when it is initialized.
4	Volume security. This field is not used by DOS/VSE. Some operating systems use it. In this case, $\emptyset$ = no security and 1 = security protected.
5	Data file directory. This field gives the disk address of the VTOC address.
6	Reserved for future use (contains blanks).
7	Control interval (CI) size for the VTOC. The term "control interval" is discussed in Chapter 10.
8	The number of blocks per control interval.
9	The number of labels per CI.
1$\emptyset$	Reserved.
11	Owner name and address. The use of this field is optional, as it was with the tape volume label.
12	Reserved (contains blanks).
13	Standard label version. 1 = a FBA device and $\emptyset$ = a non-FBA device.

IBM provides a utility program, INTDK, that is used to initialize a disk pack. Once a disk pack is initialized, it is seldom reinitialized as in the case of magnetic tapes. Therefore, disk initialization is more a computer operator's duty than a duty of the programmer. For this reason, the JCL needed for disk initialization will not be discussed in this book.

Sequential File Labels

The file label used to describe sequential disk files is the format 1 label shown in Figure 9.3. Many of the fields shown in this label are similar to the fields in tape

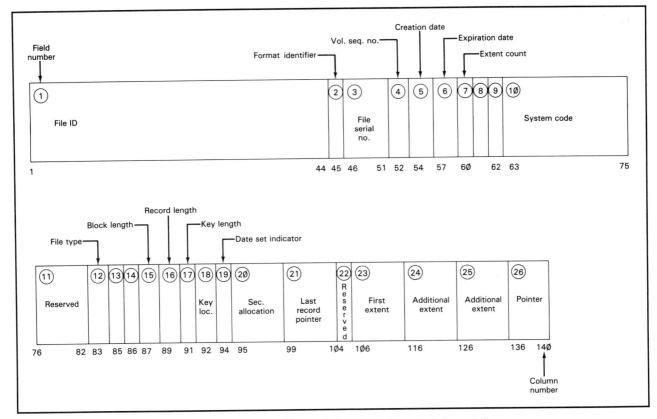

Figure 9.3 DASD file label, format 1.

header and trailer file labels. However, this is a more complex label. The fields of major importance are listed below.

Field Number	Contents
1	File-ID. A 44-character alphameric field which is a file identifier. It has nothing to do with the program name files.
2	Format identifier. This field indicates if the label is a format 1, 2, or 3 format label.
3	File serial number. This is the volume serial number given to the disk pack when it is initialized.
4	Volume sequence number. In multivolume files, this number is increased by 1. The default is 1.
5	Creation date in Julian date form.
6	Expiration date in Julian date form.
7	An extent count. This field indicates the number of extents used for this file.
8	System code. This code indicates the type of operating system used.
9	File type. This code indicates if the file organization is sequential, indexed sequential, or direct.
1Ø–26	These fields contain record and block lengths, describe extents, and so on.

THE DLBL STATEMENT

first, most import(ant)

The DLBL statement is used to provide disk file label information. The format is shown in Figure 9.4. Continuation lines are allowed for this statement by coding a nonblank character in column 72 and continuing on column 16 or to the right on the next line. Even though this statement has some keyword operands, a comma must be used for any omitted operands.

The DLBL statement operands are as follows:

Comes from Select. Statement

1. Filename   The filename can be one to seven alphameric characters, the first of which must be alphabetic. If a filename exists at the end of the COBOL ASSIGN clause, this is the name that is used. Otherwise, it defaults to the symbolic device number used *in the program* for this file.

Comes from user (supplies)

2. File-ID   This operand can be from 1 to 44 alphameric characters enclosed in apostrophes. As with the TLBL statement if this operand is omitted, the default is the filename.

USER Experation Date

3. Date   This is an expiration date in the form of:
   a. A retention period in days in the form DDDD, where DDDD may range from ∅ to 9999, *or*
   b. An absolute Julian expiration date in the form YY/DDD, where YY is the last two digits of the year (19∅∅–1999) and DDD ranges from ∅ to 366 (366 in the case of leap year). DOS/VSE versions 2 and 3 allow an absolute expiration date of 19YY/DDD or 2∅YY/DDD. YY/DDD defaults to 19YY/DDD. 2∅YY/DDD is not accepted for diskette files.
   If this operand is omitted on an output file, a seven-day retention period is assumed (from the IPL date). If this operand is present for an input file, it is ignored.

4. Code   This operand indicates the type of file label as follows:
   SD = sequential file. *This is the default.*
   DA = direct file.
   DU = diskette file.
   ISC = indexed sequential file that is being loaded or created.
   ISE = indexed sequential file that is already loaded and is being processed.
   VSAM = a virtual storage access method file. This type of file will be discussed in Chapter 1∅.

Security

5. Data secured file (DSF)   This operand, when used for an output file, creates a data-secured file. Later, when this file is accessed, a warning message is given to the operator. The operator can then decide if file access should be allowed.

6. BUFSP=n   This buffer space operand is not used for native files.

7. CAT=filename   This catalog operand is not used for native files.

8. BLKSIZE=n   This blocksize operand is valid only for sequentially organized native files on CKD devices. It allows one to specify a more efficient

```
                                                                    (JCS)

// DLBL  filename,['file-ID'],[date],[codes][,DSF]
       [,BUFSP=n][CAT=filename][,BLKSIZE=n]
       [CISIZE=n][,DISP=disposition][,RECORDS=n]
       [,RECSIZE=N]
```

Figure 9.4   The DLBL statement format.

blocksize than that specified in the program. (You will recall that in Chapter 8 we said that data is read by blocks or physical records.)

For fixed-length blocked records in an input file, n must be a multiple of the value used in the RECSIZE operand. For output files, n must = 8 + a multiple of the RECSIZE. Also, n must be ≤ 65,536.

9. CISIZE=n   The control interval size operand is used only for native sequential files on FBA devices. It is used to alter a programmed CISIZE to improve space utilization.

On FBA devices, data is *not* read by blocks. It is transferred by *control intervals*. A control interval can be 512-byte blocks or a string of 512-byte blocks. Restriction: 512 ≤ n ≤ 32,768 bytes and n must be a multiple of the FBA block size. If n is > 8K, n must be a multiple of 2K.

10. DISP=disposition   This operand is *not* used for native files.

11. RECORDS=n   This operand is *not* used for native files.

12. RECSIZE=n   The RECSIZE operand is *not* used for native files.

Normally for native files, only the first four operands are coded: the filename, file-ID, expiration date, and a file label type code. Since the file label type code default is SD, the fourth operand is sometimes omitted also. Occasionally the DSF, BLKSIZE, and CISIZE operands are used for native files.

EXAMPLE 9.1

Code a DLBL statement given the following COBOL SELECT statement:

```
SELECT OUTPUT-FILE, ASSIGN TO SYS008-UT-3350-S.
```

The file-ID for the sequential file is MAR 1988 INVENTORY MASTER FILE, and the expiration date is 50 days from the creation date.

Answer

```
// DLBL SYS008,'MAR 1988 INVENTORY MASTER FILE',50
```

(symbolic) filename   File ID   Date (Expiration)

Note that SD could follow the 50 operand, but it is the default.

EXAMPLE 9.2

Using the same SELECT statement and information as given in Example 9.1, code a DLBL statement for a direct file.

Answer

```
// DLBL SYS008,'MAR 1988 INVENTORY MASTER FILE',50,DA
```

(Symbolic) filename   file ID   Date (Expiration)   Code

EXAMPLE 9.3

Given the same SELECT statement and information as given in Example 9.2, code a DLBL statement but with the default expiration date.

Answer

```
// DLBL SYS008,'MAR 1988 INVENTORY MASTER FILE',,DA
```

(Symbolic) filename   file ID   code

Note: This means that the expiration date is seven days from the creation date.

ISAM FILE REVIEW

The parts of an ISAM file, except for a master index, are shown in Figure 9.5. The distinguishing characteristic of an indexed sequential file is that it has *indices* to help locate a record. An outline of the ISAM file arrangement would be:

1. Master index
2. Cylinder index
3. Prime data area
   a. Track index
   b. Prime data
   c. Cylinder overflow
4. Independent overflow

Examining each of these parts:

1. A *master index* is an *optional* index that contains the key (track address), which points to a track in the cylinder index. It is used only on an extremely large file (i.e., the cylinder index is longer than four tracks).

   It must be located on a cylinder separate from the prime data area and has a minimum length of one track. The location of the master index is described by a job control EXTENT statement.

2. A *cylinder index* contains the highest key for each cylinder used for an ISAM file. It also contains the disk address of the first track in the corresponding cylinder. This index has a minimum length of one track.

   It must be located on a cylinder separate from the prime data area. If a master index exists, it must follow it in location. The location of the cylinder index is also described by a job control EXTENT statement.

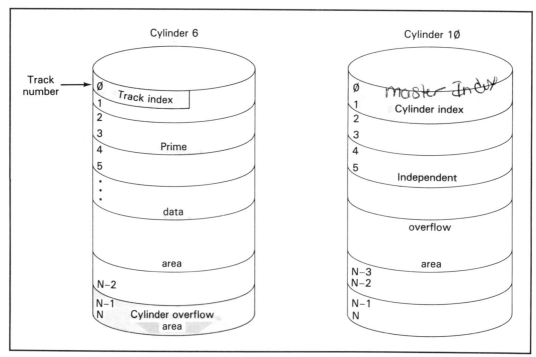

Figure 9.5 Parts of an indexed sequential file.

3. The *prime data area* in an ISAM file is an area on disk that contains a track index, the prime data, and a cylinder overflow area. It is made up of one or more complete cylinders. The area is described by a job control EXTENT statement.

   a. The *track index* is at the beginning of the first cylinder in a prime data area. It is one or more tracks in length. It contains the highest key in each track of a cylinder and the disk address of that track. It is set up automatically when a file is loaded or created.

   b. The *prime data* is composed of records that are in sequential order by a key.

   c. The *cylinder overflow* area is one or more tracks at the end of each cylinder. It contains records for which no room existed when a record was added to a track. The number of tracks used for this area is specified in the DATA DIVISION of a COBOL program or on the file description form of a RPGII program.

      The records in this area are *not* in sequential order by the key. They have an extra six-byte link field that links records from the same track.

4. The *independent overflow area* is an *optional* area used for overflow records from a cylinder. This area must be located on a cylinder separate from the prime data area. It does not need to start on a cylinder boundary (i.e., it does not need to start on the first track). Its location is described by a job control EXTENT statement.

INDEXED SEQUENTIAL FILE REORGANIZATION

Records to be deleted in an indexed sequential file are not physically deleted. Usually, room is left in the record for a delete code. For example, the first byte might be blank for an active record, but it would have a "D" in it for a deleted record.

It was mentioned earlier that records in the cylinder overflow area are longer than the original record due to a six-byte link field. The records in this overflow area are also not in sequential order; the link field directs the operating system to the next overflow record from that same track.

Therefore, several conditions arise in indexed sequential file processing:

1. The prime data areas and overflow areas fill up due to record additions and due to deleted records that are still physically present.

2. Processing time slows due to too many records in the overflow area. It takes longer to locate these records since they are not in sequential order by a key.

Therefore, the extents for the prime data area may need to be enlarged. Also, the deleted records may need to be physically deleted.

To accomplish this, a *file reorganization* needs to take place. When a file is reorganized, all undeleted records (records with no delete code) are retrieved sequentially by the keys. These records are then written out as a new indexed sequential file, possibly with larger extents. In this way, all records are placed in sequential order in the prime data area, thus improving processing time and saving space due to no link field.

✍ THE EXTENT STATEMENT

The EXTENT statement specifies where the data is located on the DASD. These statements must follow the DLBL statement for native files. Multiple EXTENT statements are possible if the data in a sequential file are located in several areas on the disk pack or if it is an indexed sequential file.

The format for this statement is shown in Figure 9.6. The operands are as follows:

1. *Logical unit.* This is the symbolic device (SYSxxx) number. If it is omitted, the default is (a) that of the preceding EXTENT statement or (b) that specified in the program if only one EXTENT statement exists.

   This is the symbolic device number of the drive where the data is located, and it must match the SYS number of the ASSGN statement. It is important to understand that the SYS number in the *EXTENT* statement specifies the disk device that the data is to be found on. Unlike card, printer, and tape input, the DLBL SYS number does *not* specify where the data is. This fact will be demonstrated in some of the examples shown after this section.

2. *Serial number.* This is the six-character volume serial number. If omitted, the volume serial number of the preceding EXTENT is used.

3. *Type.* Possible types are 1, 2, 4, and 8. The meanings are as follows:
   1 = a data area. This is the default value.
   2 = an independent overflow area for an ISAM file.
   4 = a cylinder or master index area for an ISAM file.
   8 = a data area for a SAM split cylinder file. This type cannot be used on a FBA device.

   Split cylinders allow a cylinder to contain more than one file. An example is shown in Figure 9.7. This arrangement is sometimes advantageous if sequential processing involves accessing records in two files at the same time. It lessens the movement of the read/write arm.

4. *Sequence number.* A decimal number 0–255 indicating the sequence for multiextent files. The first extent begins with the number 0. The default is 0. This operand is optional for all files except ISAM files.

   For ISAM files the extents must be in order by sequence number. That is, the order is as follows:
   a. An optional master index extent, type 4, sequence number 0
   b. Cylinder index extent, type 4, sequence number 1
   c. Prime data extent(s), type 1, sequence numbers 2, 3, 4, . . . , n
   d. An optional independent overflow extent, type 2, sequence number n + 1

   If the master index does not exist, the first extent sequence number is 1. A default cannot be used for the sequence number in this case.

5. *Relative track | block.* This number indicates the location of the beginning of the prime data area.

```
                                                              (JCS)

// EXTENT [logical-unit],[serial-number],[type]
         [sequence-number],[relative-track|block],
         [number-of-tracks|blocks],[split-cylinder-track]
```

Figure 9.6   The EXTENT statement format.

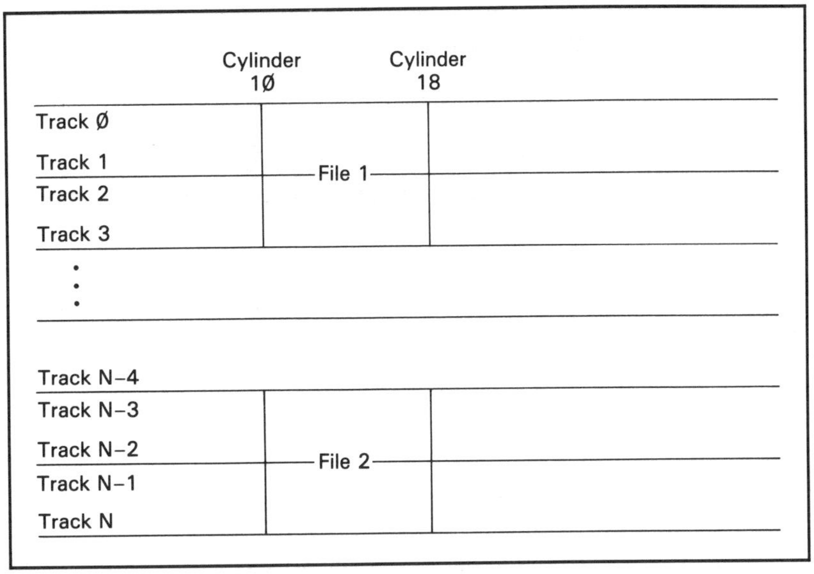

Figure 9.7 Split cylinder files.

a. For a CKD device, this number is expressed as a relative track number. The formula is RT = cylinder number * number of tracks per cylinder + track number. *Example:* If the area begins at cylinder number 8, track number 2 on a disk pack that has 12 tracks per cylinder, then RT = 8 * 12 + 2 = 98. The formula to convert from a relative track number back to the cylinder and track number is RT/tracks per cylinder = cylinder number with the remainder = track number. Example: 98/12 = 8 with a remainder of 2.

b. On FBA devices, a physical block number is used. The block number can be a number from 2 to 2,147,483,645 inclusive.

6. *Number of tracks | number of blocks.* This operand specifies the length of the area or extent in tracks for CKD devices or blocks for FBA devices.

   For indexed sequential files on CKD devices, the total number of tracks for the prime data area must be a multiple of the number of tracks per cylinder for that disk device. A chart follows to give this information:

Model	Number of tracks per cylinder
2311	1Ø
2314 or 2319	2Ø
333Ø or 3333	19
334Ø	12
335Ø	3Ø
3375	12
338Ø	15

7. *Split cylinder track.* A one- or two-digit number giving the upper track number for the split cylinder in SAM files on CKD devices. The maximum number is one less than the tracks per cylinder for that device. For example, for the 3350 the maximum value would be 29.

   Some coding examples are given below. (Track numbers begin with zero and end with one less than the number of tracks per cylinder.)

EXAMPLE 9.4

Write a data EXTENT statement for a sequential output disk file on a volume with a serial number of 111111. The extent begins with cylinder number 10, track number 0, and ends at cylinder number 29, track number 11. There are 12 tracks per cylinder. The extent is on SYS010.

Answer

```
// EXTENT SYS010,111111,1,0,120,240
```

or

```
// EXTENT SYS010,111111,,,120,240
```

Analysis

Number of cylinders used = 29 − 10 + 1 = 20 cylinders
RT number = beginning cylinder number * number of tracks per cylinder
            + beginning track number = 10 * 12 + 0 = 120
Length of extent (in tracks) = 20 cylinders * 12 tracks per cylinder
                             = 240 tracks

Note that this is a type 1 (data) extent and that the volume number is 0. Both of these values are defaults, thus the second possible answer.

EXAMPLE 9.5

Code the ASSGN, DLBL, and EXTENT statements for a sequential file with the following COBOL SELECT statement:

```
SELECT DISK-FILE, ASSIGN TO SYS015-UT-3340-S.
```

The file is stored on disk pack 226666 and occupies cylinder number 10, track number 0 through cylinder number 99, track number 11. Use a generic ASSGN statement. The file-ID is MAY 88 PAYROLL.

Answer

```
// ASSGN SYS015,DISK,VOL=226666,SHR
// DLBL SYS015,'MAY 88 PAYROLL',160,SD
// EXTENT SYS015,226666,1,0,120,1080
```

Note the SHR or share operand that has been added to the ASSGN statement. This allows more than one program to share the use of this drive.

Another possible answer

```
// ASSGN SYS016,DISK,VOL=226666,SHR
// DLBL SYS015,'MAY 88 PAYROLL',160
// EXTENT SYS016,226666,1,0,120,1080
```

Note that unlike tape, the SYS number in the EXTENT statement determines the location of the data. The SYS number in the ASSGN statement must match it. The different SYS number in the DLBL statement is there only because it is a default for the filename.

Usually in such a simple case, one makes the SYS numbers all the same. But if a file is on several different extents or several different volumes, this distinction is a necessity.

EXAMPLE 9.6 SEQUENTIAL INPUT AND OUTPUT FILES

Given the following COBOL SELECT statements:

```
SELECT DISK-INPUT-FILE, ASSIGN TO SYS010-UT-3350-S.
SELECT DISK-OUTPUT-FILE, ASSIGN TO SYS011-UT-3350-S.
```

(a) Case in which files are on the *same* volume. Both files are on a disk pack with a volume serial number of 666666. The file-ID for the input file is STUDENT MASTER IN; the expiration date is not checked; and the file begins at cylinder number 12, track number Ø and is two cylinders long.

The output file has a file-ID of STUDENT MASTER OUT; the expiration date is to be 15Ø days from the current date; and the file begins at cylinder number 7Ø, track number Ø and has a length of three cylinders.

The 335Ø drives have 3Ø tracks per cylinder. Use type generic assignments and a SYS number of 12 for the ASSGN statement.

Code the ASSGN, DLBL, and EXTENT statements for these files.

Answer

```
// ASSGN SYS012,3350,VOL=666666,SHR
// DLBL SYS010,'STUDENT MASTER IN'         INPUT FILE
// EXTENT SYS012,666666,1,0,360,60
// DLBL SYS011,'STUDENT MASTER OUT',150    OUTPUT FILE
// EXTENT SYS012,666666,1,0,2100,90
```

Note that the SYS numbers in the DLBL statements are defaults for the file name—*not* the actual SYS number. Note also that the default for SD was taken in the DLBL statements.

(b) Case in which files are on different volumes. If the output had been on a different volume with a volume serial number of 777777, we would have

```
// ASSGN SYS012,3350,VOL=666666,SHR
// DLBL SYS010,'STUDENT MASTER IN'         INPUT FILE
// EXTENT SYS012,666666,1,0,360,60
// ASSGN SYS013,3350,VOL=777777,SHR
// DLBL SYS011,'STUDENT MASTER OUT',150    OUTPUT FILE
// EXTENT SYS013,777777,1,0,2100,90
```

The second ASSGN statement for volume serial number 777777 could have followed the first ASSGN statement, but the best technique is to keep the ASSGN statement with the DLBL and EXTENT statements. However, the EXTENT statements *must* follow the corresponding DLBL statements.

✸ **EXAMPLE 9.7   MULTIPLE-EXTENT SEQUENTIAL OUTPUT FILE**

Write the ASSGN, DLBL, and EXTENT statements for an output file on volume serial number 555555. The file has a file-ID of OUTPUT MASTER FILE and an expiration date of December 31, 1988. It is to occupy three extents on the same volume. The extents are as follows:

- Cylinder number 1Ø, track number Ø, five cylinders in length
- Cylinder number 26, track number Ø, three cylinders in length
- Cylinder number 88, track number Ø, two cylinders in length

The COBOL SELECT statement is

```
SELECT MASTER-FILE-OUT, ASSIGN TO SYSØ2Ø-UT-333Ø-S.
```

The 333Ø drive has 19 tracks per cylinder. Use a specific assignment on drive 221.

Answer

```
// ASSGN SYSØ2Ø,221
// DLBL SYSØ2Ø,'OUTPUT MASTER FILE',88/365
// EXTENT SYSØ2Ø,555555,1,Ø,19Ø,95
// EXTENT SYSØ2Ø,555555,1,1,494,57
// EXTENT SYSØ2Ø,555555,1,2,1672,38
```

EXAMPLE 9.8

A sequential input file is being read from tape and an ISAM output file is being written on disk. The program CLROLL is cataloged in the system CIL (size is 3ØK). An option PARTDUMP is required. The program is to run in F6 or BG. Use a printer with a class of Z and type generic assignments.

	Tape Input	Disk Output
Volume serial number	666666	234444
File-ID	SORTED ROLL	CLASS REPORT
Expiration date	1/1/88	12/31/88
SYS number in program	SYSØ1Ø	SYSØ11
Program filename	ROLL	REPORT
Device	IBM 88Ø9	IBM 335Ø (3Ø tracks per cylinder)
Extents	—	Master index: cylinder number 1, track number Ø, one track in length
		Cylinder index: cylinder number 1, track number 1, five tracks in length
		Prime data: cylinder number 2, track number Ø, 1Ø cylinders in length
		Independent overflow: cylinder number 5Ø, track number Ø, two cylinders in length

Code the entire job stream.

Answer

```
* $$ JOB JNM=LEESON,CLASS=S
* $$ LST CLASS=Z
// JOB LEESON
// OPTION PARTDUMP
// ASSGN SYS010,8809,VOL=666666          TAPE INPUT
// TLBL ROLL,'SORTED ROLL',88/001,666666
// ASSGN SYS011,3350,VOL=234444,SHR       ISAM DISK OUTPUT
// DLBL REPORT,'CLASS REPORT',88/366,ISC
// EXTENT SYS011,234444,4,0,30,1          MASTER INDEX EXTENT
// EXTENT SYS011,234444,4,1,31,5          CYLINDER INDEX EXTENT
// EXTENT SYS011,234444,1,2,60,300        PRIME DATA EXTENT
// EXTENT SYS011,234444,2,3,1500,60       INDEPENDENT OVERFLOW EXTENT
// EXEC CLROLL,SIZE=30K
/*
/&
* $$ EOJ
```

If there were no master index, the first disk EXTENT statement would be omitted. This is the only case where the first EXTENT statement can have a volume sequence number other than 0 (1 in this case). If there were no independent overflow area, the fourth EXTENT statement would be omitted.

THE AMS PROGRAM AND INDEXED SEQUENTIAL FILES

Some types of disk drives allow only VSAM files. An example is the IBM 3370 disk drive. VSAM was not original to DOS (i.e., it is nonnative) and does not support the native indexed sequential file organization, which has been very popular. VSAM is discussed in Chapter 10.

To lure ISAM users away to VSAM, IBM provides a conversion process. This allows ISAM programs to be used on VSAM disk drives without rewriting the programs.

IBM provides an access method services (AMS) program to create and maintain VSAM files. AMS is a very large and complex program. One of its services is to convert ISAM to VSAM files. If you have VSAM disk drives, you may need to use an AMS program called IDCAMS for the ISAM end-of-chapter exercises involving actual execution.

IDCAMS will be discussed further in Chapter 11 after some of the VSAM terms are mastered.

SUMMARY

Disk requires standard labels. As with tape, the first label is an 80-byte volume label. This is written by a disk initialization program. Disks differ from tape in that they are seldom reinitialized.

All disk file or header labels (140 bytes long) are grouped together in a specific area called a VTOC. The VTOC is a directory that can be listed by an LVTOC program. The location of this directory varies according to the type of drive.

Some of the principal items of information in these file labels are a 44-character file-ID, creation and expiration dates, a volume serial number, a file type number, and an EXTENT count.

There are three types of native (original to DOS) file organization: sequential (SAM), indexed sequential (ISAM), and direct (DAM).

Records in indexed sequential files are located by the use of a set of indices. Possible indices are the master index, the cylinder index, and the track index. Records in direct files may be located by the use of an algorithm or a relative record number (RRN).

The outline of an indexed sequential file is:

1. Master index (optional)
2. Cylinder index
3. Prime data area
   a. Track index
   b. Prime data
   c. Cylinder overflow
4. Independent overflow (optional)

ISAM files must sometimes be reorganized to physically delete records (to provide more space) and/or to improve processing time. The two types of file processing are sequential and random.

Disk drives may be classified as CKD or FBA devices. Records are accessed on CKD devices by a cylinder and track number, whereas on FBA devices, records are located by a block number.

The DLBL job control statement is used to provide disk file label information to the operating system. Its main operands are a file name (which may default to a SYS number), a file-ID, an expiration date, and a code telling the type of file label.

The EXTENT job control statement is used to describe the area or areas (extents) where indices or data is located on disk. The most important EXTENT operands are the logical unit (SYS number), the volume serial number, the extent type number, an extent sequence number, the relative track number (CKD devices) or beginning block number (FBA devices), and the length of the extent in tracks or blocks.

The formula for the relative track number is

$$\text{RT number} = \text{beginning cylinder number} * \text{number of tracks per cylinder} + \text{track number}$$

Sequential file organization is good for high-activity, volatile files. It does not permit random processing. It is the only type of file organization permitted on tape.

Indexed sequential file organization (ISAM) means that:

1. Records must be fixed length.
2. All volumes must be on-line for any multivolume files.
3. The file cannot be used as input for the sort/merge program. (The file must be first converted to a sequential file.)
4. Records are not physically deleted; thus file reorganization must sometimes be done.

Direct file organization (DAM) is useful where it is not feasible to organize data sequentially by a key. DAM is not supported by some higher-level languages, and it requires that programmers write their own maintenance routines.

Some disk drives, such as the IBM 337∅, support only VSAM files. A special program, IDCAMS, in AMS will convert ISAM files to VSAM files, thus eliminating the rewriting of ISAM programs.

TERMS TO REMEMBER

Access method
Algorithm
CKD device
Count key data device
Cylinder
Cylinder index
Cylinder overflow
DAM
Direct file
Extent
FBA device
File organization
File processing
File reorganization
Fixed block architecture
High-activity file
Independent overflow
Indexed sequential file
ISAM
Key

Master index
Native file organization
Prime data
Prime data area
Random processing
Record addition
Record deletion
Record update
Relative record number
RRN
SAM
Sequential file
Sequential processing
Split cylinder
Track
Track index
Volatile file
Volume table of contents
VTOC

STUDY GUIDE

1. Contrast CKD and FBA devices in regard to how data is located.

   CKD - located within one cylindr of the device

   FBA - it is within a specifier number of blocks

2. (a) Define native file organization.

   Those types of file organization that were orginal to the first dos Release

   (b) List the three types of native file organization.

   (1) Sequential

   (2) Index

   (3) Direct file

3. Contrast the three types of native file organization as to how a record is located.

   (a) _Sequential - arranging records on a storage media in the physical Sequence that they will be processed_

   (b) ~~Index~~ - loading Records in the file Sequentially by a key & establishing at least 2 indices as the file is Load.

   (c) _Direct file - nonsequential organization method on which each record is located by an algorithm or a relative record #._

4. List the structure of an ISAM file.

   (a) _Master Index_

   (b) _Cylinder Index_

   (c) _Prime data area_

   (1) _Track index_

   (2) _Prime data_

   (3) _Cylinder overflow_

   (d) _Independent overflow_

5. What type of EXTENT statements are mandatory for an ISAM file?

   Job control Extent

6. Define an extent. _A Continuous portion of a disk defined by Some upper + lower limits_

7. Mark true or false.
   T or **(F)** **(a)** Programmers frequently write volume labels on *disk* packs.
   (T) or F **(b)** An EXTENT statement is needed for a track index in an ISAM file.
   T or **(F)** **(c)** The volume serial number can never be omitted on an EXTENT statement.
   (T) or F **(d)** It is possible to omit the volume sequence number operand on an EXTENT statement for a sequentially organized file.
   T or **(F)** **(e)** Prime data areas on an ISAM file must begin on a cylinder boundary (track number 0).
   T or **(F)** **(f)** The default value for the DLBL statement expiration date operand is zero days.

8. Give the words that the following abbreviations represent.

   (a) DAM _Direct Access Method_

   (b) VTOC _Volume Table of Contents_

(c) RRN _Relative Record Number_

(d) ISC _____

(e) DSF _____

9. Describe when split cylinders are helpful.

   Allows a cylinder to contain more the one file

10. Calculate the relative track number for cylinder number 15, track number 2 on an IBM 335∅ disk device.

    RT = _____

11. Given:

    ```
    // EXTENT SYS∅19,621348,1,∅,144,24
    ```

    If this is a CKD disk device:

    (a) The type of extent is ___1___ (what). data area

    (b) The volume sequence number is ___0___ (what).

    (c) The length of the extent is ___24___ (how many) tracks.

12. State two reasons why ISAM files sometimes need to be reorganized.

    (a) Prime data area & overflow areas fill up

    (b) Processing time slows due to too many records

CODING EXERCISES

Code the following job control exercises on coding sheets.

1. Code the ASSGN, DLBL, and EXTENT statements for a sequential disk output file with the following COBOL SELECT statement:

   ```
   SELECT DISK-FILE-OUT, ASSIGN TO SYS∅12-UT-334∅-S-OUTFLE.
   ```

   (The IBM 334∅ has 12 tracks per cylinder.)

   (a) Use a class generic assignment.
   (b) The volume serial number is 643821.
   (c) The file is stored from cylinder number 8∅, track number ∅ through cylinder number 85, track 11.
   (d) The file should be saved for 25∅ days, and the file-ID is 'SP 1988 GRADE FILE'.

2. Rewrite the DLBL statement in Exercise 1 for a direct-access file.

3. The file in Exercise 1 does *not* have OUTFLE at the end of the ASSIGN clause. It occupies two extents on the same volume instead of one extent. The first extent begins at cylinder number 68, track number Ø and extends through cylinder number 7Ø, track number 11. The second extent begins at cylinder number 84, track number Ø and extends through cylinder number 86, track number 11.

    Code the ASSGN, DLBL, and EXTENT statements for this file. Use a type generic ASSGN statement.

4. Code the ASSGN, DLBL, and EXTENT statements for a sequential disk output file with the following COBOL SELECT statement:

    ```
    SELECT SEQ-MASTER-FILE, ASSIGN TO SYSØ22-UT-334Ø-S.
    ```

    (The IBM 334Ø has 12 tracks per cylinder.)

    This file will be stored on three different volumes. The librarian has said that you may use 2Ø full cylinders of data starting at cylinder number 2 on volume serial number 111111, 15 full cylinders of data starting at cylinder number 32 on volume serial number 222222, and 16 full cylinders of data starting at cylinder number 4Ø on volume serial number 333333. Use symbolic device numbers 22, 23, and 24.

    Use a file-ID of '1988 INVENTORY FILE', and the file should be saved for 365 days. Use a type generic ASSGN statement.

5. Code the entire JCL to compile, link edit, and execute a COBOL program named SQLOAD. The program is stored in an ICCF library member by the same name. It reads 8Ø-byte records in a sequential file stored in the source library under the name P.SQDATA. (It is treated as a card input file.)

    The data is to be written as a sequential disk file on volume serial number 666666 under a file-ID of 'SP 88 CAR REGISTRATION FILE'. The data begins at cylinder number 6Ø and is 15 full cylinders in length. It should be saved for 4ØØ days. Use a class generic assignment.

    The COBOL SELECT statements are

    ```
    SELECT INPUT-FILE, ASSIGN TO SYSØØ5-UR-254ØR-S.
    SELECT DISK-OUTPUT-FILE, ASSIGN TO SYSØ14-UT-335Ø-S.
    ```

    (The IBM 335Ø has 3Ø tracks per cylinder.)

6. Code the ASSGN, DLBL, and EXTENT statements to load an indexed sequential file with the following COBOL SELECT statements:

    ```
    SELECT IS-PAYROLL-MASTER-FILE,
        ASSIGN TO SYSØ15-DA-335Ø-I-ISOUT
        RESERVE NO ALTERNATE AREA
        RECORD KEY IS CUSTOMER-NUMBER.
    ```

    (a) There will be a master index two tracks in length and a cylinder index seven tracks in length. Use the first cylinder (cylinder number Ø) for these indices.

    (b) The prime data area is 9Ø cylinders in length. Use cylinder number 2 for the beginning of the area.

    (c) There will be an independent overflow area 2Ø cylinders in length beginning in cylinder number 15Ø.

    (d) Use a File-ID of '88 PAYROLL MASTER FILE'. The file should be saved for two years and is on volume serial number 866866. Use a class generic assignment.

7. Write the ASSGN, DLBL, and EXTENT statements to create an indexed sequential file on volume serial number 666666. The file-ID is '88 INVEN-TORY MASTER FILE', and the file should be saved for one year. Use a type generic assignment. The COBOL SELECT statement is

```
SELECT INVENTORY-MASTER
    ASSIGN TO SYS020-DA-3350-I
    RESERVE NO ALTERNATE AREA
    RECORD KEY IN INV-NO.
```

(a) There will be no master index or independent overflow area.
(b) The cylinder index will require two tracks and will begin in cylinder number 3.
(c) The prime data area is 33 cylinders and is to begin in cylinder number 20.

8. Rewrite the DLBL statement in Exercise 7 showing the changes necessary if the file above is retrieved sequentially.

9. Code the entire JCL to compile, link edit, and execute a COBOL program named ISRET. The program is stored in an ICCF library member under ISRET. The program randomly *retrieves* and updates records in an indexed sequential master file on volume serial number 777888. The COBOL SE-LECT statement is

```
SELECT PAYROLL-MASTER-FILE
    ASSIGN TO SYS016-DA-3350-I
    RESERVE NO ALTERNATE AREAS
    RECORD KEY IS MASTER-KEY
    SYMBOLIC KEY IS MASTER-SYM-KEY.
```

(a) The file-ID is '88 ISAM PAYROLL FILE', and the expiration date is not checked.
(b) There is no master index.
(c) The cylinder index is one track in length and occupies the first track of cylinder number 5. The independent overflow area occupies the rest of cylinder number 5.
(d) The prime data area begins in cylinder number 6 and is five cylinders in length.

10. This exercise is to be keyed and actually run. Your instructor will give you directions as to the partition and equipment to be used and where and under what names the programs and data are stored. The entire exercise is to be done in *one* POWER job and one DOS job. Document fully and also give your full name and chapter and problem number after the DOS/VSE JOB statement.

(a) *First job.* Compile, link edit, and execute the card image to sequential disk program in Appendix D and use the data in Appendix D. Use a descriptive file ID.
(b) *Second job.* Compile, link edit, and execute the sequential disk to printer program in Appendix D.
(c) Write a report in essay style, including the following items:
  (1) Any problems that you had.
  (2) An explanation of why no data records were included in part (b).
  (3) An explanation of why these tasks should all be done in one DOS/VSE job.

11. This exercise is to be keyed and actually run. However, you must first have done Exercise 1∅. Your instructor will again give you directions. Use the same documentation as in Exercise 10 and do the work all in one POWER job and one DOS job. Document the jobs and the I/O files used.

If you have a VSAM setup, your instructor may give you some job control statements to execute an AMS program before you do this job.

(a) *First job*. Compile, link edit, and execute the sequential disk to indexed sequential disk program in Appendix D. Your input file ID must be the same as the output file ID in Exercise 1∅. Your output file ID must be the same as the one used in the AMS program if you have a VSAM setup.

(b) *Second job*. Compile, link edit, and execute the indexed sequential to printer program in Appendix D.

(c) Write a report in essay style including the following items:
    (1) A comparison of the differences involved in job control coding for the input and output files.
    (2) An explanation of why no data records were included in the job stream in either part (a) or (b).
    (3) An explanation of what would have happened if both jobs had been in the same POWER job but two different DOS jobs.
    (4) A report on any problems that you had with this exercise.

RESEARCH PROBLEMS

Answer these problems in essay style.

1. Use the IBM *System Management Guide* manual to answer the following questions. (*Hint:* Look in the index under "label information.")
   (a) Under what conditions and where can tape and DASD label information be stored?
   (b) How is the OPTION job control statement involved in storing these labels?
   (c) Is there a chart or a table that is helpful in describing these situations? If so, what page is it on?

2. Use the IBM *VSE/Advanced Functions System Control Statements* manual to answer the following questions.
   (a) On the DLBL statement, should VSAM files be declared data secured? Why or why not?
   (b) Would the DSF operand be appropriate for an input file that had not been declared data secured on output?

3. Use the *System Control Statements* manual to answer the following questions on the EXTENT statement.
   (a) Can extents on SYSLNK have multiple-extent statements? Quote the sentence in the manual that answers this question.
   (b) What happens on an EXTENT statement if an operand is coded incorrectly?

4. Use the *Systems Control Statements* manual to answer the following questions.
   (a) What is the difference in using the ASSGN statement as a JCS or as a JCC?
   (b) Can DLBL and EXTENT statements be used as JCC? Justify your answer.

    (c) Contrast the treatment of the date on the TLBL and DLBL statements in regard to *input* files.

    (d) What is the purpose of the RSTRT job control statement? Copy the format and explain each operand.

5. Use the IBM *DOS/VSE Data Management Concepts* manual and locate the section on how records are organized for processing. Answer the following questions.

    (a) When is a secondary key field helpful in processing data records?

    (b) In direct processing with disk addressing, when would organization by an index be superior to relative record number (RRN) organization?

    (c) Could RRN organization be used with variable-length records?

    (d) What is the manual's definition of a serial device?

    (e) What is a spanned record?

chapter 10

Virtual Storage and VSAM

INTRODUCTION

In multiprogramming with a fixed-partition memory, the background partition might appear as shown in Figure 1∅.1. We see that program A takes up 1∅∅K of memory and 66K of that partition is wasted. A multitasking environment could be set up. *Multitasking* is running more than one program or task at a time in the *same partition*. Multitasking is a special form of multiprogramming.

Thus a second program B could be loaded into memory in the unused portion of the partition as long as it took up 66K or less of storage. However, if the program took up more than 66K, there is a problem. Fragmenting program B into parts might be a possibility. Most programmers segment programs now, since the evolution of structured programming.

This type of reasoning led to the concepts of virtual storage and paging. IBM did not originate this concept. Burroughs had a fully operational virtual storage system on their 5∅∅∅ series in the 1960s. They just did not call it virtual storage. UNIVAC (Sperry Rand) also had such a system on their UNIVAC 11∅∅ series. RCA was the first to use the term "virtual memory" in 197∅. Then IBM took up the concept.

VIRTUAL STORAGE

Before virtual storage we were limited to the physical storage or memory in the CPU. *Real storage* is the storage from which the CPU can directly obtain instructions and data and in which results can be stored directly. *Virtual storage*, on the other hand, is addressable storage on a DASD that *appears* as real storage. (The word "virtual" means "not in actual fact.") Since addresses on a DASD are sequential, the storage appears to be like real storage.

The instructions of a program and the related data must be in the CPU to be executed. But only *one* instruction can be executed at a time. Therefore, all

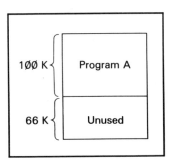

Figure 10.1 Background partition.

instructions do not have to be in the CPU at the same point of time. Thus virtual storage can be divided up into segments called *pages*. A *page* is a fixed block length of instructions and/or data that can be transferred between real and virtual storage. For DOS/VSE, a page is 4K bytes of storage. (2K in E mode.)

The pages that are not needed for execution are kept on a DASD until needed. They are kept in an area called a *page data set*. When a segment or page is no longer needed, it is transferred from real storage to the DASD. When it is needed, it is transferred from the DASD to main storage.

To *page-in* is the process of transferring a page (that is needed) from the page data set to real storage. To *page-out* is the process of transferring a page (that is no longer needed) from real storage to the page data set on the DASD. This paging process is shown in Figure 10.2.

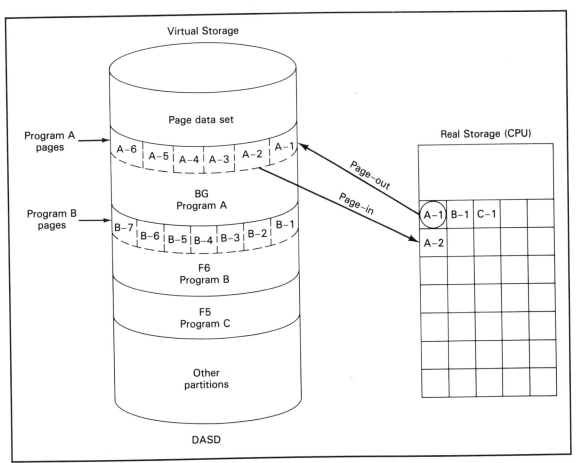

Figure 10.2 Virtual storage and paging.

Sometimes a situation called thrashing occurs. *Thrashing* is a condition in which the system is so busy paging that it cannot do any useful work. This occurs when real storage is almost full, and something must go out for a page to come in. This takes time. Systems programmers are used to fine-tune these systems to prevent such situations. Sometimes thrashing is the fault of the program, and the program must be thrown out. A poorly designed program that branches all over the place can be a disaster in virtual storage conditions.

Virtual storage does *not* make a computer run faster. It just makes better use of real storage and increases multiprogramming capabilities.

THE VIRTUAL STORAGE ACCESS METHOD

The *virtual storage access method (VSAM)* is *nonnative*, that is, not original to the DOS operating system. Unfortunately, the terms that IBM chose to assign to VSAM concepts are different from the *native* terms, although they are similar in concept. We will try to relate these new terms to the ones that we already know as we go along. This should make the new concepts easier to understand.

VSAM files are called *data sets*. Thus the page data set, referred to above in the virtual storage section, is an extent on a DASD where pages are stored.

There are three types of nonnative or VSAM file organization.

Type	Abbreviation	Native (non-VSAM) Equivalent
1. *Entry-sequenced data set*	*ESDS*	Sequential (SAM)
2. *Key-sequenced data set*	*KSDS*	Indexed sequential (ISAM)
3. *Relative record data set*	*RRDS*	Direct (DAM)

The indices setup for the KSDS organization is different from that of the indexed sequential organization, but records are still loaded by a key and retrieved by the use of an index.

The advantages of VSAM, as enumerated by the manufacturer, are:

1. It does not necessitate as much file reorganization since records are physically deleted.
2. It is device independent, freeing the programmer of being concerned about where the data is located.
3. It is CICS compatible. (It works well with the CICS terminal software.)
4. It offers more data security.
5. It automatically allocates space on the DASD, controlling all blocking and deleting.
6. Job control is somewhat easier in that you do not usually need to code ASSGN and EXTENT job control statements.

Some disadvantages are:

1. The software is expensive.
2. Its sequential files are not as effective in most batch-processing environments. That is, SAM files are more effective.
3. VSAM sometimes wastes disk space on some disk drive models because of its large block sizes. For example, typical VSAM blocks are 4K and must be in multiples of 4K. On the IBM 3350 disk drives (19K bytes per track), 4 * 4K = 16K. Therefore, 3K bytes are wasted on each track.

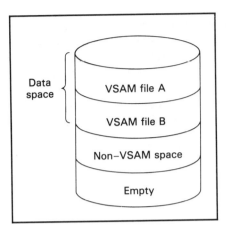

Figure 10.3 Data space configuration.

VSAM AREA

VSAM uses data spaces as an area on a DASD to set up a VSAM file. This *data space* is similar to an extent and is usually set up in the VTOC area by a systems programmer or data base manager. It is defined by the DLBL and EXTENT statements. After this process, VSAM manages the activities.

VSAM and non-VSAM files can occupy the same disk packs on some drives as shown in Figure 10.3. VSAM records are arranged in an area called a *control interval* as shown in Figure 10.4. A control interval is similar to a physical record. Records can be fixed or variable length and are accessed by a key. The index points to the correct key.

Both ESDS and RRDS have only a data component. *But* records are accessed by a relative record number in the RRDS, and the records must be *fixed-*

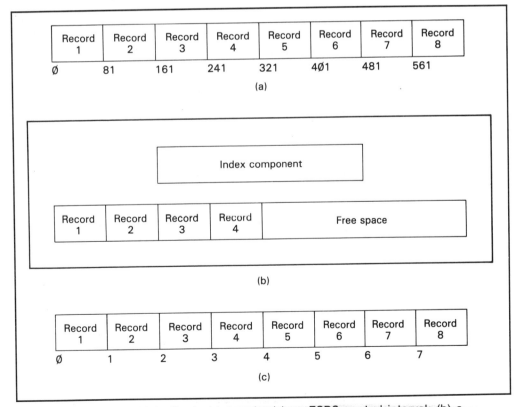

Figure 10.4 Control intervals: (a) an ESDS control interval; (b) a KSDS control interval; (c) a RRDS control interval.

length records. In contrast, ESDS records are referenced by the relative *byte* address, and ESDS records can be fixed or *variable-length records.* Notice these differences in Figure 1Ø.4. Note also that the KSDS control interval has an index component as well as a data component. A KSDS, just as with an ISAM file, can be processed sequentially or randomly.

Control intervals are grouped into an area called a *control area* or a *cluster.* Examples of data areas are shown in Figure 1Ø.5. Note in the case of a KSDS that the cluster also contains an index component, as mentioned above. This index is created and maintained automatically by VSAM just as the track index is for ISAM. This index is called the *sequence set.* There is also an *index set* that could be compared to the ISAM cylinder index.

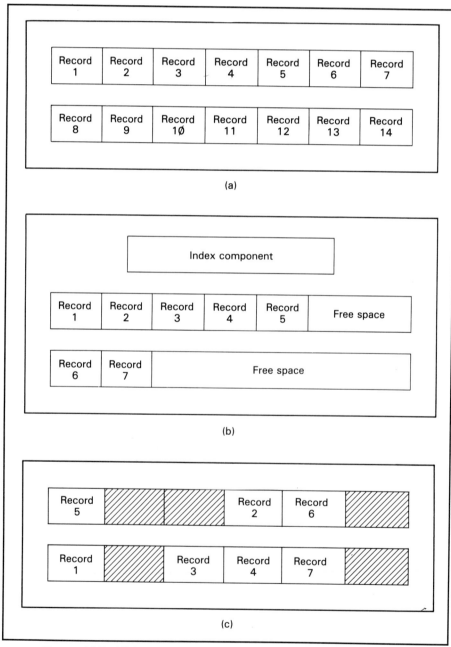

Figure 10.5 VSAM control areas or clusters: (a) an ESDS cluster; (b) a KSDS cluster; (c) a RRDS cluster.

VSAM CATALOGS

Native files are identified in a VTOC area. Nonnative or VSAM files are identified by *catalogs*. The contents of these catalogs can be listed by the use of a program called LISTCAT. There are two kinds of catalogs: the master catalog and one or more user catalogs.

The SYS device number for the master catalog is *SYSCAT*. The *master catalog* contains label information for all user catalogs and possibly some VSAM files. Usually, though, the information for VSAM files is stored in the *user catalog*. These user catalogs can act as backup for the master catalog.

THE KSDS CONTROL SPLIT

Figure 1∅.6 demonstrates what happens when a record is added to a control interval in which there is no more room. This condition is called a *control interval split* and corresponds to the ISAM overflow case. VSAM splits about half of the

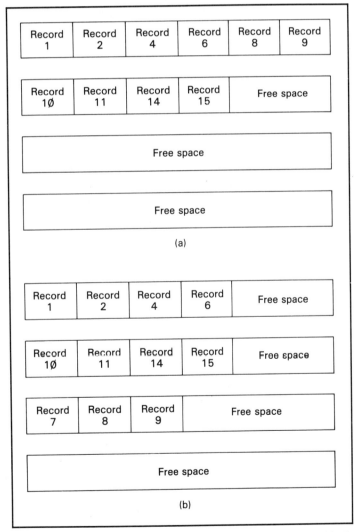

Figure 10.6 KSDS control interval split: (a) a control interval before a control split; (b) a control interval after adding record 7, which caused a control interval split.

```
NATIVE (NON-VSAM)                 NONNATIVE (VSAM)
      TERM                          EQUIVALENT TERM

SAM                               ESDS
ISAM                              KSDS
DAM                               RRDS
File                              Data set (made up of control
                                           areas)
Extent                            Data space
Physical record or block         Control interval
Overflow space                   Free space
Track overflow                   Control interval split
Cylinder overflow                Control area split
VTOC                             Catalog
LVTOC program                     LISTCAT program
Indexed sequential indices        VSAM cluster
 and prime data area
```

Figure 10.7 Native versus nonnative term equivalencies.

control interval and moves the remainder of the records to a new control interval at the end of the control area. This *free space* corresponds to the overflow area at the end of an ISAM cylinder.

A condition called a *control area split* also exists. This occurs when a record is added and the control area has no room for these additional records. In this case, VSAM creates a new control area at the end of the file and shifts about half of the control intervals to this new area. This condition could be compared to overflow into an ISAM independent overflow area.

VSAM files are maintained by an access method services (AMS) program, which is discussed in Chapter 11.

A summary of native versus nonnative term equivalencies is shown in Figure 1Ø.7.

THE VSAM DLBL STATEMENT

Since the VSAM catalog structure locates VSAM files, the only job control statement required for a VSAM file is a DLBL statement for the VSAM master catalog. Your systems programmer will have arranged for this master catalog label to be stored as a standard label. Review the format of the DLBL statement as shown in Figure 9.4.

A typical VSAM DLBL statement might appear as follows:

```
// DLBL ISFILE,'CDP251.IHL1492.MASTER.FILE',Ø,VSAM
```

Notice that the file ID (the area enclosed in apostrophes) has periods instead of spaces. The rules for forming VSAM file-IDs is as follows:

1. The ID may be 1 to 44 characters (A–Z, Ø–9, @, #, or &), as in the case of native files.

2. If a word used is greater than eight characters, it must be broken down into eight-character (or less) segments separated by periods.

3. The segments must begin with a letter and cannot end with a period.

Examples of illegal VSAM IDs would be

```
INVENTORY.1988   (Inventory has too many characters;
                  1988 does not start with a letter.)
```

```
INVENTRY.MAY+APR   (No + or special character is
allowed.)
INVENT.MASTER.FILE.   (An ID cannot end in a period.)
```

Five operands appearing in the DLBL statement shown in Figure 9.4, and not discussed in Chapter 9 because they dealt with VSAM files, are as follows:

1. BUFSP=N This operand specifies the size in bytes of the buffer VSAM uses for file I/O operations. Usually, the standard buffer size is adequate, and this operand is not used. We will not be using the BUFSP operand.
2. CAT=catalog name This operand specifies the filename of the DLBL statement, defining the catalog owning this file. This operand should not be used unless you wish to override certain system assumptions about who owns the file. We will not be using this operand.
3. DISP= NEW (NEW,KEEP) (NEW,DELETE) (NEW,DATE) OLD *(OLD,KEEP)* (OLD,DELETE) (OLD,DATE) (,KEEP) (,DELETE) (,DATE) Note that the default is (OLD,KEEP). This operand specifies the disposition of the data set and is used for reusable files. A *reusable file* is a file that can be used as a work file.

    Briefly, NEW deletes all previous contents of the area when the file is opened. OLD keeps all previous contents when the file is opened. KEEP keeps the contents of the file when it is closed and DELETE does not. DATE will keep the contents if the expiration date has not occurred; otherwise, the contents are deleted.
4. RECORDS=n (where n = a number) This operand is used if you want a SAM ESDS file. You must use the RECSIZE operand also.
5. RECSIZE=n (where n = a number) This operand specifies the record size for a SAM ESDS file.

VSAM CATALOGS AND THE DLBL STATEMENT

You may have one or more catalogs in the VSAM environment. One of these catalogs must be chosen as a master catalog, and the rest are called user catalogs. These catalogs are areas on disk that act much as a VTOC does in the native file environment. They contain information about VSAM files. Much of this information is taken from the DLBL statement.

Having user catalogs in addition to a master catalog is helpful because you can reduce the time required to search a given catalog for file information. In such a case, the master catalog has a pointer or information that points to the user catalog containing the required information.

All VSAM files, except SAM ESDS files, must have an entry (be defined) in a master catalog or a user catalog. The system's programmer defines the master catalog for the system and user catalogs, if desired.

It is possible to specify a user catalog as the catalog to be used to reference all the files for a current job. In this case the user catalog is called the job catalog. This is done by using IJSYSUC as a filename in the DLBL job control statement.

Definitions

1. A *master catalog* is a file with extensive file and volume information that assists in locating files. If a user catalog exists, it has entries that point to the user catalogs. It is identified by the filename IJSYSCT.

2. A *user catalog* is an optional catalog (pointed to be the master catalog) that lessens the required search time when many file entries exist.

3. A *job catalog* is a user catalog that has been declared *the* catalog to be used for all files in a current job. It is identified by the filename IJSY-SUC.

DLBL and EXTENT statements for the master catalog must be placed in the job stream unless the system's programmer has placed the DLBL as a permanent label in the LIA. An example of such a master catalog DLBL is

```
// DLBL IJSYSCT,'MASTER CATALOG LABEL',,VSAM
```

where IJSYSCT is the filename for the master catalog. We will assume that the system's programmer has placed the DLBL as a permanent label in the LIA unless stated otherwise.

A user catalog DLBL statement must be defined in the job stream. This is then used as the job catalog unless it is overridden by the CAT = filename operand on the DLBL statement. (We will see in Chapter 11 that a catalog may also be defined using the AMS feature.)

An example of defining a user catalog as a job catalog would be the following DLBL statement

```
// DLBL IJSYSUC,'USER1.CATALOG',,VSAM
```

Then the following files are owned by IJSYSUC:

```
(a) // DLBL VSAMIN,'MARCH88.PAYROLL',,VSAM
(b) // DLBL VSAMOUT,'APRIL88.PAYROLL',,VSAM,DISP=NEW
```

If (b) were to be owned by another user catalog, it could be overridden by the following:

```
// DLBL PRIVCAT,'USER2.CATALOG',,VSAM
// DLBL VSAMOUT,'APRIL88.PAYROLL',,VSAM,DISP=NEW,CAT=PRIVCAT
```

The hierarchy of catalog searching is as follows:

1. An explicit user or master catalog specified by the AMS CATALOG parameter or the CAT = filename operand in the DLBL statement
2. The user or job catalog, IJSYSUC, specified as the filename of a DLBL statement
3. The master catalog, IJSYSCT, specified as the filename of a DLBL statement

SAM ESDS FILES

SAM ESDS files may be set up or defined:

1. By explicitly defining the space with an AMS CLUSTER command (see Chapter 11), *or*
2. By implicitly defining it with job control statements using the VSAM Space Management feature. *VSE/VSAM Space Management* is a program that allows you to define and process SAM files within a VSAM data space.

An example of option 2 might be

(a) `// DLBL IJSYSUC,'USER1.CATALOG',,VSAM`

This defines USER1.CATALOG as the job catalog.

(b) `// DLBL INVFILE,'MARCH88.INVTRY.FILE',,VSAM,RECORDS=150,RECSIZE=80`

Notice that an estimate must be made of the number of records, and that the record size must be stated.

If the user catalog and the SAM ESDS model have already been defined by AMS commands, only the DLBL statement in case (b) need be used.

EXAMPLE 10.1

Code a DLBL statement for a VSAM file that is to be loaded. The master and user catalogs have already been defined using the AMS program. The file name is PAYFLE; it has an expiration date of 30 days from the date it is loaded. The cluster name is MAY1988.PAYROLL.MASTER.FILE.

Answer

`// DLBL PAYFLE,'MAY1988.PAYROLL.MASTER.FILE',30,VSAM,DISP=NEW`

EXAMPLE 10.2

Code the file in Example 10.1 as an input file to be processed.

Answer

`// DLBL PAYFLE,'MAY1988.PAYROLL.MASTER.FILE',30,VSAM`

EXAMPLE 10.3

Code the file in Example 10.1 as a SAM ESDS input file that has already been defined. It has a maximum of 125 110-byte records.

Answer

`// DLBL PAYFLE,'MAY1988.PAYROLL.MASTER.FILE',30,VSAM,RECORDS=125,RECSIZE=110`

EXAMPLE 10.4

Code a job catalog DLBL statement for the user catalog STU-DENT.USER.CATALOG. Take the default on the date.

Answer

`// DLBL IJSYSUC,'STUDENT.USER.CATALOG',,VSAM`

SUMMARY

Virtual storage allows the execution of segments of a program. Individual segments or pages are brought into real storage as needed.

Real storage is in the CPU, whereas virtual storage is on a DASD in a page data set (an extent). The process of transferring pages back and forth between the CPU and the DASD is called paging, or paging in and out.

VSAM is nonnative; that is, it is not original to the DOS system. VSAM terms and facts to be remembered are:

1. The types of file organization are ESDS, KSDS, and RRDS.
2. A data space or extent is an area set up on disk for a VSAM file.
3. Records are stored in an area called a control interval (similar to a physical record).
4. Control intervals are grouped into a control area or cluster.
5. A KSDS has indices just as an ISAM file has indices. It has a sequence set similar to an ISAM track index and a sequence set similar to an ISAM cylinder index.
6. VSAM file information is registered in a catalog (similar to the native VTOC area).
7. KSDS control splits are caused by overflow. A control interval split is similar to an ISAM track overflow. A control area split is similar to an ISAM cylinder overflow.
8. VSAM file names are formed by the following rules:
   a. No segment can be longer than eight letters, and it must begin with a letter.
   b. Segments are separated by periods. No period may be used at the end of the name.
   c. Segments may be formed using the characters A–Z, Ø–9, @, #, or $.
9. Usually, the only JCS needed for VSAM files is the DLBL statement as long as the master catalog and user catalogs have been predefined. Operands are about the same as with native files except for the DISP=operand. If a new file is created, DISP=NEW is used. (The file must have been defined through IDCAMS, or the AMS program, as a reusable file.) If an SAM ESDS file is created, the RECORDS= and RECSIZE= operands must be used.
10. VSAM files are maintained by the AMS service program.

TERMS TO REMEMBER

Cluster	Job catalog
Control area	Key-sequenced data set
Control area split	KSDS
Control interval	Master catalog
Control interval split	Multitasking
Data set	Native
Data space	Nonnative
Entry sequenced data set	Page
ESDS	Page data set
Fixed-length record	Page in
Free space	Page out
Index set	Pointer

Real storage
Relative record data set
Reusable file
RRDS
Sequence set
Thrashing
User catalog

Variable-length record
Virtual storage
Virtual storage access method
VSAM
VSAM catalog
VSE/VSAM Space Management

STUDY GUIDE

1. Distinguish between real and virtual storage.

   Virtual storage is on a DASD as Real storage is in CPU

2. State the advantage of using virtual storage.

   makes better use of real storage + increases multiprogramming capability

3. Contrast the meaning of the terms "native" and "nonnative."

   nonnative - not original to DOS operating system

4. State the three types of VSAM file organization and give the non-VSAM equivalent.

   (a) *Entry-Sequenced data set - Sequential*

   (b) *Key-Sequenced data set - Index Sequential*

   (c) *Relative Record data set - Direct*

5. State at least three advantages of using VSAM and two disadvantages.
   (a) Advantages:

   (1) *does not necessitate as much file organization*

   (2) *device independent*

   (3) *CICS compatible*

   (b) Disadvantages:

   (1) *Software is expensive*

   (2) *VSAM sometimes waste disk space*

6. Contrast multitasking and multiprogramming.

   more than one program is executed at a time - multiprogramming is in the CPU, multitasking is in the partition

7. Complete the blanks using VSAM terms.

(a) Logical records are stored in a control ___Intervals___ .

(b) The equivalent of a control interval in native terms is a ___physical___ (physical, logical) record.

(c) Control intervals and free space make up a control ___split___ .

(d) A control interval split is similar to an ISAM ___Independent___ overflow.

(e) A control area split is similar to an ISAM ___Case___ overflow.

(f) The two KSDS indices are called a(n) ___Sequence___ set and a(n) ___Index___ set.

(g) *True or False:* VSAM and non-VSAM files can exist on the same DASD.

(h) A VSAM ___file___ is equivalent to the native VTOC area.

8. (a) State the filename of the master catalog. ___ISGSPT___

(b) State the filename of the user catalog being defined as a job catalog. ___ISYSUC___

9. Mark the following VSAM file IDs as correct (C) or incorrect (I). If incorrect, say why.

C or I (a) VSAM.OUTPUT.MASTER.FILE ___C___

C or I (b) DEC.19.1988.PAYROLL ___I___

C or I (c) ACCOUNTS.RECEIVABLE.FILE ___C___

C or I (d) STUDENT.GRADE.FILE. ___I___

C or I (e) STUDENT.PERSONAL.INF.FILE ___C___

C or I (f) AC.REC.FILE ___C___

10. Give the hierarchy of VSAM catalog searching.

(1) ___Explicit user or master catalog___

(2) ___user or job catalog___

(3) ___Master Catalog___

CODING EXERCISES

1. Code a DLBL statement for a SAM ESDS file named SQDISK. The file-ID should identify the file as a parts file for March of the current year. The expiration date should be the end of the current year. This file is being loaded and will have no more than 1ØØ records, 12Ø bytes in length. The master and user catalogs have already been defined.

2. Code a DLBL statement for a sales file for the month of April of the current year. The file name is SLSFILE. It is a VSAM file that is being loaded. Its expiration date is 6Ø days from the current date. The master and user catalogs have already been defined.

3. Rewrite the DLBL statement in Exercise 2 for an input file to be processed.

4. Assume that the master catalog file has been predefined. Write a DLBL statement to define the job catalog as a user catalog named STU-DENT.USER.CATALOG. (Take the default on date.) Define the DLBL statement for a VSAM student grade file (owned by the user catalog above). It is an input file. Take the default on the expiration date. The file-ID should identify it as a student grade file for the current semester and year. The filename is STFILE.

5. This exercise will be keyed and actually run. An ESDS cluster will need to be defined before you do this. (See Example 11.14 for an example of defining an ESDS cluster. Your instructor may help you with this definition.)

    Continue documentation procedures as before, using a comment to identify you, the chapter, and exercise. Also use comments to label the jobs and the DLBL and ASSGN statements used as to input or output.

    (a) *First job.* Compile, link edit, and execute the card image to VSAM ESDS disk program and data in Appendix D. The output file-ID must be that used when you defined the VSAM ESDS cluster.

    (b) *Second job.* Compile, link edit, and execute the ESDS to printer program in Appendix D. The file-ID should be the same as the one used in part (a).

    (c) Write a report in essay style, including the following items:
        (1) Describe any problems that you had.
        (2) How did this problem differ from the creation of a SAM file in Chapter 9?

6. This exercise will be keyed and actually run. A KSDS cluster will need to be defined before you do this. (See Example 11.15 for an example of defining a KSDS cluster. Your instructor may help you with this definition.)

    Continue documentation procedures as before using a comment to identify you, the chapter, and exercise. Also document your DLBL and ASSGN statements with comments, identifying them as input or output.

    (a) *First job.* Compile, link edit, and execute the ESDS to VSAM KSDS disk program in Appendix D. The input file-ID must be the same as your output file-ID in Exercise 5. The output file-ID should be the one that you used when you defined your KSDS cluster.

    (b) *Second job.* Compile, link edit, and execute the KSDS to printer program in Appendix D. The input file-ID should be the same as the one used in part (a).

    (c) Write a report in essay style, including the following items:
        (1) Describe any problems that you had.
        (2) How did this problem differ from the creation of an ISAM file in Chapter 9?

RESEARCH PROBLEMS

Use the *VSE/VSAM Commands and Macros* manual to answer the following questions in essay style.

1. What is an alternate index, and why is it useful?
2. What does the DEFINE PATH command do? Where is the path located?
3. How are catalog entries altered? How does this involve file reorganization?

chapter 11

Service Programs

INTRODUCTION

In Chapter 1 we defined a service program as one that assists in the successful execution of problem programs without directly controlling the system or production results.

The **LIBRARIAN**, a service program, is a group of programs used to maintain and service system and private libraries. They are used to:

1. Display the contents of a library entry
2. Display the names of the entries in a library
3. Catalog an entry in a library
4. Delete entries from a library
5. Update entries in the source and procedure libraries
6. Condense libraries
7. Copy and merge libraries

The *linkage editor program* is a service program used to link the main object program to any subroutines or macros needed from the relocatable library. It produces a program in executable form.

The *Access Method Services (AMS) program* is a service program that maintains nonnative or VSAM files. It allows you to create, delete, update, or list these files.

The purpose of this chapter is to learn how to use some features of these programs. Applications programmers normally must consult with librarians and/or the systems programmers before using the librarian and AMS programs. You, as a student, will use them only with the permission of your instructor (who normally consults with the computer center personnel).

It is very important that adequate backup and protection is exercised when using these programs to maintain the libraries. Most computer centers accomplish this protection by:

1. Keeping tape or disk copies on-site in fireproof safes and off-site in protected areas
2. Limiting access to storage areas for backups
3. By the use of expiration dates on internal file labels
4. By the use of passwords and user labels

THE LINKAGE EDITOR PROGRAM

This program prepares a program for execution or for being cataloged in the core image library. It links the main object program with any subroutines or macros needed from the RL, producing an executable program.

The linkage editor itself has four control statements: the ACTION, ENTRY, INCLUDE, and PHASE statements. The format for these statements is: ƀopcodeƀoperands separated by commas (where ƀ = a blank). The operands cannot extend past column 71. The operand field is ended by the first blank position. The statement must *not* begin in column 1, but it can start anywhere past column 1.

Placement of these control statements must follow the following rules:

1. The ACTION statement must be the first linkage editor control statement in the job stream. (A good place to put it is after the OPTION statement, if used.)
2. The PHASE statement must precede or come before each object module. It should be placed before the source or object program to be compiled. For example, in the case of a COBOL program, it should be placed before the // EXEC FCOBOL and CBL statements.
3. *All* linkage editor control statements must precede the // EXEC LNKEDT statement.
4. A /* statement must follow any object module read in from SYSIPT. (You will recall that SYSIPT is the device that reads the source program statements and data.)
5. If the linkage editor is to be used, LINK must be specified as an operand in the OPTION statement.

The Action Control Statement. This linkage editor control statement allows you to alter certain options built into the linkage editor program. The format of this statement is shown in part (a) of Figure 11.1.

MAP Indicates that a storage map and linkage editor diagnostic messages be printed for use in case of debugging problems. Many applications programmers use an ACTION NOMAP statement after the OPTION statement when compiling and executing.

NOAUTO Suppresses the AUTOLINK feature. The AUTO feature automatically links any subroutines needed with the program. The NOAUTO option should *not* be used by the COBOL programmer. If you do use it, you will need to use the INCLUDE statement described below for anything needed from the RL.

```
    (a)   ACTION [MAP|NOMAP][,NOAUTO][,CANCEL][,SMAP]
    (b)   ENTRY entry-point-name
    (c)   INCLUDE [module name][,(namelist)]
    (d)   PHASE name,origin [,NOAUTO][,SVA][,PBDY]
              Note:  The op code in all statements must begin to the
                     right of column 1.
```

Figure 11.1 The LINKAGE EDITOR control statement formats.

CANCEL   Will cancel the job if any serious linkage editor problems are encountered.

SMAP   Causes control section names to be listed alphabetically in the storage map produced by the MAP option.

The Entry Control Statement.   This linkage editor control statement is used if a program has several possible entry points and the first entry point (that is, the first phase entry) is not desired. The format of this statement is shown in part (b) of Figure 11.1.

The Include Control Statement.   This control statement is used if an object module is to be included for editing by the linkage editor. The format is shown in part (c) of Figure 11.1.

If no operands are present, the object module is assumed to be on SYSIPT. In former days, the INCLUDE statement was frequently used to include an object program that had been punched on cards.

If a module-name is present, the object module is assumed to be in the RL. (The object name is one to eight alphameric characters.) The name-list operand can be used to specify up to five phases to be extracted from a program.

However, the INCLUDE statement is seldom used because the linkage editor can determine through its AUTOLINK feature what modules are needed by the main object module.

The Phase Control Statement.   This control statement is used in cataloging or placing a program in the core image library (version 1 DOS/VSE) or in a virtual I/O area (versions 2 and 3). It gives the program a phase name and an origin point for the phase. The format of this statement is shown in part (d) of Figure 11.1.

The name operand gives the phase name. It must be one to eight alphameric characters long (A–Z, Ø–9, @, # or $). The name may not be ALL, $, or ROOT. Each single phase name should be unique in the first four characters of its phase name.

ORIGIN specifies the load address of the name. An asterisk (*) is usually used for the origin to allow the phase to be loaded into any partition.

PHASE name,* is all that you will probably use.

THE LIBRARIAN PROGRAM (DOS/VSE VERSION 1)†

The LIBRARIAN is a set of programs used to maintain service and copy the system and private libraries. The libraries you wish to act on are usually defined

---

† See the LIBRARIAN section in Chapter 12 if you have DOS/VSE SP version 2 or 3.

```
Function               Core-image library        Relocatable library

List Directory         // EXEC DSERV,SIZE=20K     // EXEC DSERV,SIZE=20K
   Entries                DSPLY CD                    DSPLY RD
                       /*                        /*

List the contents      // EXEC CSERV,SIZE=20K     // EXEC RSERV,SIZE=20K
   of an entry            DSPLY phase name           DSPLY module name
                       /*                        /*

   Note:   DSPLYS can be used with a DSERV to sort the directory
           entry names.

=================================================================

Function               Source-statement library  Procedure library

List Directory         // EXEC DSERV,SIZE=20K     // EXEC DSERV,SIZE=20K
   Entries                DSPLY SD                    DSPLY PD
                       /*                        /*

List the Contents      // EXEC SSERV,SIZE=20K     // EXEC PSERV,SIZE=20K
   of an entry            DSPLY book name            DSPLY procedure name
                       /*                        /*

=================================================================

Function               All Libraries

List directory         // EXEC DSERV,SIZE=20K
   Entries                DSPLY ALL
                       /*
```

Figure 11.2 DOS/VSE ICS for displaying entries in or the contents of a library.

by DLBL, EXTENT, and LIBDEF statements, although in most cases, an ASSGN statement can be used instead of the LIBDEF.

The sets of programs in the LIBRARIAN are:

1. *The service programs: DSERV, CSERV, RSERV, SSERV, PSERV, and ESERV*
2. *The maintenance program: MAINT*
3. *The organizational programs: COPYSERV and CORGZ*

The LIBRARIAN has control statements. The general format is

```
bop codeboperands separated by commas
```

where b = blank. The statement must *not* start in column 1, but it can start anywhere to the right of column 1. The operands cannot extend past column 71. Continuation statements are not allowed except for the special cases of CORGZ ALLOC or the NEWVOL statements.

```
DSPLY    {directory[,directory, ...]|CD(phasename[,nn])
  or
DSPLYS

  Note:   The op code, DSPLY, must start in column 2 or
          to the right of column 2.
```

Figure 11.3 The DISPLAY control statement format.

The Service Programs

These programs are used to service the libraries. The ones that we will be using are as listed below.

Name	Function
DSERV	Displays the entries in the directories
CSERV	Prints or punches the contents of an entry in the core image library
RSERV	Prints or punches the contents of an entry in the relocatable library
SSERV	Prints or punches the contents of an entry in the source statement library
PSERV	Prints or punches the contents of an entry in the procedure library

(handwritten margin notes:)
- *(Phase Name) Goes in — CSERV*
- *module! Goes in — RSERV*
- *(BOOKS) Goes in — SSERV*
- *(Procedure Goes in) — PSERV*

Applications programmers are seldom interested in the *contents* of an entry in the core image library or the relocatable library (provided by the CSERV and RSERV programs) since the contents are in machine language. However, it is often helpful to be able to print the contents of an entry in the source statement library or procedure library.

A summary of some of the job control statements needed for the service programs is shown in Figure 11.2. (See page 142.)

The format for the DSPLY control statement is shown in Figure 11.3.

The op code DSPLYS, when used with the DSERV program, displays the phase names sorted alphabetically. Possible operands you may be using are

CD	Core image directory
RD	Relocatable directory
SD	Source statement directory
PD	Procedure directory
ALL	All possible directories

Therefore, the control statement for displaying the entries in the core image library in sorted order would be DSPLYS CD. If phases (programs) were cataloged beginning with your initials and you wished to display only your programs, you could use the control statement DSPLY CD(III), where III represents your initials.

If you are displaying the contents of a *private* library, you will need to use the LIBDEF JCS in the job stream.

EXAMPLE 11.1

Code the statements necessary to display the entries of the system relocatable directory in sorted order.

Answer

```
* $$ JOB JNM=FREYE,CLASS=J
* $$ LST CLASS=Z
// JOB FREYE    DSERV ON SYSTEM RL
// EXEC DSERV,SIZE=20K
   DSPLYS RD
/*
/&
* $$ EOJ
```

EXAMPLE 11.2

Code the statements necessary to display the private student core image directory entries beginning with IHL. Write the DLBL, EXTENT, and LIB-DEF statement using the following information:

1. The filename is STUCIL; the file-ID is MCC.STUDENT.PVT.CLB; the expiration date is the 135th day of 1999.
2. Take the default on the SYS number; the volume serial number is SYSWK1; it is a data area; the beginning block number is 150242 (this is a FBA disk device); and the length of the extent is 10648 blocks.
3. The name used in the LIBDEF statement is STUCIL.

Answer

```
* $$ JOB JNM=BUCK,CLASS=J
* $$ LST CLASS=Z
// JOB BUCK     DISPLAY IHL ENTRIES IN A PRIVATE CIL
// OPTION LOG   (Would be omitted if system default is
                 LOG)
// LIBDEF CL,SEARCH=STUCIL,TO=STUCIL,FROM=STUCIL
// DLBL STUCIL,'MCC.STUDENT.PVT.CLB',99/135
// EXTENT ,SYSWK1,1,0,150242,10648
// EXEC DSERV,SIZE=20K
   DSPLY CD(IHL)
*
/&
* $$ EOJ
```

Note that the LIBDEF statement could have had just one operand, FROM = STUCIL. Sometimes it is easier to code all operands rather than worrying about whether the SEARCH, TO, or FROM operand should be used.

EXAMPLE 11.3

Code the statements necessary to display the contents of a data file in the system source library under the name AJCL1.

Answer

```
* $$ JOB JNM=PRATT,CLASS=J
* $$ LST CLASS=Z
// JOB PRATT   DISPLAY CONTENTS OF AJCL1 IN SYSTEM SL
// EXEC SSERV,SIZE=20K
   DSPLY AJCL1
/*
/&
* $$ EOJ
```

The Maintenance Program

This 80K program named MAINT is used to maintain system or private libraries. It can do one or more of the following functions in one job: catalog, condense, delete, set condense limit, rename, or update.

The maintenance program does not physically delete programs from a li-

Function	Core-image library	Relocatable library

Catalog	`// OPTION CATAL`
	`   PHASE ....,*`
	`// EXEC FCOBOL,SIZE=100K`
	`   (Source Program)`
	`/*`
	`// EXEC LNKEDT,SIZE=64K`
	`/*`
		`// EXEC MAINT,SIZE=80K`
		`   CATALR modulename`
		`(object deck of module)`
		`/*`
		
		`(Or see method of punching`
		`            to tape)`

Delete	`// EXEC MAINT,SIZE=80K`
	`   DELETC phasename...`
	`/*`
		`// EXEC MAINT,SIZE=80K`
		`   DELETR modulename...`
		`/*`

Rename	`// EXEC MAINT,SIZE=80K`
	`   RENAMC oldname, newname`
	`/*`
		`// EXEC MAINT,SIZE=80K`
		`   RENAMR oldname,newname`
		`/*`

Condense	`// EXEC MAINT,SIZE=80K`
	`   CONDS CL`
	`/*`
		`// EXEC MAINT,SIZE=80K`
		`   CONDS RL`
		`/*`

Function	Source-statement library	Procedure library

Catalog	`// EXEC MAINT,SIZE=80K`
	`   CATALS sublib.bookname..`
	`   BKEND`
	`   (book to be cataloged)`
	`   BKEND`
	`/*`
		`// EXEC MAINT,SIZE=80K`
		`   CATALP procedurename`
		`(procedure to be cataloged)`
		`/+ (end of procedure)`
		`/*`

Delete	`// EXEC MAINT,SIZE=80K`
	`   DELETS sublib.bookname...`
	`/*`
		`// EXEC MAINT,SIZE=80K`
		`   DELETP procedurename..`
		`/*`

Rename	`// EXEC MAINT,SIZE=80K`
	`   RENAMS oldname,newname..`
	`/*`
		`// EXEC MAINT,SIZE=80K`
		`   RENAMP oldname,newname`
		`/*`

Condense	`// EXEC MAINT,SIZE=80K`
	`   CONDS SL`
	`/*`
		`// EXEC MAINT,SIZE=80K`
		`   CONDS PL`
		`/*`

Figure 11.4 DOS/VSE JCS for library maintenance.

brary. It just removes the directory entry for that directory. If this space is needed, the library is *condensed* to physically delete this area and reformat the library.

Another method exists for reformatting a library. It is called the *backup and restore* method. This method is usually used by the computer operator.

Figure 11.4 shows a summary of some of the job control needed for library maintenance. Note that the only function *not* using the // EXEC MAINT program is the situation of cataloging in the CIL. The statements following the // EXEC MAINT statement are librarian control statements.

The first six letters of the control statement op code represents the following:

CATAL = catalog   RENAM = rename
DELET = delete   COND = condense

The last letter of the control statement op code represents the following:

C = CIL   S = SL
R = RL   P = PL

Therefore, DELETC IHLLAB1 means "delete the program (phase name) IHLLAB1 from the core image library."

EXAMPLE 11.4

Code the statements necessary to delete program PAYROL1 from the system core image library and condense the library.

Answer

```
* $$ JOB JNM=LOW,CLASS=J
* $$ LST CLASS=B
// JOB LOW    DELETE PAYROL1 FROM THE CIL AND CONDENSE
// EXEC MAINT,SIZE=80K
   DELETC PAYROL1
   CONDS CL
/*
/&
* $$ EOJ
```

Deleting and condensing in the other libraries uses the same procedures except that you would change the last letter of the control statement op code to the appropriate letter (e.g., R for relocatable) and the appropriate library abbreviation in the CONDS statement (e.g., RL for relocatable).

Renaming entries in the libraries is a simple process.

EXAMPLE 11.5

Rename an entry in the procedure library called IHLJCL. The new name is to be CLJCL.

Answer

```
* $$ JOB JNM=ANDERS,CLASS=J
* $$ LST CLASS=B
// JOB ANDERS    RENAME IHLJCL TO CLJCL
// EXEC MAINT,SIZE=80K
   RENAMP IHLJCL,CLJCL
/*
/&
* $$ EOJ
```

Cataloging. Cataloging in the core image and relocatable libraries is not as straightforward as using the other MAINT functions. In fact, on some systems, cataloging in the equivalent of the CIL is automatic each time you compile. Unfortunately, this is not true in DOS/VSE. Examples of cataloging in these libraries follow.

EXAMPLE 11.6

Code the statements necessary to catalog the COBOL program GRREP in the system CIL.

Answer

```
* $$ JOB JNM=HARRIS,CLASS=S
* $$ LST CLASS=Z
// JOB HARRIS    CATALOG PROGRAM GRREP IN THE CIL
// OPTION CATAL
```

```
                      PHASE GRREP,*
                      ACTION NOMAP
                     // EXEC FCOBOL,SIZE=100K
                      CBL APOST
                     /INCLUDE GRREP
                     /*
                     // EXEC LNKEDT,SIZE=64K
                     /*
                     // EXEC DSERV,SIZE=20K    PROVE THAT PROGRAM IS IN THE CIL
                      DSPLY CD(GRREP)
                     /*
                     /&
                     * $$ EOJ
```

EXAMPLE 11.7

Code the statements necessary to catalog an assembler program named
JDATE in the system RL.

In former days, an object program was punched in a deck of cards.
Then it was used with an INCLUDE statement and the MAINT program
to place it in the RL. Now a tape is assigned as SYSPCH. The following
job stream shows how this is done.

Answer

```
* $$ JOB JNM=JOHNS,CLASS=S
* $$ LST CLASS=Z
// JOB JOHNS                    CATALOG THE PROGRAM JDATE IN THE RL
// OPTION DECK                  PUNCH OBJECT PROGRAM
// ASSGN SYS021,300             REWIND TAPE ON DRIVE 300 AND WRITE TAPE MARK
// MTC REW,SYS021
// MTC WTM,SYS021
// MTC REW,SYS021
// ASSGN SYS021,UA              UNASSIGN TAPE AND ASSIGN IT AS SYSPCH
// ASSGN SYSPCH,300
// EXEC ASSEMBLY,SIZE=100K      ASSEMBLE SUBROUTINE JDATE AND PUNCH
   PUNCH 'CATALR JDATE'         OBJECT PROGRAM ON TAPE
/INCLUDE JDATE                  BRING IN PROGRAM FROM ICCF LIBRARY
/*
// MTC WTM,SYSPCH               WRITE TM AND REWIND TAPE
// MTC REW,SYSPCH
// ASSGN SYSPCH,02D             REASSIGN SYSPCH TO NORMAL ASSIGNMENT
// ASSGN SYSIPT,300             ASSIGN DEVICE THAT READS PROGRAMS TO 300
// EXEC MAINT,SIZE=80K          CATALOG OBJECT PROGRAM ON TAPE IN RL
/*                              (CATALR JDATE CONTROL STATEMENT IS ON TAPE)
// ASSGN SYSIPT,02C             REASSIGN SYSIPT TO NORMAL ASSIGNMENT
// EXEC DSERV,SIZE=20K          PROVE JDATE IS IN RL
   DSPLY RD(JDATE)
/*
/&
* $$ EOJ
```

The PUNCH 'CATALR JDATE' statement in the job stream is an
assembler statement that punches what is in apostrophes. Since this was the
first statement on tape, we did not have to have it following the // EXEC
DSERV statement in the job stream.

When entries are cataloged in the source library, they are called books. They are given names of the form "sublib.bookname." The sublibrary is represented by one alphabetic character. The general conventions used for the sublibrary name are

- C for COBOL programs
- R for RPG programs
- A for assembler programs
- P for data or Pl/1 programs

The bookname can be one to eight alphameric characters (∅–9,A–Z, #, $, and @). The first character must be alphabetic (A–Z) and the name ALL is invalid.

Books being cataloged must be preceded and followed by BKEND statements. The BKEND statements must start to the right of column 1.

EXAMPLE 11.8

Code the statements necessary to catalog a COBOL source program in the source library under the name IHLLAB1. This program has been keyed in the ICCF library.

Answer

```
      * $$ JOB JNM=SAMS,CLASS=J
      * $$ LST CLASS=B
      // JOB SAMS   CATALOG A COBOL PROGRAM IN THE SL
      // EXEC MAINT,SIZE=80K
        CATALS C.IHLLAB1
        BKEND
      /INCLUDE IHLLAB1
        BKEND
      /*
      /&
      * $$ EOJ
```

To retrieve this book in a job stream, we use the POWER statement * $$ SLI C.IHLLAB1.

EXAMPLE 11.9

Catalog a stream of data in an ICCF library member in the system SL under the name P.PAYDATA and do a SSERV to show what was cataloged.

Answer

```
* $$ JOB JNM=MIMS,CLASS=J
* $$ LST CLASS=Z
// JOB MIMS   CATALOG DATA IN THE SL
// EXEC MAINT,SIZE=80K
  CATALS P.PAYDATA
/INCLUDE PAYDATA (BKENDs are in PAYDATA)
/*
// EXEC SSERV,SIZE=20K   DISPLAY WHAT WAS CATALOGED IN THE SL
  DSPLY P.PAYDATA
/*
/&
* $$ EOJ
```

EXAMPLE 11.10

Catalog a stream of JCL (in an ICCF library under the name JCL) in the
PL under the name of PROC1. Do a PSERV to show what was cataloged.

Answer

```
* $$ JOB JNM=JONES,CLASS=J
* $$ LST CLASS=Z
// JOB JONES   CATALOG IN THE PL
// EXEC MAINT,SIZE=80K
  CATALP PROC1
/INCLUDE JCL
/*
// EXEC PSERV,SIZE=20K
   DSPLY PROC1
/+ (End of procedure)
/*
/&
* $$ EOJ
```

Notice that a new / + delimiter statement has been used. To retrieve
and include this JCL in a job stream, the following job control statement is
used:

```
// EXEC PROC=PROC1
```

If cataloging is done in a private library, LIBDEF, DLBL, and EX-
TENT statements for the private library must be inserted before the // EXEC
MAINT statement.

Entries in the SL and PL can be updated, although most programmers
simply recatalog and condense.

The Organizational Programs

The *organizational programs* in the LIBRARIAN are used to organize or create
libraries.

The CORGZ *copy program* in the LIBRARIAN is used to:

1. Copy system resident volumes
2. Create private libraries
3. Transfer entries between libraries of the same type

This program is executed by use of the job control statement

```
// EXEC CORGZ,SIZE=80K
```

It has control statements which are:

1. ALLOC This creates new systems packs.
2. NEWVOL This creates private libraries.
3. MERGE This transfers elements between existing libraries of the same
   types.

The COPYSERV program compares the contents of two libraries and will
generate input for the CORGZ program.

Systems programmers usually work with these programs, so we will not use them. However, you should know that these programs exist and what they are used for.

THE AMS PROGRAM

The Access Method Services program is a service program used to create and maintain VSAM files. Some, but not all, of the ways in which it can be used are to:

1. Define and copy VSAM catalogs
2. Allocate space for a VSAM file
3. Create, print, copy, or reorganize VSAM files
4. Create a backup copy of a file
5. Alter, delete, or list catalog entries
6. Convert a sequential or indexed-sequential file to VSAM format

Command	Use
ALTER	Used to alter existing catalog entries
BLDINDEX	Used to build alternate indexes
DEFINE	Used to define catalogs, alternate indexes, data spaces, VSAM and non-VSAM files, and paths
DELETE	Used to delete catalogs, data spaces, VSAM and non-VSAM files, alternate indexes, passwords, and paths
EXPORT	Used to create a copy of a file for backup or to make a file or user catalog portable so that it can be used on another system
EXPORTA	Used to recover data independent of the status of a catalog by means of duplicate catalog entries in catalog recovery areas (CRAs)
IMPORT	Used to read a backup copy of a file or to make available for use in one system a file or user catalog that was previously exported from another system
IMPORTRA	Used to make data recovered via the EXPORTRA function available again
LISTCAT	Used to list catalog entries
LISTCRA	Used to list catalog recovery areas or make comparisons with another catalog
PRINT	Used to print VSAM and non-VSAM files
REPRO	Used to copy files and to convert sequential files on tape or disk and ISAM files to VSAM format; used to convert ISAM files to sequential format, to create backup copies of VSAM catalogs, and to reload a VSAM catalog from a backup copy.
RESETCAT	Used to reset a recoverable catalog to the level of its owned volumes
VERIFY	Used to cause a catalog to correctly reflect the end of file

Figure 11.5 AMS functional commands and their uses.

```
DELETE    (entryname[/password][ entryname[/password]...]|volsr)

          [ALTERNATEINDEX|CLUSTER|MASTERCATALOG|NONVSAM|PATH|
              SPACE|USERCATALOG]

          [CATALOG(catname[/password][ dname])]

          [ERASE|NOERASE]

          [FILE(dname)]

          [FORCE|NOFORCE]

          [PURGE|NOPURGE]

          [SCRATCH|NOSCRATCH]
```

Figure 11.6   The AMS DELETE command format.

The AMS program is loaded by the use of the job control statement

```
// EXEC IDCAMS,SIZE=AUTO
```

The program has two types of commands: functional and modal. *Functional commands* are used to request that actual work be done (e.g., defining a file). *Modal commands* specify options and allow the conditional execution of functional commands.

Figure 11.5 shows a summary of the functional commands and the functions that they perform. (See page 150.)

The modal commands, which we will not be concerned with, are the IF, DO, END, SET, and PARM commands. The general format for these statements is

```
ḃVerbḃḃparametersḃterminator
```

1. The verb specifies the service requested.
2. The parameters further describe the verb.
3. The terminator (a semicolon or simply the absence of a continuation symbol) indicates the end of the command.

Verbs can be separated by one or more blanks, a comment, or both. Comments are made up of a string of characters preceded by a /* and followed by a */. (Comments can contain any character but a */.)

A few AMS commands and their use are demonstrated below.

Figure 11.6 shows the DELETE command format. The meaning of the notation is similar to DOS/VSE commands:

1. Brackets [ ] represent an optional field or parameter.
2. The vertical bar | separating parameters means "choose one."
3. Braces { } represent a field or parameter that must be chosen.
4. Elipsis (. . .) indicate that multiple entries are allowed.
5. Underscores indicate a default.
6. Parentheses, commas, and spaces must be entered as shown.
   ḃ = blank.
7. A minus sign at the right indicates a continuation.

EXAMPLE 11.11

Code the job stream to delete a VSAM file named
@MCC.CDP251.MASTER.FILE from the SIPOE.USER.CATALOG.

Answer

```
* $$ JOB JNM=KLINE,CLASS=J
* $$ LST CLASS=B
// JOB KLINE    DELETE A VSAM FILE
// EXEC IDCAMS,SIZE=AUTO
   DELETE (@MCC.CDP251.MASTER.FILE)    -
   CLUSTER                             -
   PURGE                               -
   CATALOG(SIPOE.USER.CATALOG)
/*
/&
* $$ EOJ
```

The continuation or minus sign can be coded in any column through
column 72.

The name in parentheses after the verb DELETE specifies the object
to be deleted. CLUSTER specifies that all components of the cluster (i.e.,
index, data components, etc.) are deleted. PURGE specifies the object is
to be deleted regardless of the retention date. CATALOG gives the name
of the catalog that defines the object to be deleted.

Many persons favor coding only one operand per line. However, the DE-
LETE statement could have been coded as follows:

```
DELETE (@MCC.CDP251.MASTER.FILE) CLUSTER PURGE -
   CATALOG(SIPOE.USER.CATALOG)
```

The DEFINE CLUSTER command format is shown in Figures 11.7, 11.8,
and 11.9. As can be seen, this command is quite complex. Briefly,

1. The CLUSTER NAME (   ) parameter gives the name of the CLUSTER
    being defined.
2. The MODEL (   ) parameter says that what is in the parentheses is to
    be used as a model for this entry being built. This parameter is required
    if you are using a model that already exists in the catalog for the entry
    being built in this command.
3. The DATA (   ) parameter specifies the attributes of the data component
    cluster.
4. The INDEX (   ) parameter gives the attributes of the index component
    (KSDS). NONINDEXED here would indicate an ESDS file and NUM-
    BERED would indicate an RRDS file. The default is INDEXED.
5. The CATALOG parameter identifies the catalog in which the cluster is
    defined. The only time that this parameter needs to be included is (a) if
    it is needed for password specification, or (b) if the catalog is not the
    default catalog.

```
DEFINE   CLUSTER
         (
             NAME(entryname)
             [ATTEMPTS(number)]
             [AUTHORIZATION(entrypoint[♭string])]
             [BUFFERSPACE(size)]
             [CODE(code)]
             [CONTROLINTERVALSIZE(SIZE)]
             [CONTROLPW(password)]
             [CYLINDERS(primary[♭secondary])|
                BLOCKS(primary[♭secondary])|
                RECORDS(primary[♭secondary])|
                TRACKS(primary[♭secondary])]
             [ERASE|NOERASE]
             [EXCEPTIONEXIT(mname)]
             [FILE(dname)]
             [FOR(days)|TO(date)]
             [FREESPACE(cipercent[♭capercent])]
             [IMBED|NOIMBED]
             [INDEXED|NONINDEXED|NUMBERED]
             [KEYRANGES((lowkey♭highkey)
                [♭lowkey♭highkey)...])]
             [KEYS(length♭offset)]
             [MASTERPW(password)]
             [MODEL(entryname[/password]
                [♭catname[/password][♭dname]])]
             [ORDERED|UNORDERED]
             [OWNER(ownerid)]
             [READPW(password)]
             [RECORDFORMAT(FORMAT)]
             [RECORDSIZE(average♭maximum)]
             [RECOVERY|SPEED]
             [REPLICATE|NOREPLICATE]
             [REUSE|NOREUSE]
             [SHAREOPTIONS(value[♭reserved])]
             [SPANNED|NONSPANNED]
             [UNIQUE|SUBALLOCATION|NOALLOCATION]
             [UPDATEPW(password)]
             [USECLASS(primary[♭secondary])]
             [VOLUMES(volser[♭volser...])|
                DEFAULTVOLUMES]
             [WRITECHECK|NOWRITECHECK]
         )
```

Figure 11.7 DEFINE CLUSTER component.

```
[DATA
 (
     [ATTEMPTS(number)]
     [AUTHORIZATION(entrypoint[♭string])]
     [BUFFERSPACE(size)]
     [CODE(code)]
     [CONTROLINTERVALSIZE(SIZE)]
     [CONTROLPW(password)]
     [CYLINDERS(primary[♭secondary])|
       BLOCKS(primary[♭secondary])|
       RECORDS(primary[♭secondary])|
       TRACKS(primary[♭secondary])]
     [ERASE|NOERASE]
     [EXCEPTIONEXIT(mname)]
     [FILE(dname)]
     [FREESPACE(cipercent[♭capercent])]
     [IMBED|NOIMBED]
     [INDEXED|NONINDEXED|NUMBERED]
     [KEYRANGES((lowkey♭highkey)
       [♭lowkey♭highkey)...])]
     [KEYS(length♭offset)]
     [MASTERPW(password)]
     [MODEL(entryname[/password]
       [♭catname[/password][♭dname]])]
     [NAME(entryname)]
     [ORDERED|UNORDERED]
     [OWNER(ownerid)]
     [READPW(password)]
     [RECORDSIZE(average♭maximum)]
     [RECOVERY|SPEED]
     [REUSE|NOREUSE]
     [SHAREOPTIONS(value[♭reserved])]
     [SPANNED|NONSPANNED]
     [UNIQUE|SUBALLOCATION|NOALLOCATION]
     [UPDATEPW(password)]
     [USECLASS(primary[♭secondary])]
     [VOLUMES(volser[♭volser...])|
        DEFAULTVOLUMES]
     [WRITECHECK|NOWRITECHECK]
 )]
```

Figure 11.8 DEFINE DATA component.

```
[INDEX
(
   [ATTEMPTS(number)]
   [AUTHORIZATION(entrypoint[ốstring])]
   [CODE(code)]
   [CONTROLINTERVALSIZE(SIZE)]
   [CONTROLPW(password)]
   [CYLINDERS(primary[ốsecondary])|
      BLOCKS(primary[ốsecondary])|
       RECORDS(primary[ốsecondary])|
       TRACKS(primary[ốsecondary])]
   [EXCEPTIONEXIT(mname)]
   [FILE(dname)]
   [IMBED|NOIMBED]
   [MASTERPW(password)]
   [MODEL(entryname[/password]
       [ốcatname[/password][ốdname]])]
   [NAME(entryname)]
   [ORDERED|UNORDERED]
   [OWNER(ownerid)]
   [READPW(password)]
   [REPLICATE|NOREPLICATE]
   [REUSE|NOREUSE]
   [SHAREOPTIONS(value[ốreserved])]
   [SPANNED|NONSPANNED]
   [UNIQUE|SUBALLOCATION|NOALLOCATION]
   [UPDATEPW(password)]
   [USECLASS(primary[ốsecondary])]
   [VOLUMES(volser[ốvolser...])|
       DEFAULTVOLUMES]
   [WRITECHECK|NOWRITECHECK]
)]

[CATALOG(catname[/password][ốdname])]
```

Figure 11.9 DEFINE INDEX and CATALOG components.

EXAMPLE 11.12

Define a default model for a SAM ESDS file. There will be a maximum of 1000 80-byte records. The name of the object being defined DEFAULT.MODEL.ESDS.SAM, and the volume serial number of the volume to be used is SYSWK3.

Answer

```
* $$ JOB JNM=REED,CLASS=J
* $$ LST CLASS=B
// JOB REED    DEFINE A DEFAULT MODEL FOR A SAM ESDS FILE
// EXEC IDCAMS,SIZE=AUTO
   DEFINE CLUSTER (NAME(DEFAULT.MODEL.ESDS.SAM) -
       VOLUMES(SYSWK3) -
       RECORDS(1000) -
       RECORDSIZE(80 80) -
       RECORDFORMAT(UNDEF) -
       REUSE -
       NOALLOCATION -
       NONINDEXED)
   LISTCAT -
       ENTRIES(DEFAULT.MODEL.ESDS.SAM) -
       ALL
/*
/&
* $$ EOJ
```

The RECORDSIZE operand specifies the average and maximum length in bytes of the data record. These values are used by AMS to compute the control interval and control area sizes.

The REUSE operand means that it is permissible to reload or use this area as a work file.

The LISTCAT verb is used to list entries in a catalog. The format of the LISTCAT command is shown in Figure 11.10. The ALTERNATEIN-DEX through USERCATALOG entries specify the type of entries to be listed. The ENTRIES operand simply indicates that we wish to see any entries with the name in parentheses. The default for ENTRIES is all entries in the catalog. The ALL operand specifies that all fields in the entry are to be listed, the default being NAME.

The CATALOG entry is not used here because it is the default catalog.

```
LISTCAT   [ALTERNATEINDEX]
          [ƀCLUSTER]
          [ƀDATA]
          [ƀINDEX]
          [ƀNONVSAM]
          [ƀPATH]
          [ƀSPACE]
          [ƀUSERCATALOG]
          [CATALOG(catname[/password][ƀdname])]
          [ENTRIES(entryname[/password]
             [ƀentryname[/password][ƀ...]])]
          [NAME|VOLUME|ALLOCATION|ALL]
          [NOTUSABLE]
```

Figure 11.10 The AMS LISTCAT command format.

This example implies the use of what is called a ''VSAM space management for SAM'' feature provided by IBM. It allows you to define and process SAM files in a VSAM data space. A SAM ESDS file is not identical to a VSAM ESDS file. A SAM ESDS file is a SAM file within a VSAM data space. It is defined using the space management feature, and its name is entered in the VSAM catalog. A VSAM ESDS file is defined using *IDCAMS*.

EXAMPLE 11.13

Define an area for converting an ISAM file to a VSAM file. The cluster name is CDP251.MASTER.FILE and the user catalog name is SIPOE.USER.CATALOG. The DATA name is the cluster name plus DATA, and the index name is the cluster name plus INDEX. Where you see IIISSSS, the user is to key his or her initials and the last four digits of the person's social security number.

Answer

```
* $$ JOB JNM=MANN,CLASS=J
* $$ LST CLASS=B
// JOB MANN    DEFINE A VSAM FILE FOR ISAM CONVERSION
// EXEC IDCAMS,SIZE=AUTO
   DELETE (CDP251.IIISSSS.MASTER.FILE) CLUSTER PURGE -
      CATALOG(SIPOE.USER.CATALOG)
   DEFINE CLUSTER (NAME(CDP251.IIISSSS.MASTER.FILE) -
      MODEL(@MCC.CDP251.MASTER.FILE SIPOE.USER.CATALOG)) -
      DATA (NAME(CDP251.IIISSSS.MASTER.FILE.DATA)) -
      INDEX (NAME(CDP251.IIISSSS.MASTER.FILE.INDEX)) -
      CATALOG(SIPOE.USER.CATALOG)
/*
/&
* $$ EOJ
```

EXAMPLE 11.14

Define an ESDS cluster to be named CDP251.LEE.ESDS.FILE. It will have a maximum of 250 records, fixed length, and 140 bytes in length. Use a volume named SYSWK1. The user catalog name is SIPOE.USER.CATALOG.

Answer

```
* $$ JOB JNM=ROWE,CLASS=J
* $$ LST CLASS=B
// JOB ROWE    DEFINE AN ESDS CLUSTER
// EXEC IDCAMS,SIZE=AUTO
   DEFINE CLUSTER (NAME(CDP251.LEE.ESDS.FILE) -
         VOLUMES(SYSWK1) -
         RECORDS(250) -
         RECORDSIZE(140 140) -
         NONINDEXED) -
         DATA (NAME(CDP251.LEE.ESDS.FILE.DATA)) -
         CATALOG(SIPOE.USER.CATALOG)
/*
/&
* $$ EOJ
```

A RRDS file could be defined as in Example 11.14 except that NUMBERED would be substituted for the NONINDEXED entry.

EXAMPLE 11.15

Define the same file as in Example 11.14 as a KSDS file. The key is four bytes long and begins in the first position of the record. Allow 15 percent of the control interval for free space and 20 percent of the control area for free space.

Answer

```
* $$ JOB JNM=HAMM,CLASS=J
* $$ LST CLASS=B
// JOB HAMM    DEFINE A KSDS CLUSTER
```

```
// EXEC IDCAMS,SIZE=AUTO
   DEFINE CLUSTER (NAME(CDP251.LEE.KSDS.FILE) -
          VOLUMES(SYSWK1) -
          RECORDS(250) -
          RECORDSIZE(140 140) -
          FREESPACE(15 20) -
          KEYS(4 0) -
          INDEXED) -
          DATA (NAME(CDP251.LEE.KSDS.FILE.DATA)) -
          INDEX (NAME(CDP251.LEE.KSDS.FILE.INDEX)) -
          CATALOG(SIPOE.USER.CATALOG)
/*
/&
* $$ EOJ
```

The INDEXED entry could have been omitted since it is the default.

This AMS section has shown you how to define a cluster or file. Each data space that contains these clusters must be defined, but the system's programmer usually defines the data space and any catalogs that are used (i.e., the SIPOE.USER.CATALOG in Examples 11.13, 11.14, and 11.15. You need only be concerned with defining the area for your VSAM file or cluster.

Group	Program Name	Functions	Size
Maintenance	MAINT	Catalog (in RL, SL, and PL) Delete Rename Condense Update for SL	80K
Service	DSERV	Display the contents of the library directories	20K
	CSERV RSERV SSERV PSERV	Display and/or punch the contents of an element in the CIL, RL, SL, or PL	20K
	ESERV	Convert edited macros to source format; display and/or punch converted macros	64K
Organization	CORGZ	Allocate a new SYSRES Create a private library Transfer elements between two libraries of the same type	80K
	COPYSERV	Compare library contents and generate input for CORGZ	20K

Figure 11.11 A summary of the LIBRARIAN programs (version 1 DOS/VSE).

SUMMARY

Service programs assist in the successful execution of problem programs without directly controlling the system or production results.

A service program, the linkage editor, links the output of translators with any subroutines or I/O routines needed to produce an executable program. The linkage editor program has control statements: the ACTION, PHASE, ENTRY, and INCLUDE statements.

Another service program is the LIBRARIAN program. The DOS/VSE version 1 LIBRARIAN has three sets of programs: the maintenance, service, and organization programs. These programs and their functions are summarized in Figure 11.11.

Another service program is the AMS (Access Method Services) program. It is used to create, maintain, and delete VSAM files (ES, KS, and RR data sets). It can also be used to define and copy VSAM catalogs and data spaces, list the entries in a VSAM catalog, create SAM ESDS space, and convert native ISAM files to VSAM form. The program has functional and modal commands. The functional commands available are summarized in Figure 11.5.

TERMS TO REMEMBER

AMS program	LIBRARIAN
Backup and restore	Linkage editor program
Condense	Maintenance or MAINT program (LIBRARIAN)
COPYSERV program	Modal AMS command
CORZ copy program	Organizational program (LIBRARIAN)
CSERV	PSERV
DSERV	Reusable file
ESERV	RSERV
Functional AMS command	SSERV
IDCAMS	SYSCAT

STUDY GUIDE

1. State the three librarian programs and give the purpose of each.

(a) _Linkage editor Program - used to link the main object program to any subroutine_

(b) _Librarian Program - Group of programs used to maintain & service system & Private Library_

(c) _Access Method Services - maintains nonnative or vsam files_

2. State the purpose of the following service programs.

   (a) DSERV _Displays the entries in the directory_

   (b) CSERV _Prints or Punches the contents of an entry in the core image Library_

   (c) RSERV _Prints or Punches the contents of an entry in the relocatable Library_

   (d) PSERV _Prints or Punch the contents of an entry in the objective Library_

3. State at least five functions of the maintenance program.

   (a) _Catalog_

   (b) _Condense_

   (c) _Delete_

   (d) _Set Condense Limit_

   (e) _Rename_

4. State a purpose of the organizational set of LIBRARIAN programs.

   Organize or Create Libraries

5. State the purpose of the linkage editor program.

   Prepares the output from language Translators for execution

6. Name the four linkage editor control statements and give the purpose of each.

   (a) _Action - Alter certain options_

   (b) _Phase - Cataloging or placing a program in the core image Libraries_

   (c) _Include to include object module_

   (d) _Origin - Specifies the load address of the_

7. State the general format of the linkage editor control statements.

   b opcode b operands Separated by Commas

8. State the purpose of the ACTION NOMAP linkage editor control statement.

9. State the purpose of the AMS program.

   Used to Create + maintain VSAM files.

10. State the general format of the AMS commands.

Verb parameter terminator (handwritten)

11. State the purpose of the following functional AMS commands.

(a) LISTCAT *List catalog entries* (handwritten)

(b) DEFINE *Define catalog, Alternate Index, data spaces, VSAM, nonVSAM files & paths* (handwritten)

(c) DELETE *Delete catalogs, data spaces, VSAM, nonVSAM files, passwords* (handwritten)

12. What is the meaning of a SAM ESDS file?

CODING EXERCISES

Code the following job control exercises on coding sheets.

1. Code the job stream to catalog a COBOL program being compiled in the CIL under the name IIIEX1, where III = your initials. Also, do a DSERV on III to show that it has been cataloged. The program has already been keyed and is in your ICCF library under the name IIIEX1.

2. Code the job stream to rename the program in Exercise 1 under the name XXXEX1.

3. Code the job stream to delete the program XXXEX1 from the CIL.

4. Code the job stream to delete a cataloged procedure named PAYPROC and condense the PL.

5. Code the job stream to catalog 25 data records in the SL. The records are in your ICCF library under the name DATALB1. Display the contents of the entry cataloged to show what 25 records are there.

6. Code the job stream to display all the entries in the SL directory in sorted order.

7. Rename an RPG program entry in the SL. The old name is R.INVFILE. The new name is to be R.INVMAS. Do a DSERV to prove that is has been properly renamed.

8. Code the job control statements necessary to delete the VSAM file in the ESDS example in this chapter (Example 11.14).

9. Use the operands CLUSTER, NAME, and CATALOG to code the commands necessary to run a LISTCAT on the catalog name given to you by your instructor. Key and run this program. Circle any of your own files in the output.

10. This exercise is to be keyed and actually run.

    (a) *First job*. Code the statements necessary to catalog the programs used in Coding Exercise 1∅ of Chapter 9 or Coding Exercise 5 of Chapter 1∅ in the CIL. Your instructor will tell you what type of phase names and what library to use.

    (b) *Second job*. Code the statements necessary to do a DSERV to prove that the programs are there.

    (c) *Third job*. Code the statements necessary to execute these programs from the CIL using data set 2 in Appendix D.

    (d) Write a report in essay style discussing:

        (1) Any problems that you had.

        (2) The reason why a DSERV is used instead of a CSERV.

11. This exercise is to be keyed and actually run. Catalog the source statements in the ENVIRONMENT DIVISION of the program GSLIST (statements 1∅13∅∅–2∅∅8∅∅) in Appendix D in the source library. Your instructor will tell you what type of book names to use and the location of the library. Then do a DSERV on the SL to prove that the entry is there. Also, do a SSERV to show what is there.

RESEARCH PROBLEMS

Use the *DOS/VSE System Control Statements* manual for the following questions.

1. Look up the DSPLY or DSPLYS control statement for the DSERV program.

    (a) Do the DSPLY and DSPLYS op codes for the core image directory produce different results?

    (b) What does the SDL operand do?

2. Look up source library updating.

    (a) Describe how a statement can be:

        (1) Replaced without recataloging.

        (2) Added without recataloging.

        (3) Deleted without recataloging.

    (b) Why is this method difficult on the terminal or with 8∅-position records?

3. Look up updating a cataloged procedure.

    (a) Describe how a statement can be:

        (1) Replaced without recataloging.

        (2) Added without recataloging.

        (3) Deleted without recataloging.

    (b) Is this a temporary or permanent update?

Use the *Using VSE/VSAM Commands and Macros* manual to answer the following questions.

4. When must a MASTER catalog be defined?

5. Can a file be defined at the same time as the data space that will contain it? What is meant by calling the type of file UNIQUE?

6. What is a recoverable catalog?

chapter 12

DOS/VSE/SP (DOS/VSE Versions 2 and 3) Additions and Changes

INTRODUCTION

DOS/VSE/SP (SP = systems package) actually consists of two new versions of DOS/VSE. The original DOS/VSE is referred to by IBM as version 1. The first version of DOS/VSE/SP is termed version 2 of DOS/VSE and the second version is termed version 3 of DOS/VSE. In this chapter we deal with the changes involved between the original version (1) of DOS/VSE and the last version (3). Version 2 is very similar to version 3.

IBM lists the advantages of DOS/VSE/SP as:

1. Virtual storage is extended from a 16-megabyte (MB) limit to 4Ø MB.
2. A new LIBRARIAN program is available which combines the core image, relocatable, source, and procedure libraries into one large library. This library is subdivided into sublibraries which have member types: phases, relocatable modules, source books and macros, and procedures.
3. An interactive interface exists in which all users are presented with a single view of the system. Users may have access to all or some of these components as controlled through user profiles.
4. New conditional job control statements have been introduced.
5. Procedures may be cataloged with variable parameters. Values for these parameters may be supplied at job execution time.
6. Intelligent workstation support via personal computers is enhanced (or improved).
7. Problem determination and service and installation procedures are said to be improved.

For the purposes of this book, only items 2, 4, and 5 are of great importance to us.

CONDITIONAL JOB CONTROL STATEMENTS

The use of conditional job control statements in the job stream can eliminate many decisions that operators must make. Normally, job control statements are read and executed in the sequence in which they are entered on SYSRDR or SYSLOG. *Conditional job control statements* allow the system to execute or bypass parts of the job stream conditionally, depending on the result of previously executed steps within the same job.

To do this, a *return code* is used whose value may range from $\emptyset$ to $4\emptyset95$. This return code is set by a previously executed program and stays in effect until the next EXEC statement. The code is placed in the rightmost two bytes of general register 15 by the programmer, by an EOJ macro, or by a DUMP macro. Then its value can be tested by the use of a conditional job control statement. Return code standards recommended by IBM are shown in Figure 12.1.

If job control receives a return code greater than 16, it terminates the job unless the conditional job control ON statement is used to specify a different action for the return code given. Five conditional job control statements (the /., ON, IF, GOTO, and PWR statements) are discussed in individual sections below.

RC	Meaning
$\emptyset$	Function was executed normally. (This is the default.)
4	Function was executed, but the end result may not be as expected.
8	Some functions were not (or partly) executed, but processing continued.
12	Function could not be performed.
16	Severe error; the job stream is terminated.

Figure 12.1   Return code standards.

PARAMETERS AND PARAMETERIZED PROCEDURES

A *symbolic parameter* is a name that is one to seven alphabetic or numeric characters, the first of which must be alphabetic. When it is used in job control, it must be preceded by an ampersand (&) and is ended by a period or another character that is not numeric or alphabetic.

As will be seen, the values of these parameters can be assigned:

1.   In a PROC statement in a catalogued procedure. (A *cataloged procedure* is a stream of job control statements that have been placed in a library.)
2.   In a // EXEC PROC statement. As mentioned in Chapter 11, this is a version of the EXEC job control statement that brings a cataloged procedure into the job stream rather than executing an object program in a library.
3.   By a SETPARM command or statement in the job stream (discussed later in the chapter).
4.   By a SETPARM command or statement entered by the operator.

The values assigned to a symbolic parameter can be a character string $\emptyset$–$5\emptyset$ characters long. If special characters are included in the string, the string must be enclosed in apostrophes.

For example, if an ASSGN statement is written as follows:

```
// ASSGN SYS001,&UNIT.&VOLUME.
```

and in a cataloged procedure UNIT = 8809 and VOLUME = ',VOL = 666666', the ASSGN statement would be executed as

```
// ASSGN SYS001,8809,VOL=666666.
```

A job control operand can be all or part of a symbolic parameter.

Examples

Parameter	Assignment	Executed As
SYS&NUM	NUM = 008	SYS008
&C&UU	C=0, UU=2F	02F
&LIBNAM.LIB	LIBNAM=USER	USERLIB
&LIBNAM..LIB	LIBNAM=USER	USER.LIB
&SIZE.(132)	SIZE=BLKSIZE	BLKSIZE(132)
&SIZE(132)	SIZE=BLKSIZE	BLKSIZE(132)
&OPERAND	OPERAND='REW,300'	REW,300

THE LABEL STATEMENT

The format of the label statement is shown in Figure 12.2. The *label job control statement* is a fourth delimiter statement. It defines a point in the job stream up to which job control statements are to be skipped. The GOTO statement or the GOTO action of the ON statement is used in conjunction with this statement.

Label is a name consisting of one to eight alphanumeric characters, the first of which must be alphabetic. Symbolic parameters are not allowed in this statement.

Figure 12.2   The label statement format.

THE GOTO STATEMENT

The *GOTO job control statement* causes all statements in the following job stream to be skipped, up to the specified label statement. The format for this statement is shown in Figure 12.3. The label specifies (the operand of the /. statement) the point at which execution of the current job stream is to be continued. A GOTO $EOJ statement will cause all statements to be skipped up to the end-of-job or /& statement. The job stream *cannot* be searched backward. If *nested procedures* (procedures within procedures) are being used, the target label statement must be in the same procedure or an outside one. This rule is similar to the rule in FORTRAN on branching in a nested DO loop.

Figure 12.3   The GOTO statement format.

No check is made on duplicate labels. If duplicate labels exist, the branch will be made to the first duplicate label encountered.

THE IF STATEMENT

The *IF conditional statement* is used to check a given condition. If the condition is true, the following statement is executed; if not, the following statement is skipped. The format of this statement is shown in Figure 12.4. Continuation lines are accepted for the IF statement. The "THEN" is *not* optional as in the COBOL IF statement.

The condition operands specify a condition to be checked. An explanation of the condition operands follows:

1. $RC specifies the return code of a preceding job step. It is set by the last program executed and is in effect until the next job step (the next program executed).
2. $MRC specifies the maximum return code of all preceding job steps in the current job.
3. The operand "pname" specifies the name of a parameter to be compared.
4. The operand "n" specifies a decimal integer from 0 to 4095.
5. The operand "value" specifies a character string of $0-50$ characters. If the string has any special characters, it must be enclosed in apostrophes. This operand can also be a symbolic parameter.

If both items being compared are numbers, an arithmetic comparison is made. If one or both items being compared are nonnumeric, a logical comparison is made using the length of the longer operand and padding the shorter one on the right with blanks.

An example of using the IF and LABEL conditional job control statements follows:

```
(1)    * $$ JOB JNM=AMICK,CLASS=S
(2)    * $$ LST CLASS=Z
(3)    // JOB AMICK
(4)    // EXEC PROG1,SIZE=AUTO
(5)    // IF $RC = 0 THEN
(6)    // EXEC PROG2,SIZE=AUTO
(7)    /&
(8)    * $$ EOJ
```

```
              condition              condition
             ⌒‾‾‾‾‾‾‾‾⌒            ⌒‾‾‾‾⌒
[//] IF {$RC|$MRC|pname} c {n|val} [j...] THEN            (JCS,JCC)


    where c = comparators            and j = logical operators

          = or EQ                          OR or |
        ¬= or NE                           AND or &
         > or GT
         < or LT
        >= or GE
        <= or LE
```

Figure 12.4 The IF statement format.

If program 1 in statement 4 is not canceled and does not terminate abnormally, a return code of $0-4095$ will be returned. Program 2 in statement 6 is executed only if the statement 5 condition is true (i.e., the return code is $= 0$).

The IF statement checks *local conditions*, that is, conditions in that job step only. Therefore the IF statement is said to be a local conditional function.

THE ON STATEMENT

The *ON statement* tests a specified condition at the end of each job step following the ON statement. If the condition is true, the specified action is taken; otherwise, processing continues with the next statement. This statement is said to be a *global conditional* function. That is, it has the same value for several job steps.

The format of the ON statement is shown in Figure 12.5. Conditions and comparators have the same meanings as in the IF statement. However, you will note that there are two new conditions: $CANCEL and $ABEND.

- $CANCEL specifies that the action is to be taken if the CANCEL command has been used on the job (the operator canceled the job).
- $ABEND specifies that the action is to be taken if the step terminates abnormally.
- CONT or CONTINUE specifies that processing should continue if the specified condition is true. CONTINUE is not valid with the conditions $CANCEL or $ABEND.

Whenever a job starts, the default ON conditions are

```
ON $RC <  16 CONTINUE
ON $RC >= 16 GOTO $EOJ
ON $ABEND GOTO $EOJ
ON $CANCEL GOTO $EOJ
```

An example of the use of the IF, ON, and GOTO statements follows:

```
(1)  * $$ JOB JNM=LEA,CLASS=S
(2)  * $$ LST CLASS=Z
(3)  // JOB LEA
```

```
                     (conditions)
[//] ON {$RC c n|$CANCEL|$ABEND} [j...]              (JCS,JCC)
       {GOTO label|CONT[INUE]}

                     (actions)


   where c = the comparators        and j = the logical operators

          = or EQ                           OR or |
         ¬= or NE                           AND or &
          > or GT
          < or LT
         >= or GE
         <= or LE
```

Figure 12.5 The ON statement format.

```
(4)   // ON $ABEND GOTO CANRTN
(5)   // EXEC PROG1,SIZE=AUTO
(6)   // IF $RC > 4 THEN
(7)   // EXEC PROG2,SIZE=AUTO
(8)   // GOTO $EOJ
(9)   /. CANRTN
(10)  // EXEC CANPROG,SIZE=AUTO
(11)  /&
(12)  * $$ EOJ
```

Statement 4 says: "If there is an abnormal ending, skip all statements until the label statement CANRTN." Otherwise, if there is no abnormal ending, statement 5 is executed.

Statement 6 says: "If the return code from PROG1 is >4, execute the next statement (i.e., execute PROG2 in statement 7)." If the return code is not >4, statement 7 is skipped and only statement 8 is processed. Note that in both return code cases, statement 8 is processed and statements 9 and 10 are bypassed.

THE PWR STATEMENT

The format of the PWR statement is shown in Figure 12.6. The *PWR statement* allows the programmer rather than the operator to issue a PRELEASE or PHOLD console POWER command at any point in the job stream.

Example

```
// PWR PRELEASE RDR,LEEJOB
```

The underlined part of the statement is considered a console POWER command. (In this case, R cannot be used as an abbreviation for PRELEASE or H for PHOLD as is the custom on the console.)

This feature allows the programmer to release a program on HOLD in the RDR queue to run on the basis of what happens in a job step of the job *currently* running.

Example

```
* $$ JOB JNM=DUKE,CLASS=S
* $$ LST CLASS=Z
// JOB DUKE
// EXEC PROG1,SIZE=AUTO
// IF $RC=1 THEN
// PWR PRELEASE RDR,LEEJOB
// EXEC PROG2,SIZE=AUTO
/*
/&
* $$ EOJ
```

```
[//] PWR {PRELEASE...|PHOLD...}                        (JCS,JCC)
```

Figure 12.6 The PWR job control statement format.

THE LIBRARIAN PROGRAM (DOS/VSE/SP, VERSIONS 2 AND 3)

This service program replaces the version 1 LIBRARIAN program. It too services, copies, and provides access to system and printer libraries. It takes over the version 1 functions of the MAINT, COPYSERV, CORGZ, DSERV, CSERV, RSERV, SSERV, PSERV, BACKUP, and RESTORE programs. Its facilities are now invoked by *one* // EXEC LIBR job control statement. If the SIZE option is used, at least 256K should be used in the SIZE operand of the EXEC statement. After this EXEC statement, the action to be taken is described by the use of further commands called *LIBRARIAN commands*. The actions to be taken are ended by a /* end-of-session command (in batch mode).

The following facts should be noted:

1. The system library is no longer the default.
2. Several of the "old" programs, such as the DSERV program, are *emulated* for compatibility reasons. (To emulate means to imitate.)
3. Any comment on a LIBRARIAN command must begin with a /* and end with a */.
4. SYSCLB, SYSRLB, and SYSSLB are no longer supported in ASSGN statements and commands.
5. There is a new format for the LIBDEF, LIBDROP, and LIBLIST statements, but the old versions are automatically converted. However, the LIBDEF statement is *not* needed with LIBRARIAN commands.
6. Return codes (see Figure 12.1) are now returned by the LIBRARIAN program, and the code can be tested.
7. The structure of the libraries is different and is described in the following section.

The DOS/VSE/SP Library Organization

All data (programs, procedures, data, subroutines, macros, etc.) exists in libraries that are divided into *sublibraries*. These libraries have data in units called *members*.

Each member can be identified by one or more of the following items:

1. A *library name*, identified by LIB = 1., where 1 is a library name of one to seven characters (A–Z, Ø–9, $, #, @) and LIB is a keyword.
2. A *sublibrary name*, identified by SUBLIB = 1.s, where s is a sublibrary name of one to eight characters, 1 has the meaning in item (1) above, and SUBLIB is a keyword. (IJSYSRS, IJSYSRn, and SYSLIB should not be used as a sublibrary name since they are reserved for SYSRES files and the system sublibrary, respectively.)

Most LIBRARIAN commands that act on members require a further identification of mn.mt, where:

1. A *member name* (mn) is one to eight alphameric characters (A–Z, Ø–9, $, #, @) in length, and
2. A *member type* (mt) is one to eight alphameric characters (A–Z, Ø–9, $, #, @) in length.

Member Type	MT	Old Version 1 Library
Phases (executable programs)	PHASE	CIL
Modules (output from a language translator—not link edited)	OBJ	RL
Procedures (cataloged job control statements)	PROC	PL
Books (source programs, data)	Any characters (A–Z, 0–9, $, #, @) Suggestions: use C for COBOL R for RPG A for assembler P for data	SL
Dumps	DUMP	Not applicable

Figure 12.7 Member type usage.

Member type usage is shown in Figure 12.7. Note that:

1. Library members, called *phases*, are executable programs that have been compiled or translated and link edited.
2. Library members, called *modules*, are subroutines or macros that have been compiled but *not* link edited.
3. Library members, *books*, are source programs or parts of source programs or data records.
4. Library members, called *procedures*, are streams of job control statements.

LIBRARIAN Commands

LIBRARIAN commands follow the // EXEC LIBR,SIZE = 256K statement. The format of these commands is

```
 bop codeboperands separated by a blank or comma
```

A summary of possible LIBRARIAN command op codes and their functions is shown in Figure 12.8. Note the following:

1. The op code can start anywhere after column 1. The command should not extend past column 71.
2. Allowed separators (comma, blank, equal sign, colon, two periods, parentheses, or comments) may be surrounded by one or more blanks.
3. Comments may be used where a blank is allowed. Comments must begin with a /* and end with a */.

Op Code	Function
ACCESS	Specifies the sublibrary, qualified by the library name, to be used in any following commands
BACKUP	Causes libraries, sublibraries, or SYSRES files to be copied to tape
CATALOG	Causes the data following it to be cataloged under the name and type specified
CHANGE	Can be used to change the REUSE attribute of a sublibrary
COMPARE	Used to compare libraries, sublibraries, or members and provide a listing of the differences
CONNECT	Must be used before COPY, MOVE, or COMPARE commands to provide the names of the sublibraries in which members are to be found or placed
COPY	Used to copy libraries, sublibraries, or members
DEFINE	Used to create system and private libraries and sublibraries
DELETE	Used to delete members, sublibraries, or libraries
GOTO	Causes the LIBRARIAN to skip all LIBRARIAN commands up to the LIBRARIAN label command
INPUT	Causes the LIBRARIAN to read any following commands from SYSIPT instead of SYSLOG until the end of the current job step (has no effect if SYSIPT is already defined as the input device)
LIST	Causes the *contents* of one or more members to be displayed on SYSLST or SYSLOG
LISTDIR	Displays the contents of a library *directory*
MOVE	Moves data from one library or sublibrary to another
ON	Allows the conditional execution of LIBRARIAN command streams in batch mode
PUNCH	Causes the contents of one or more members to be "punched" to SYSPCH
RELEASE	Used to override the AUTOMATIC attribute of a library or sublibrary
RENAME	Used to change the name and/or type of one or more members, or the names of one or more sublibraries
RESTORE	Causes libraries, sublibraries, and members or SYSRES files which were backed up to be restored to disk
TEST	Used to check the structure and contents of a library, sublibrary, or member for consistency and corrections
UPDATE	Allows the contents of a member to be modified by adding, deleting, or replacing lines

Figure 12.8   Summary of LIBRARIAN commands.

```
{LISTDir|LD}  {Lib=1...|Sublib=1.s,...|mn,mt...|SDL}        (LIBR)
              {Output={Full|Normal|SHort|STatus}]
              [Unit={SYSLST|SYSLOG}]
```

Figure 12.9   The LIBRARIAN LIST DIRECTORY (LISTDIR) command format.

4. Statements may be continued by the use of a minus sign (−) *anywhere* in the statement if it is the *last nonblank character* on the line. Otherwise, the minus sign is considered a separator.

In regard to command syntax notation:

1. Command op codes can be shortened by leaving off one or more letters from right to left, as long as the name is unique. For example, COMPARE could be coded COMPARE, COMPAR, COMPA, COMP, or COM. But CO could *not* be used because CONNECT and COPY start with CO. Operands can be shortened in the same manner.

2. Operands may be positional or keyword (as with POWER commands), but positional operands must come first.

3. Some commands perform the function on several targets at once. This is indicated in the syntax as three dots. Example: LIB = 1 . . . Here, for example, you could code:

```
    LIB = LIB1 LIB2 LIB3
 or LIB = LIB1, LIB2, LIB3
 or LIB = (LIB1 LIB2 LIB3)
 or LIB = (LIB1,LIB2,LIB3)
```

4. As in microcomputer DOS commands, the sequence of the operands for commands that require two targets determines how the command is carried out. In a COPY command if you use LIB = LIB1:LIB2 or LIB1:LIB2, the action is from LIB1 to LIB2.

5. As in microcomputer DOS commands, generic references are allowed for member names and types within a sublibrary. AB*.OBJ means all object modules beginning with the letters AB. LEE.* means all types with the name LEE.

It would be possible to organize the libraries into phase, module, book, and procedure sublibraries as in version 1 of DOS/VSE. However, centers often organize the libraries according to task (i.e., all payroll source, object, data, and procedures in the same library).

These libraries have directories that can be listed by the use of the LISTDIR LIBRARIAN command. Individual library members can be listed by the use of the LIST LIBRARIAN command.

The LISTDIR or LD LIBRARIAN Command. The format of the LISTDIR LIBRARIAN command is shown in Figure 12.9. The *LISTDIR command* is used to list the contents of a library directory. The output is a list sorted in alphanumeric order. The command can be used to see if a library, sublibrary, or member exists. If it does not exist, a return code of 4 is set; and this code can be tested by an ON command.

An explanation of the LISTDIR operands follows.

First Operand

1. A choice of Lib = 1 indicates the directory of a library or libraries (and all sublibrary contents) are to be displayed.

2. A choice of Sublib = 1.s indicates that the directory contents of a specific sublibrary or sublibraries is to be displayed.

3. A choice of mn.mt specifies that only the parts of the sublibrary directory relevant to the member or members is to be displayed. If this choice is used, an ACCESS LIBRARIAN command naming the sublibrary must precede.

4. SDL specifies that the system directory is to be displayed. In this case the OUTPUT operand cannot be used.

Second Operand. This operand controls the type and amount of information to be displayed. As can be seen in the format, NORMAL is the default. STATUS cannot be used for member displays.

Third Operand. The UNIT operand specifies the output device for the display. If the LISTDIR command is issued from SYSIPT (batch), the default is SYSLST. If the command is issued from SYSLOG, the default is SYSLOG.

EXAMPLE 12.1

Display the contents of the system library directory.

Answer

```
* $$ JOB JNM=BALL,CLASS=J
* $$ LST CLASS=B
// JOB BALL
// EXEC LIBR,SIZE=256K
  LISTD SDL
/*
/&
* $$ EOJ
```

Note the use of the /* command to end the LIBRARIAN commands. Its format is shown in Figure 12.10.

```
Format for SYSIPT        Format for SYSLOG           (LIBR)
    /*                         END
```

Figure 12.10 The LIBRARIAN End-of-session command format.

EXAMPLE 12.2

Display the directory of a sublibrary named USER.STUDENT.

Answer

```
* $$ JOB JNM=LOPEZ,CLASS=J
* $$ LST CLASS=B
// JOB LOPEZ
// EXEC LIBR,SIZE=256K
  LISTD SUBLIB=USER.STUDENT
/*
/&
* $$ EOJ
```

EXAMPLE 12.3

Display the phase members beginning with LEE in the sublibrary named USER.STUDENT.

Answer

```
* $$ JOB JNM=COLE,CLASS=J
* $$ LST CLASS=B
// JOB COLE
// EXEC LIBR,SIZE=256K
   ACCESS SUBLIB=USER.STUDENT
   LISTD LEE*.PHASE
/*
/&
* $$ EOJ
```

Note the ACCESS LIBRARIAN command shown in Example 12.3.

The ACCESS Command. The format of the ACCESS command is shown in Figure 12.11. The ACCESS command is used to specify the sublibrary, qualified by the library name, where a member used in the following command can be found.

```
Access {Sublib=1.s|?}                                          (LIBR)
```

Figure 12.11   The LIBRARIAN ACCESS command format.

It remains in effect until one of the three following occurs:

1. Another ACCESS command is given.
2. The sublibrary in the command is deleted or renamed.
3. The library containing the sublibrary is deleted by a DELETE command or a MOVE or RESTORE command is used.

A question mark used as an operand instead of a sublibrary name causes the name of the sublibrary currently accessed to be displayed on SYSLST (or on SYSLOG if operations are on the console).

The LIST LIBRARIAN Command. The format of the LIST command is shown in Figure 12.12. The *LIST command* is used to list library member contents on SYSLST or SYSLOG. If the command is issued from SYSLST (batch), the default is output on SYSLST. If the command is issued from SYSLOG, the output will be the first 68 positions of each record on SYSLOG.

The operand "mn.mt" indicates the member to be displayed. The sublibrary for this member must be specified in a preceding ACCESS command.

```
List    mn.mt...[Unit={SYSLIST|SYSLOG}][Format=Hex]    (LIBR)
```

Figure 12.12   The LIBRARIAN LIST command format.

The operand "FORMAT=HEX" has no effect on types PHASE and DUMP. On other members, it causes a one-line type character and two-line type hex display similar to that often seen in DITTO dumps.

EXAMPLE 12.4

List the contents of a phase named LEE and all phases beginning with AB in a sublibrary named USER.STUDENT. Also list a COBOL source program named SMITH.C and a procedure named HURST.

Answer

```
* $$ JOB JNM=HORN,CLASS=J
* $$ LST CLASS=B
// JOB HORN
// EXEC LIBR,SIZE=256K
  ACCESS SUBLIB=USER.STUDENT
  LIST LEE.PHASE, AB*.PHASE, SMITH.C, HURST.PROC
/*
/&
* $$ EOJ
```

Note that the commas could have been omitted in the LIST command.

Cataloging Library Members   As in version 1 of DOS/VSE, cataloging phases is a different process than cataloging other member types. To catalog *phases*, the LIBRARIAN is *not* used. The linkage editor program and a LIBDEF statement must be used to catalog PHASE and DUMP types.

The DOS/VSE/SP LIBDEF Job Control Statement

The new format for the LIBDEF statement is shown in Figure 12.13. This *LIBDEF statement* specifies:

1. Which libraries are to be searched for specific member type(s), *or*
2. The sublibrary in which new phases or dumps are to be stored

The libraries to be searched can be concatenated or chained. Different chains can be established for different member types or a common chain can be established for all member types except type DUMP.

First Operand.   This operand indicates the type of member that is to be accessed. Possible types are PHASE, OBJ, SOURCE, PROC, DUMP, or *. An * means "all member types except type DUMP."

Second Operand.   If a type OBJ, SOURCE, or PROC is used in the first operand, the SEARCH operand is required. If a type PHASE or * operand is used, the SEARCH or CATALOG operand or both must be used.

```
[//] LIBDEF {type|*}[,SEARCH=(lib.sublib,...)]        (JCC, JCS)
            [,CATALOG=lib.sublib][{,TEMP|PERM}]
```

Figure 12.13   The DOS/VSE/SP LIBDEF job control statement format.

Except with system phases, the system sublibrary is added at the end of the library chain by default (unless you specify it in another position of the chain).

Third Operand. CATALOG= specifies the sublibrary in which a PHASE or DUMP is to be cataloged. With the version 1 LIBRARIAN, cataloging takes place in the system library as a default if no LIBDEF statement is present. This is *not* true in DOS/VSE/SP.

Fourth Operand. This operand indicates if the library definition is to be permanent or temporary. The default is temporary. A temporary assignment is in effect until:

1. An EOJ.
2. Another LIBDEF statement occurs in the same job.
3. A LIBDROP statement occurs in the job.

EXAMPLE 12.5

Compile, link edit, and catalog a COBOL program named PAYROLL in a sublibrary named USER.STUDENT. The program is in an ICCF library under the name PAYROLL. Also display the member to show that it is actually in the library.

Answer

```
(1)   * $$ JOB JNM=REJCEK,CLASS=S
(2)   * $$ LST CLASS=Z
(3)   // JOB REJCEK
(4)   // LIBDEF PHASE,CATALOG=USER.STUDENT
(5)   // OPTION CATAL
(6)      PHASE PAYROLL,*
(7)   // EXEC FCOBOL,SIZE=125K
(8)   /INCLUDE PAYROLL
(9)   /*
(10)  // EXEC LNKEDT,SIZE=64K
(11)  /*
(12)  // EXEC LIBR,SIZE=256K
(13)     ACCESS SUBLIB=USER.STUDENT
(14)     LISTDIR PAYROLL.PHASE
(15)  /*
(16)  /&
(17)  * $$ EOJ
```

Note that the operand CATAL is used in statement 5. It implies the operand LINK. Note also that the linkage editor PHASE command, discussed at the beginning of Chapter 11, is used in statement 6.

If the program is to be executed in the same job with a // EXEC PAYROLL,SIZE=AUTO command after statement 11, the operand SEARCH=USER.STUDENT must be added to the LIBDEF statement (4).

EXAMPLE 12.6

Code the statements necessary to catalog an assembler subroutine named JDATE as a relocatable module.

In former days, an object program was punched in a deck of cards. Then it was used with an INCLUDE statement and the MAINT program to catalog it as a relocatable module. Now a tape is assigned as SYSPCH. The following job stream shows how this is done now.

Answer

```
* $$ JOB JNM=HORN,CLASS=S
* $$ LST CLASS=Z
// JOB HORN                     CATALOG THE PROGRAM JDATE IN THE RL
// OPTION DECK                  PUNCH OBJECT PROGRAM
// ASSGN SYS021,300             REWIND TAPE ON DRIVE 300 AND WRITE TAPE MARK
// MTC REW,SYS021
// MTC WTM,SYS021
// MTC REW,SYS021
// ASSGN SYS021,UA              UNASSIGN TAPE AND ASSIGN IT AS SYSPCH
// ASSGN SYSPCH,300
// EXEC ASSEMBLY,SIZE=100K      ASSEMBLE SUBROUTINE JDATE AND PUNCH
   PUNCH ' ACCESS SUBLIB=USER.STUDENT'  /*OBJECT PROGRAM ON TAPE*/
   PUNCH ' CATALOG JDATE.OBJ REPLACE=YES EOD=/*'
/INCLUDE JDATE                  BRING IN PROGRAM FROM ICCF LIBRARY
/*
// MTC WTM,SYSPCH               WRITE TM AND REWIND TAPE
// MTC REW,SYSPCH
// ASSGN SYSPCH,02D             REASSIGN SYSPCH TO NORMAL ASSIGNMENT
// ASSGN SYSIPT,300             ASSIGN DEVICE THAT READS PROGRAMS TO 300
// EXEC LIBR,SIZE=256K          CATALOG OBJECT MODULE ON TAPE
/*        (ACCESS AND CATALOG STATEMENTS ARE ON TAPE)
// ASSGN SYSIPT,02C             REASSIGN SYSIPT TO NORMAL ASSIGNMENT
// EXEC LIBR,SIZE=256K          PROVE JDATE MODULE IS CATALOGED
   ACCESS SUBLIB=USER.STUDENT
   LISTDIR JDATE.OBJ
/*
/&
* $$ EOJ
```

The PUNCH statements in the job stream are assembler statements that punch what is in apostrophes. Since these are the first two statements on tape, it is not necessary to have them following the // EXEC LIBR statement in the job stream.

The second statement punched

```
CATALOG JDATE.OBJ EOD=/* REPLACE=YES
```

is a LIBRARIAN CATALOG command. This command is used when cataloging object modules, books, or procedures.

Library Maintenance

The CATALOG, DELETE, RENAME, and UPDATE commands are used to create and maintain library, sublibrary, or library members.

The CATALOG LIBRARIAN Command.   The *CATALOG command* is used when cataloging any member type (except PHASE and DUMP) in a sublibrary. Its format is shown in Figure 12.14. The data following up to the end-of-data (*EOD*) statement will be cataloged under the name and type specified.

First Operand.   The first operand, mn.mt, specifies the name and type of data to be cataloged. The sublibrary to be used must have been specified in a previous ACCESS command.

The library directory has a put-in-library time-stamp and a last-replaced time-stamp. If this is the first time the member has been placed in the library, both time-stamps will have the current data placed there. If it is a replacement (a re-catalog), only the last-replaced time-stamp will be changed.

```
CATalog  mn.mt[Eod=xx][DATA={YES}][REPLACE={YES}]         (LIBR)
                             NO             NO
```

Figure 12.14 The LIBRARIAN CATALOG command format.

Second Operand.   The *end-of-data* or *EOD operand* specifies what two characters indicate the end of the input to be cataloged. The default is a /+. Do not use a /* or a comma and blank for the EOD. In Example 12.7 below, the default is taken. The EOD statement itself is not cataloged.

Third Operand.   The default for the DATA operand is NO. The only time that the option YES is used is when procedures are to be cataloged that contain SYS-IPT data. (In Example 12.7 below, the input was a book, so the default was taken.)

Fourth Operand.   The default for the REPLACE operand is NO. If RE-PLACE = NO is used, a member of the same name and type cannot be recataloged. In Example 12.7 below, REPLACE = YES was used, which implies that this is new or a corrected version. If an old version exists, it will be replaced with the new.

When source statements or data are cataloged in a library, they are called books. They are given names of the form bookname.c, where c represents one alphabetic character. The general conventions used for this character are

- C for COBOL programs
- R for RPG programs
- A for assembler programs
- P for data or P1/1 programs

The rules for forming a bookname are those described for forming a member name.

Books being cataloged were preceded and followed by BKEND statements in version 1 of DOS/VSE. The BKEND statements had to start to the right of column 1. Now this is not longer necessary, although the statements are still accepted for compatibility reasons. All that is needed is a /+ at the end of the data or source program to be cataloged.

EXAMPLE 12.7

Code the statements necessary to catalog a COBOL source program under the name IHLLAB1 in a library named USER.STUDENT. This program has been keyed in the ICCF library under the name IHLLAB1.

Answer

```
* $$ JOB JNM=MILLS,CLASS=J
* $$ LST CLASS=B
// JOB MILLS   CATALOG A COBOL PROGRAM
// EXEC LIBR,SIZE=256K
  ACCESS SUBLIB=USER.STUDENT
  CATALOG IHLLAB1.C REPLACE=YES
/INCLUDE IHLLAB1
/+
/*
/&
* $$ EOJ
```

To retrieve this book in a job stream, we use the POWER statement
* $$ SLI MEM = IHLLAB1.C.

EXAMPLE 12.8

Catalog a stream of data in an ICCF library member as a source type under the name PAYDATA.P and display the member to show what was cataloged. The sublibrary to be used is USER.STUDENT.

Answer

```
* $$ JOB JNM=SCOTT,CLASS=J
* $$ LST CLASS=Z
// JOB SCOTT   CATALOG DATA
// EXEC LIBR,SIZE=256K
   ACCESS SUBLIB=USER.STUDENT
   CATALOG PAYDATA.P REPLACE=YES
/INCLUDE PAYDATA
/+
   ACCESS SUBLIB=USER.STUDENT
   LIST PAYDATA.P
/*
/&
* $$ EOJ
```

EXAMPLE 12.9

Catalog a stream of JCL (in an ICCF library under the name JCL) in the USER.STUDENT sublibrary. Catalog it under the name PAY.PROC and prove that it was cataloged.

Answer

```
* $$ JOB JNM=WEST,CLASS=J
* $$ LST CLASS=Z
// JOB WEST    CATALOG A PROCEDURE
// EXEC LIBR,SIZE=256K
  ACCESS SUBLIB=USER.STUDENT
  CATALOG PAY.PROC REPLACE=YES
/INCLUDE JCL
/+
  ACCESS SUBLIB=USER.STUDENT
  LIST PAY.PROC
/*
/&
* $$ EOJ
```

To retrieve and include this JCL in a job stream, the following job control statement is used: // EXEC PROC=PAY.

The DELETE LIBRARIAN Command. The format of the DELETE command is shown in Figure 12.15. The *DELETE command* is used to delete members, sublibraries, or libraries. You will probably be deleting only library members. Therefore, you will be using the mn.mt operand choice. An ACCESS command must precede the DELETE statement.

```
DELete    {Lib=1...|Sublib=1.s...|mn.mt...}                 (LIBR)
```

Figure 12.15   The LIBRARIAN DELETE command format.

EXAMPLE 12.10

Code the statements necessary to delete a program PAYROL1.PHASE from the USER.STUDENT sublibrary.

Answer

```
* $$ JOB JNM=CHINN,CLASS=J
* $$ LST CLASS=B
// JOB CHINN    DELETE PAYROL1.PHASE
// EXEC LIBR,SIZE=256K
   ACCESS SUBLIB=USER.STUDENT
   DELETE PAYROLL.PHASE
/*
/&
* $$ EOJ
```

If you wanted to delete all procedures from the library above, the delete statement would be changed to DELETE *.PROC.

The RENAME Librarian Command.   Renaming entries in the libraries is a simple process. The format for the RENAME LIBRARIAN command is shown in Figure 12.16. The *RENAME command* changes the name and/or type of one or more members, or the names of one or more sublibraries. If the new name already exists, the renaming will not take place. You will probably only be renaming members and/or types.

```
REName    {Sublib=1.s[:]1.s...|mn.mt[:]mn.mt...}           (LIBR)
```

Figure 12.16   The LIBRARIAN RENAME command format.

When you use the "mn.mt[:]mn.mt" choice, this means that the first operand will be renamed to the second operand. If the second operand is specified generically, the first operand must also be generic. If a name or type is not to be changed, an = sign may be used in the second operand. Example:

```
RENAME LEE.PHASE:LEELAB.=.
```

The RENAME command must be preceded by an ACCESS command when a member is to be renamed. Renaming a type cannot imply a change of internal representation (i.e., you cannot change a PHASE to a PROC).

EXAMPLE 12.11

Rename a procedure called IHLJCL.PROC. The new name is to be CLJCL.PROC. The procedure is in the USER.STUDENT sublibrary.

Answer

```
* $$ JOB JNM=LEWIS,CLASS=J
* $$ LST CLASS=B
// JOB LEWIS   RENAME THE IHLJCL PROCEDURE TO CLJCL
// EXEC LIBR,SIZE=256K
  ACCESS SUBLIB=USER.STUDENT
  RENAME IHLJCL.PROC:CLJCL.PROC
/*
/&
* $$ EOJ
```

Updating in Libraries.   Updating can be done to source and procedure entries. Usually, most programmers simply recatalog with a REPLACE = YES. The format of the UPDATE LIBRARIAN command is shown in Figure 12.17. The *UPDATE command* is used to alter or modify the contents of a member by adding, deleting, or replacing lines. If you wish, you can save the unmodified version. Details on this command will be left to a research problem at the end of this chapter.

```
UPDATE   mn.mt[SAve=mn.mt][SEquence={n|FS|NO}           (LIBR)
         [Column=start[:]end]
```

Figure 12.17   The UPDATE LIBRARIAN command format.

The Organizational LIBRARIAN Commands

The organizational programs in the LIBRARIAN are used to organize or create libraries. Examples of such commands are:

1. The COPY command, which is used to copy libraries, sublibraries, or members
2. The MOVE command, which is used to move data from one library or sublibrary to another
3. The COMPARE instruction, which can compare the contents of libraries, sublibraries, or members

When any of these commands are used, the CONNECT command precedes them to provide the names of the sublibraries in which the members are to be found or placed.

Systems programmers usually work with these commands, so we will not use them. However, you should know that these commands exist and what they are used for.

The SLI POWER Statement

A new format, unique to DOS/VSE/SP, for the POWER SLI statement is shown in Figure 12.18. The format makes the SLI statement compatible with the new DOS/VSE/SP library arrangement but retains the old option for compatibility reasons.

```
* $$ SLI     {MEM=membername[.membertype]|[sublib.]bookname}

             ICCF=(membername[,password])
             LIB=(libnumber[,libnumber,libnumber])
```

Figure 12.18 The DOS/VSE/SP SLI PWR statement format.

The first format in Figure 12.18 is used if data is a library member is being used. MEM = membername[.membertype] should be used for DOS/VSE/SP. To avoid default problems on membertype, it is best to use the format

```
* $$ SLI MEM=mn.mt.
```

That is if a set of data had been cataloged under LAB01.P, you should code

```
* $$ SLI MEM=LAB01.P.
```

Operating under version 1 DOS/VSE, the second option (sublib. bookname) would be used. The second format, the ICCF format, is used if you are introducing data into the job stream from an ICCF library. There are two advantages of using this format instead of the /INCLUDE ICCF statement that we have been using previously. They are:

1. You do not have to be signed on in the ICCF library being used to submit the run.
2. The data is not brought into the POWER queue until execution time, thus saving POWER queue space.

In this format the membername is the ICCF library name. A password can be coded if the library is password protected. The library number is the ICCF library number, which is displayed at the top of the screen when the /LIB ICCF command is used.

The PROC (PROCEDURE) Job Control Statement

The format of the PROC statement is shown in Figure 12.19. This statement, unique to DOS/VSE/SP, allows the programmer to use symbolic parameters in a procedure that has been cataloged. This statement is *not* used in a procedure unless symbolic parameters are used in the procedure. (Symbolic parameters can be used without procedures.)

If symbolic parameters are used in a procedure, the PROC statement must be the first statement in the procedure when it is cataloged.

```
[//] PROC [parname=[value]][,...]                        (JCS,JCC)
```

Figure 12.19 The DOS/VSE/SP PROC JOB control statement format.

Example

```
      MONTHPAY.PROC
// PROC RESTART=MONTH01
// GOTO &RESTART
/. MONTH01
// EXEC JOB01
/. MONTH02
// EXEC JOB02
/. MONTH03
// EXEC JOB03
/. MONTH04
// EXEC JOB04
      .
      .
      .
/. MONTH12
// EXEC JOB12
/+
```

In the case above, the jobs executed in the procedure depend on the value assigned to the symbolic parameter RESTART.

The term "parname" in the format represents the name of the symbolic parameter, *without a leading* &, to which the value is to be assigned.

The term "value" represents the value to be assigned to the symbolic parameter. This arrangement allows a job to be started at any month assuming the value assigned to the symbolic parameter RESTART in the // GOTO &RESTART statement of the procedure. The RESTART=MONTH01 in the // PROC statement of the procedure simply establishes a default value for RESTART.

A Third Format of the EXEC Job Control Statement

The value assigned to a symbolic parameter can be assigned using a new form of the EXEC job control statement. The new form of the EXEC statement is shown in Figure 12.20. In version 1 DOS/VSE, the possibility of having a parameter name as an operand did not exist. It is not shown in Figure 5.3.

There are three methods of addressing symbolic parameters in an EXEC PROC statement:

1. parname1 = value1
2. parname2
3. parname3 = &parname3

In case 1, the EXEC statement can be coded as shown in the restart job stream shown below.

Example

```
* $$ JOB JNM=DUNN,CLASS=J
* $$ LST CLASS=Z
// JOB DUNN    RESTART JOB STREAM
// EXEC PROC=MONTHPAY,RESTART=MONTH04
/*
/&
* $$ EOJ
```

```
[//] EXEC PROC=procname[,parname[=[value]]][...]          (JCS,JCC)
```

Figure 12.20   The DOS/VSE/SP EXEC PROC job control statement format.

This causes value1 or MONTH∅4 to be passed to the procedure. It is possible for value1 to be nothing or quotes. This indicates a null value for RESTART. It causes the specified parameter in the procedure (in this case, RESTART) to be ignored.

In case 2, if the EXEC statement is coded as

```
// EXEC PROC MONTH∅4
```

then MONTH∅4 is the value passed to the procedure. If the value is changed in the procedure, it is passed back and may be assumed for later use in the job stream.

In case 3, if the EXEC statement is coded as

```
// EXEC PROC RESTART=&MONTH∅4
```

then MONTH∅4 will be passed to the procedure. It will *not* be passed back to the calling level if it is changed in the procedure. The new value cannot be assumed for later use in the job stream.

The SETPARM Job Control Statement

The format of the SETPARM statement is shown in Figure 12.21. This job control statement, unique to DOS/VSE/SP, can be used only within a job. It provides another way of defining and/or assigning a value to a symbolic parameter. The value can then be tested in an IF statement and used later by job control statements, or it can be used in a procedure.

The operand "pname" represents the symbolic parameter to be defined. Possible assignment for pname are PNAME=

1.   Value, a string of 1–5∅ characters. As indicated at the beginning of the chapter, if this string contains any special characters, the value must be enclosed in apostrophes. Example:

```
// SETPARM RESTART=MONTH∅1
```

2.   Nothing or " is coded. This indicates a null value. Example:

```
// SETPARM RESTART="
```

or

```
// SETPARM RESTART=
```

```
[//] SETPARM pname=[{value|$RC|$MRC}][,...]          (JCS,JCC)
```

Figure 12.21   The DOS/VSE/SP SETPARM job control statement format.

3. $RC indicates that the return code of the last job step executed should be used as a value. This return code is assigned as a string of four characters. Example:

```
// SETPARM RESTART=$RC
```

4. $MRC indicates that the maximum return code of all the preceding job steps executed should be used as a value (again a string of four characters). Example:

```
// SETPARM RESTART=$MRC
```

SUMMARY

DOS/VSE/SP is a new version of the DOS/VSE operating system. Among other things, it has the following new concepts:

1. Conditional job control statements
2. Return codes
3. A new librarian program and a new library structure
4. Variable parameters
5. Other new job control statements, such as the PWR, SETPARM, and PROC statements, and an enhanced SLI statement

Conditional job control statements allow the system to bypass parts of a job stream. New conditional job control statements are the IF, GOTO, ON, and the /. label statements. The IF statement is said to be a local conditional function, whereas the GOTO is a global conditional function.

Procedures may now be nested. This means that a procedure can be within a procedure.

Return codes allow the programmer, rather than the operator, to decide if a program should be executed or certain actions should take place. Return codes used in conjunction with the new PWR and IF job control statements allow the programmer, rather than the operator, to release jobs in a queue. Return code standards have been set up and are shown in Figure 12.1.

Symbolic parameters allow changes to be made in the job control at execution time. Symbolic parameters may be used in conjunction with cataloged procedures beginning with a new PROC job control statement.

There are three methods of assigning values to symbolic parameters:

1. Through the use of the PROC job control statement
2. Through the use of the EXEC PROC job control statement
3. Through the use of the SETPARM job control statement

TERMS TO REMEMBER

Book	Global condition
Conditional job control statement	Label job control statement
EOD	LIBRARIAN

Library	Parameterized procedure
Local condition	Phase
Member	Procedure
mn	Return code
Module	Sublibrary
mt	Sublibrary member
Nested procedure	Symbolic parameter

STUDY GUIDE

1. State three advantages of the new versions of DOS/VSE (DOS/VSE/SP).

   (a) _____

   _____

   (b) _____

   _____

   (c) _____

   _____

2. State a purpose or function of the following new job control statements.

   (a) IF THEN statement _____

   _____

   (b) GOTO statement _____

   _____

   (c) /. statement _____

   _____

   (d) ON statement _____

   _____

   (e) PWR statement _____

   _____

   (f) SETPARM statement _____

   _____

   _____

3. State three ways that values may be assigned to symbolic parameters.

(a) _____

(b) _____

(c) _____

4. Explain the meaning of $RC and the action to be taken in the following coding example.

```
// IF $RC > Ø THEN
// GOTO ERRORRT
// EXEC PAYROLL,SIZE=AUTO
        .
        .
        .
/. ERRORRT
        .
        .
        .
```

(a) IF $RC = Ø _____

_____

_____

(b) IF $RC = 8 _____

_____

_____

5. Explain the meaning of the following code.

```
// EXEC PROG1,SIZE=AUTO
// ON $ABEND GOTO LISTIT
// EXEC PROG2,SIZE=AUTO
// IF $RC > Ø THEN
// GOTO LISTIT
// GOTO $EOJ
/. LISTIT
// EXEC LISTIT,SIZE=AUTO
/*
/&
* $$ EOJ
```

_____

_____

_____

_____

_____

6. Distinguish between a phase and an object module.

_____

_____

_____

7. Distinguish between a book and a procedure.

_____

_____

_____

8. How is the LIBRARIAN program invoked?

_____

_____

9. Distinguish between how the LISTD and LIST LIBRARIAN commands are

used. _____

_____

_____

10. State the purpose or function of the following LIBRARIAN commands.

    (a) ACCESS _____

    _____

    (b) DELETE _____

    _____

    (c) CATALOG _____

    _____

    (d) BACKUP _____

    _____

CODING EXERCISES

Code the following job control exercises on coding sheets.

1. Code the job stream to catalog an *executable* COBOL program being compiled
   in a sublibrary named USER.STUDENT. Catalog it under the name IIIEX1,

where III = your initials. Also, display the directory to show that it has been cataloged. The program has already been keyed and is in your ICCF library under the name IIIEX1. Use the ICCF form of the SLI statement to bring the program into the job stream.

2. Code the job stream to rename the program in Exercise 1 to the name XXXEX1.

3. Code the job stream to delete the program XXXEX1 from its sublibrary (USER.STUDENT).

4. Code the job stream to delete a cataloged procedure named PAYPROC from a sublibrary named USER.BUSOFF.

5. Code the job stream to catalog 25 data records as a source entry. The records are in your ICCF library under the name DATALB1. Display the *contents* of the entry cataloged to show what 25 records are there.

6. Code the job stream to display the directory of a sublibrary named USER.STUDENT for *all* the *source* entries with a member type of P.

7. Rename an RPG program source entry (member type of R). The old name is INVFILE.R. The new name is to be INVMAS.R. Display the directory of USER.STUDENT to prove that it has been properly renamed.

8. This exercise is to be keyed and actually run.

   (a) *First job*. Code the statements necessary to catalog the programs used in Coding Exercise 1∅ of Chapter 9 or Coding Exercise 5 of Chapter 1∅ in a sublibrary. Your instructor will tell you what type of phase names and what sublibrary to use. Code the statements necessary to prove that the programs are in the specified library.

   (b) *Second job*. Code the statements necessary to execute these programs from the sublibrary above using data set 2 in Appendix D.

   (c) Write a report in essay style.
       (1) Discuss any problems that you had.
       (2) Circle the place in your output that proves that the programs are actually in the sublibrary.

9. This exercise is to be keyed and actually run.

   (a) *First job*. Key the source statements in the ENVIRONMENT DIVISION of the program GSLIST (statements 1∅13∅∅–2∅∅8∅∅) in Appendix D into your ICCF library unless instructed by your teacher to use another method.

   (b) *Second job*. Catalog the ENVIRONMENT DIVISION of the program GSLIST as a source entry in the sublibrary specified by your instructor. Your instructor will tell you what type of book names to use. Then display the *contents* of this book in the same job to prove that the entry is there.

   (c) *Third job*. Display the directory of the entire contents of your student library. Circle all entries in the output that are yours from this class. Run it twice, first using the NORMAL option for the output operand and then using the SHORT option.

   (d) Write a report in essay style.
       (1) Explain any problems that you had.
       (2) Explain the meaning of each column of the NORMAL directory listing.
       (3) Explain the differences you see between the output for the NORMAL and the SHORT listings.

RESEARCH PROBLEMS

Use the *Systems Control Statements* manual for the following problems.

1. What happens if the LISTDIR LIBRARIAN command is being used while the sublibrary is being updated from another partition?

2. Look up the UPDATE LIBRARIAN command and subcommands.
   (a) Describe how a source statement in a cataloged book could be:
      (1) Replaced without recataloging.
      (2) Added without recataloging.
      (3) Deleted without recataloging.
   (b) Why is this method difficult on the terminal or with 8∅-position records?

3. Quote the source under the UPDATE command that indicates if an entry in a cataloged procedure could be updated.

4. (a) How do the ON condition and GOTO function if they occur in a lower-level procedure in a nested procedures situation?
   (b) If the operator cancels your job with the FORCE operand, what happens to ON statement actions?

5. What is the maximum number of libraries that can be in a search chain of the LIBDEF statement?

6. (a) Look up the COPY LIBRARIAN command and write down the two LIBRARIAN commands required to copy members from one library to the other with no duplicate versions.
   (b) What is the difference between the action of the COPY and MOVE LIBRARIAN commands?

chapter 13

Utility Programs

INTRODUCTION

In Chapter 1 a utility program was defined as a program that performs day-to-day tasks. Some examples of such tasks are:

1. Initializing a tape or disk with a standard volume label
2. Displaying the contents of the VTOC (volume table of contents)
3. Backing up and restoring the system libraries
4. Sorting files in sequential order by some key field
5. Copying files of data from one I/O device to another
6. Printing a hard copy of the log

In this chapter we discuss some utility programs that are useful to the programmer.

THE LVTOC PROGRAM

The purpose of the *LVTOC* utility *program* is to display the file labels contained in the VTOC. The file labels are listed in alphabetical order along with each file's creation and expiration dates and extent information. The program also lists:

1. The volume label identifier (e.g., VOL1)
2. The starting address of the VTOC area
3. The volume serial number
4. The beginning and ending addresses and size of the unused disk space

The job control arrangement for a typical VTOC is shown below.

```
     * $$ JOB JNM=LEE,CLASS=J
     * $$ LST CLASS=Z
     // JOB LEE                    SAMPLE VTOC OF DRIVE 224
(1)  // ASSGN SYS004,224          ASSIGNS DISK INPUT
(2)  // ASSGN SYS005,PRINTER      ASSIGNS PRINTER OUTPUT
(3)  // PAUSE                      REPLY NO IF MSG 8V96D IS ISSUED
(4)  // EXEC LVTOC,SIZE=64K
(5)  /&
     * $$ EOJ
```

Note that:

1. Statements 1, 2, 4, and 5 are required. There are no utility control statements.
2. Statement 1. The disk input must be assigned to SYS004.
3. Statement 2. The symbolic device number assigned to the printer must be SYS005. However, output can be on tape or disk. If the output is on disk, a filename, UOUT, must be used on the DLBL statement. Usually, the output is on the printer.
4. Statement 3. This statement allows a choice of listing data secured files. It is optional.

A VTOC shows the entries for non-VSAM or native files (or data sets) and the VSAM data spaces if any exist. However, if information is desired for the entries in the VSAM data spaces, the AMS LISTCAT feature must be used. This is because information on individual VSAM data sets is stored in the VSAM catalog.

THE LISTLOG UTILITY PROGRAM

If the // EXEC LISTLOG,SIZE = 3K statement is placed after the /& statement in a job stream, it will cause all console communications to be printed regarding that job (the JOB statement preceding the LISTLOG). This list includes all AR messages. Such a list often produces helpful information to the programmer.

DITTO

The DITTO (*d*ata *i*nterfile *t*ransfer, *t*esting, and *o*perations) utility program provides a set of functions allowing the programmer to:

1. Display files
2. Print files
3. Copy files
4. Change files

These files may be on cards, tape, disk, and diskettes. DITTO is particularly helpful to the programmer who is debugging or testing a program. It can be used in either console or batch mode. Console operators usually use the console mode, whereas programmers use the batch mode. To use the batch mode, the UPSI job

```
// UPSI nnnnnnnn                                                    (JCS)
```

Figure 13.1 The UPSI statement format.

control statement is needed. The format of this statement is shown in Figure 13.1. The UPSI statement allows for the setting eight bits in a byte (the n's in the format). These bits act as eight switches which may be tested by problem programs. No UPSI statement implies a default value of zero for all eight switches.

Values allowed for these switches are Ø, 1, and X. If you code a Ø for a switch, it sets the corresponding bit off. If you code a 1 for a switch, it sets the corresponding bit on. If you code an X for a switch, it leaves the corresponding bit unchanged. Unspecified rightmost positions in the operand are assumed to be X. Job control clears the UPSI byte at the end of the job.

In RPG these switches are tested by the use of the U1–U8 indicators. In COBOL the switches are defined as UPSI-Ø through UPSI-7 condition names in the SPECIAL-NAMES paragraph in the ENVIRONMENT DIVISION. These switches allow options to be built into a program.

DITTO expects the first switch to be 1 for batch-mode operations. Therefore, a // UPSI 1 statement must precede the // EXEC DITTO statement.

A job control plan for coding a batch DITTO job follows. Code:

1. The POWER JOB and LST statements
2. The DOS/VSE JOB statement
3. The // UPSI 1 statement
4. Any tape, disk, or diskette ASSGN, TLBL, DLBL, and EXTENT statements needed
5. The // EXEC DITTO,SIZE = 15ØK statement
6. The $$ DITTO control statements needed
7. Possible card image data if card image input
8. A /* statement
9. A /& statement
10. The POWER * $$ EOJ statement

The basic functions of DITTO are grouped according to the type of input device. The groups are:

1. Card functions
2. Tape functions
3. Disk functions
4. Diskette functions

These functions and their associated control statements can be listed by the use of the following job control.

```
* $$ JOB JNM=JOHNSON,CLASS=J
* $$ LST CLASS=Z
// JOB JOHNSON    LIST DITTO FUNCTIONS AVAILABLE
// UPSI 1
// EXEC DITTO,SIZE=15ØK
$$DITTO XXX
$$DITTO EOJ
/&
* $$ EOJ
```

Key the job control above and obtain your own listing of the available DITTO control statements. Examine the list under batch operations. Note the following characteristics.

The card functions allow you to:

1. Duplicate (punch) card records
2. List card records
3. Interpret card records if this feature is available on the punch
4. Copy card records to tape or disk

The tape functions allow you to:

1. Print all or part of the records in a tape file
2. Initialize a tape
3. Position a tape (as the MTC commands do)
4. Copy from one tape to another
5. Scan a tape for data on the tape
6. Punch tape records
7. Copy tape records to disk

The disk functions allow you to:

1. Print the VTOC
2. Change VTOC entries
3. Print disk records
4. Change disk records
5. Change the volume serial number
6. Scan a sequence of disk records for a given string of data
7. Write an end-of-file record

DITTO supports all CKD and FBA devices that are supported by DOS/ VSE. The diskette functions allow you to:

1. Initialize a diskette
2. Print the index track and the diskette records
3. Scan a sequence of records for a given string of data
4. Eject or feed in a diskette
5. Change records
6. Change the volume serial number
7. Punch diskette records into cards
8. Copy diskette records to tape or disk

Examples of the use of some DITTO utility functions follow.

EXAMPLE 13.1

Copy 125 records in the your ICCF library under the name CLUBLIST to a tape with a volume serial number of 666666. Rewind the tape and print these records. Then unload the tape. The tapes are 88Ø9s, and any symbolic device number may be used above SYSØØ7. Standard header labels will be used in this case.

Answer

```
* $$ JOB JNM=MAY,CLASS=J
* $$ LST CLASS=Z
// JOB MAY
// UPSI 1
// ASSGN SYS008,8809,VOL=666666              TAPE OUTPUT DEVICE
// TLBL SYS008,'CLUB LIST FOR 1988',88/365,666666
// EXEC DITTO,SIZE=150K
$$DITTO REW OUTPUT=SYS008                     REWIND TAPE
$$DITTO CT OUTPUT=SYS008,BLKFACTOR=5          CARD TO TAPE
/INCLUDE CLUBLIST   (DATA FROM ICCF LIBRARY)
/*
$$DITTO REW OUTPUT=SYS008                     REWIND TAPE
$$DITTO TP INPUT=SYS008,NBLKS=26,NFILES=1     TAPE TO PRINTER
$$DITTO RUN OUTPUT=SYS008                     REWIND AND UNLOAD TAPE
$$DITTO EOJ
/&
* $$ EOJ
```

Note that when DITTO writes a file on tape or disk, it automatically writes a tape mark at the end.

EXAMPLE 13.2

Dump an ESDS disk file in character and hex format on the printer. The file ID is 'PAYROLL.ESDS.MASTER.FILE', and the symbolic device number used was SYS007. All the fixed-length 100-byte records are to be printed. (Look in your DITTO summary run at the VDP batch op code.)

Answer

```
* $$ JOB JNM=JONES,CLASS=J
* $$ LST CLASS=Z
// JOB JONES    DUMP AN ESDS PAYROLL MASTER FILE
// UPSI 1       BATCH DITTO
// DLBL SYS007,'PAYROLL.ESDS.MASTER.FILE',,VSAM
// EXEC DITTO,SIZE=150K
$$DITTO VDP FILEIN=SYS007
$$DITTO EOJ
/*
/&
* $$ EOJ
```

THE SORT/MERGE PROGRAM

The IBM utility program has two functions: sort and merge. The program can be used to:

1. Reorder or sort records in a file using one or more fields as sort keys
2. Merge records in previously sequenced files in sequential order
3. Reorder and merge records in multiple files in a specified order

The sort/merge program can be executed in two ways:

1. By the // EXEC SORT,SIZE = 150K statement in the job stream, *or*
2. By invoking it from a user application program such as the use of the SORT verb in a COBOL program

We will be concerned with the first method.

The *sort/merge program* uses three types of files: input, output, and *work files*. There can be one to nine input files (one to eight in the case of a merge only) and one output file. Input records may be blocked or unblocked and fixed or variable length (but not mixed). Input files must be SAM files or SAM ESDS files. There can be only one output file.

Records may be sorted on 1–12 control fields in each record, and these control fields may be sorted in ascending or descending order. Control field data may be in several data formats, some of which are unsigned binary (BI), EBCDIC character (CH), zoned decimal (ZD), packed decimal (PD), and unsigned ASCII characters (AC).

The Sort/Merge program uses control statements to tell it the type of operation to be performed, the I/O data sets, the control field parameters, and any selected options. The format for these control statements is

ƀop codeƀoperands separated by commasƀcomment

Some operands may have keywords. A nonblank character in column 72 indicates a continuation, and column 1–15 of the continued statement must be blank.

Control statements can appear in any order, but the END control statement must be the last. A summary of possible control statement opcodes is shown in Figure 13.2. Of these, we discuss the SORT, OPTION, RECORD, INPFIL, OUTFIL, and END control statements.

Operation Code	Purpose
SORT	Describes the control fields and input files to be sorted.
MERGE	Describes the control fields and the number of input files to be merged.
RECORD	Gives the record length and the format of the fields.
MODS	Associates user-written routines with certain sort/merge exits.
INPFIL	Defines the input files to be sorted or merged and specifies the procedures to be used when the files are opened or closed.
OUTFIL	Defines the output file and specifies the procedures that will be used when the file is opened or closed.
INCLUDE/ OMIT	Allows the exclusion of certain input records from the sort.
ALTSEQ	Defines an alternative collating sequence to be used on control fields.
OUTREC	Specifies what portions of the input record are to be included in the output record. If omitted, the output record is identical to the input record.
SUM	Designates specified numeric input fields as summary fields.
OPTION	Specifies the options that have been selected for this sort/merge operation. Default values are assumed if this statement is omitted.
END	Signifies the end of the sort/merge control statements.

Figure 13.2 Sort/merge control statement operation codes.

The Sort/Merge program reads the control statements in phase 0, the assignment phase. The sort is terminated if there are any errors in the control statements.

Phase 1 of the sort, the internal sort phase, sorts the records into ordered groups called *strings* and writes them on an intermediate storage device in *work areas*. The work areas may be on disk or tape.

The work area on disk needs to be at least twice the area required to hold the input records. If tape is being used, three to nine tapes may be assigned for work tapes. It is possible to have an *incore sort* with no storage device being used for a work area if a small number of records is being sorted.

Phase 3, the external sort phase, gradually merges the strings of data into two strings.

Phase 4, the final merge phase, merges the last two strings and writes the output on the specified output device.

The following example is used to discuss the sort control statements.

EXAMPLE 13.3

Sort two payroll files on the employee name fields. The last name is in columns 3–17 of the record, the first name is in columns 18–27, and the middle initial is in column 28. There are two input SAM ESDS files, and the output is to be a sorted ESDS file. Records are 100 bytes in length, blocked 10.

The input files have file-IDs of FIRST JAN PAYROLL and SECOND JAN payroll. The output file is to be kept a year and should have a file-ID of JAN MONTHLY PAYROLL REPORT. The input and output device is a FBA disk device.

Answer

```
      * $$ JOB JNM=LEE,CLASS=J
      * $$ LST CLASS=Z
      // JOB LEE    SORT TWO PAYROLL INPUT FILES AND OUTPUT ON DISK
(1)   // DLBL SORTOUT,'JAN.MONTHLY.PAYROLL.REPORT',365,VSAM,DISP=NEW
(2)   // DLBL SORTIN1,'FIRST.JAN.PAYROLL',,VSAM
(3)   // DLBL SORTIN2,'SECOND.JAN.PAYROLL',,VSAM
(4)   // EXEC SORT,SIZE=64K
(5)   SORT FIELDS=(3,15,A,18,10,A,28,1,A),FORMAT=CH,FILES=2,WORK=0
(6)   RECORD TYPE=F,LENGTH=100
(7)   INPFIL BLKSIZE=1000
(8)   OUTFIL BLKSIZE=1000,ESDS
(9)   END
      /*
      /&
      * $$ EOJ
```

```
  (A)   SORT FIELDS={(start position,length,format,sequence...)    }
             FIELDS={(start position,length,sequence...),FORMAT=format}

        [,SIZE=n] [,WORK=n ]  [,CHDPT]  [,FILES=1]
                  [,WORK=DA]  [,CKPT ]  [,FILES=n]

  (B)   MERGE FIELDS={(start position,length,format,sequence...)}
              FIELDS={(start position,length,sequence...)       }

              {,FILES=n}
```

Figure 13.3 The SORT and MERGE control statements formats.

Explanation

Statements 1–3. Here, default file names are used in the DLBL statement. No ASSGN statements are used since these are VSAM-managed files.

Default values for file names and symbolic device numbers are shown below.

Files	File names	Symbolic device numbers
Output	SORTOUT	SYS001
Input	SORTIN1 . . . 9	SYS009 . . . SYS(n + 1)
Work	SORTWK1 . . . 9	SYS(n + 2) . . . SYS(n + m + 1)
Checkpoint	SORTCKP	SYS000

Thus the first DLBL statement for the output file has a file name of SORTOUT, the second DLBL statements for the first input file has a filename of SORTIN1, and the third DLBL statement for the second input file has a filename of SORTIN2. No DLBL statement exists for a *work file* because this is to be an incore sort.

Statement 4, the EXEC SORT statement. Statement 4 loads the sort/merge program. The sort control statements 5–9 then follow.

Statement 5, the SORT control statement. The format of the SORT control statement is shown in part (a) of Figure 13.3. The top format of the SORT control statement is used for sorts in which the type of data in the control fields is not the same. That is, the control field formats are different. The bottom format in the SORT control statement is used if the control fields are all the same type of data.

The MERGE control statement is used if the merging of two previously sorted files is all that is needed. Our example requires the use of the bottom SORT format.

Our SORT control statement is

```
SORT FIELDS=(3,15,A,18,10,A,28,1,A),FORMAT=CH,FILES=2,WORK=0
```

In the FIELDS parameter, the first three entries describe the last name, which begins in column 3 and is 15 positions long. It is to be sorted in ascending order. The next three entries describe the first name, which begins in column 18 and is 10 positions long. It is also to be sorted in ascending order. The last three entries in the FIELDS parameter describe the middle initial, which is in column 28 and is to be sorted in ascending order.

The FORMAT option, FORMAT = CH, indicates that the data fields are in EBCDIC character format.

The FILES option, FILES = 2, indicates that two files are to be sorted. Possible values for n are 1–9. The default is one file.

The WORK option, WORK = 0, indicates that an incore sort will occur. This means that the work area for the sort will be in main storage. WORK = DA indicates that a DASD will be used for the work file. It allows the use of a multiextent work file, if desired. WORK = DA is the default. If WORK = n is used for this option, n indicates the number of work tapes (3–9) or sequential disk work files (1–9) to be used. A DLBL statement must be used for each work file.

The SIZE option, SIZE = n, is optional. It indicates the number of logical records to be sorted. Its use is shown in the second example below.

The CHKPT (or CKPT) option allows checkpoints to be taken. A *checkpoint* is a point in the Sort/Merge program where a check is made. A recording of data can be made for restart purposes. We will not be using this option.

Statement 6, the RECORD control statement. The RECORD control statement has a format of

$$\text{RECORD TYPE=} \begin{Bmatrix} F \\ V \\ D \end{Bmatrix} \text{,LENGTH=(record-length),[DEBLANK=} \begin{bmatrix} (p,q) \\ p \end{bmatrix} \text{]}$$

For variable-length records, the length operand is maximum length, minimum length, modal length, where modal length is the most frequently occurring length.

Our RECORD control statement in this example is

```
RECORD TYPE=F,LENGTH=100
```

The TYPE operand can have a value of F for fixed-length records, V for variable-length records, and D for variable-length ASCII records. In this example, F is used for fixed-length records.

The LENGTH operand gives the length in bytes of the record. In this case, all the records are 100 bytes in length.

The DELBLANK = p or (p,q) parameter can be used to indicate that records containing a certain character can be omitted from the sort of merge. Thus if deleted records had the character D in position 1, an operand of DEBLANK = (D,1) would indicate that records flagged as deleted are not to be included in the sort. An operand of DEBLANK = 1 would indicate that records with a *blank* in position 1 are to be omitted from the sort.

Statement 7, the INPFIL control statement. The format for the INPFIL control statement is shown in part (a) of Figure 13.4. As can be seen, the INPFIL control statement format is rather long. It defines the input files.

In our example, the statement was

```
INPFIL BLKSIZE=1000
```

Here the BLKSIZE = 1000 operand specifies the maximum block size, in bytes, of the input records. (100-byte logical records blocked 10 = 1000.)

The VSAM option, the fifth operand in the INPFIL format shown in Figure 13.4, is the default for FBA devices. On CKD device SAM is the default.

```
(A)   INPFIL   [BLKSIZE=n][,BYPASS][,EXIT][,PRESEQ][,VSAM][,TOL]

               [,VOLUME=n      ] [,OPEN=RWD  ] [,CLOSE=RWD   ]
               [,VOLUME=(N,...)] [,OPEN=NORWD] [,CLOSE=UNLD  ]
                                               [,CLOSE=NORWD ]

               [,DATA=E] [,BUFOFF=N]
               [,DATA=A]
(B)   OUTFIL   [BLKSIZE=n][,EXIT][,NOTPMK] [,OPEN=RWD  ] [,CLOSE=RWD   ]
                                           [,OPEN=NORWD] [,CLOSE=UNLD  ]
                                                         [,CLOSE=NORWD ]

               [,KSDS]
               [,RRDS] [,TOL][,BUFOFF=N][,REUSE]
               [,ESDS]
```

Figure 13.4 The INPFIL and OUTFIL Sort/merge control statements formats.

Notice that the defaults for the OPEN and CLOSE operands in Figure 13.4 are RWD (rewind). Here RWD means rewind; UNLD means unload; and NORWD means no rewind. In our example we are taking the defaults.

Other INPFIL operands that are not used are examined in the research questions at the end of the chapter.

Statement 8, the OUTFIL control statement. The format for the OUTFIL control statement is shown in part (b) of Figure 13.4. This statement defines the output files and is also lengthy.

In our example the statement

```
OUTFIL BLKSIZE=1000,ESDS
```

BLKSIZE = 1000 specifies the maximum block size, in bytes, of the output records.

The OPEN and CLOSE operands have the same meanings as in the INPFLE control statement, and we are taking the defaults.

The ESDS operand indicates that the output is to be a VSAM ESDS file. It is assumed that the output area has already been defined by the AMS program.

Other operands are examined in the research problems at the end of the chapter.

Statement 9, the END control statement. This statement indicates the end of all the Sort/Merge control statements. It is a required statement and has no operands.

EXAMPLE 13.4

Code the job control to sort a JAN MONTHLY PAYROLL FILE (the ID) on the employee name. The location of the name fields is the same as in Example 13.3. Input consists of one SAM disk file of 5000 records, and the CALCAREA option in the sort OPTION control statement is to be used. The output is to be on the printer. The device used is a 3340 CKD disk device. There will be one disk work file.

The volume serial number is 666666, and the data is in an extent beginning at cylinder number 4, track number 0 and ending in cylinder number 6, track number 11 (12 tracks per cylinder). The records are 100-byte records, blocked 10.

Before the actual sort, the CALCAREA option is to be used to check the job control and calculate the area needed for the disk work file. If it is too large or small, the extent will be changed. The librarian says that extents 7-10 could be used as a work area.

Answer

```
     * $$ JOB JNM=RAY,CLASS=J
     * $$ LST CLASS=Z
     // JOB RAY    SORT TWO PAYROLL INPUT FILES AND PRINT
(1)  // ASSGN SYS001,PRINTER
(2)  // ASSGN SYS002,3340,VOL=666666,SHR
(3)  // DLBL SORTIN1,'JAN MONTHLY PAYROLL FILE',,SD
(4)  // EXTENT SYS002,666666,1,0,48,36
(5)  // ASSGN SYS003,3340,VOL=666666,SHR
(6)  // DLBL SORTWK1
(7)  // EXTENT SYS003,666666,1,0,84,24
(8)  // EXEC SORT,SIZE=64K
```

```
(9)    SORT FIELDS=(3,15,A,18,10,A,28,1,A),FORMAT=CH,FILES=1,WORK=DA
(10)   RECORD TYPE=F,LENGTH=100
(11)   INPFIL BLKSIZE=1000
(12)   OUTFIL BLKSIZE=132
(13)   OPTION CALCAREA
(14)   END
/*
/&
* $$ EOJ
```

Note that ASSGN and EXTENT statements are used since these are native file organizations.

Statement 1 describes the printer output file. Statements 2–4 describe the input file that is to be sorted. Statements 5–7 describe the work file. Statement 7 may be changed after examining the result of the run with the CALCAREA option. This option executes only phase 0 of the sort, checks for errors in job control, and calculates the work area needed.

The OPTION control statement is discussed further in the research problems at the end of the chapter.

SUMMARY

Utility programs perform day-to-day tasks. The LVTOC program prints entries in the disk table of contents (VTOC). The list consists of native file entries and VSAM data spaces. If it is desired to print the entries in the VSAM data spaces, the AMS LISTCAT utility program must be used.

The LISTLOG program will cause console communications to be listed for a job if it is used after the /& statement.

DITTO allows the programmer to display, print, copy, or change information in files. These files may be on card, tape, disk, or diskettes. DITTO may be used in console or batch mode.

The UPSI job control statement is used to indicate batch mode (// UPSI 1). The format of batch DITTO statements is

```
$$DITTOboperands separated by commas
```

DITTO is invoked or loaded by coding // EXEC DITTO. A DITTO function summary may be listed by the use of the $$DITTO XXX statement. The last DITTO statement is always $$DITTO EOJ.

The Sort/Merge program is used to reorder records in files or merge records in previously sequenced files. It is invoked by the use of the // EXEC SORT statement. Sort control statements have the format

```
bop codeboperands separated by commas
```

They may be continued by a nonblank character in column 72.

The most commonly used SORT control statements are:

1. The SORT statement, which describes the sort control fields and input files to be sorted

2. The RECORD statement, which describes the record length and field formats

3. The INPFIL statement, which defines the files to be sorted and open and close procedures

4. The OUTFIL statement, which defines the output files and open and close procedures

5. The OPTION statement, which allows alteration of options built into the SORT program

6. The END statement, which indicates the end of the Sort/Merge program control statements

TERMS TO REMEMBER

Checkpoint	Phase
DITTO program	Sort/Merge program
Incore sort	String
LISTLOG program	Work area
LVTOC program	Work file

CODING EXERCISES

1. Code the job control to do a VTOC on a volume designated by your instructor. Include a LISTLOG statement. Key the JCL and run it. Go to the console after it is submitted, if so instructed, to see if you need to respond to any console messages. Code the same job using DITTO and submit it.

2. Use your DITTO summary printout to code the job control to read the data set 1 records in Appendix D and print them (card image to printer).

3. Use your DITTO summary printout to code the job control statements to dump the output disk file in either Coding Exercise 1∅ of Chapter 9 or Coding Exercise 5 of Chapter 1∅, as indicated by your instructor. Key the job control and run the job (disk to printer, character format).

4. Use your DITTO summary printout to code the job control to copy data set 2 to a scratch tape, rewind the tape, and dump the tape file in character and hex format. Also rewind and unload the tape at the end of the job (card image to tape and tape to printer).

5. Code the job control to sort data set 1 in Appendix D by the social security number (columns 1–9) and print the records. Key and run this job.

6. Code the job control to read the sequential disk file written in lab 3 or 5 (as designated by your instructor), sort it by name (columns 1∅–29), and print the records. Key and run this job.

RESEARCH PROBLEMS

Use the DITTO manual to answer the following problems.

1. Describe the two ways of viewing information stored on FBA disk devices: the physical view and the logical view.

2. Define deblocking.

3. What does the disk record scan function do?

4. Can DITTO always be run in 15∅K for the partition space requirement? If not, explain.

Use the Sort/Merge manual to answer the following questions.

5. In Figure 13.4, what is the PRESEQ option on the INPFIL sort control statement used for?

6. Why was the volume operand of the INPFIL control statement not used in the examples in this chapter?

7. What is the reuse option used for in the OUTFIL control statement?

8. What is the BYPASS option used for in the INPFIL control statement?

9. How is the ALTSEQ statement used in relation to foreign languages?

10. Why would the OUTREC control statement be used? Give a practical example.

11. Look up the MERGE control statement. What are the two major differences between the SORT and the MERGE control statements? Write a MERGE control statement to merge the input records from two input files into ascending order. The control field will be a nine-position social security number that begins in column 6.

DOS/VSE Logical Unit Names

Logical Unit	I/O Device Type Allowed	Function
System logical units		
SYSRDR	Card reader, tape, disk, diskette	Used for reading job control statements
SYSIPT	Card reader, tape, disk, diskette	Used for program input
SYSIN	Card reader, tape, disk, diskette	*Can* be used to assign SYSRDR and SYSIPT to the same card reader or tape; *must* be used if both are assigned to a DASD
SYSPCH	Card punch, tape, disk, diskette	Used for punched output
SYSLST	Printer, tape, disk, diskette	Used for printed output
SYSOUT	Tape	*Must* be used when SYSPCH and SYSLST are assigned to the same tape; *cannot* be used on disk.
SYSLOG	Operator console, printer	Used for communication between the operator and the system and for logging job control statements
SYSRES	Disk	Used as the system residence device
SYSREC	Disk	Used as an extent for the system recorder, system history, and hard-copy files
SYSDUMP[a]	Disk	Used as an extent for the dump files
SYSCLB[b]	Disk	Used as an extent for a private core image library
SYSRLB[b]	Disk	Used as an extent for a private relocatable library
SYSSLB[b]	Disk	Used as an extent for a private source statement library
SYSLNK	Disk	Used as an extent for the input to the linkage editor
SYSCAT	Disk	Used as an extent for the VSAM master catalog
Programmer logical units		
SYS000 SYS001 ... SYS255	Any device of the system	Used for program input/output

[a] SYSDMP in DOS/VSE version 1.
[b] No longer exists in DOS/VSE/SP (versions 2 and 3).

Appendix B

The COBOL CBL Statement*

As we have learned, some options are specified at SYSGEN time. These can be changed at run time by the use of the DOS OPTION JCL statement. The options specified at SYSGEN time are the default options.

Certain *COBOL compile time options* have been built into the COBOL compiler. These options can be changed at compile time by the use of the CBL statement. This CBL statement is unique to COBOL.

The format for *some*, but not all, of the operands is

$$
\texttt{bCBLb[BUF=NNNNN]}
\begin{bmatrix} \texttt{,SEQ} \\ \texttt{,\underline{NOSEQ}} \end{bmatrix}
\begin{bmatrix} \texttt{,FLAGW} \\ \texttt{,\underline{FLAGE}} \end{bmatrix}
\begin{bmatrix} \texttt{,SPACEN} \\ \texttt{,\underline{SPACE1}} \end{bmatrix}
\begin{bmatrix} \texttt{,CLIST} \\ \texttt{,\underline{NOCLIST}} \end{bmatrix}
\begin{bmatrix} \texttt{,QUOTE} \\ \texttt{,\underline{APOST}} \end{bmatrix}
$$

$$
\begin{bmatrix} \texttt{,TRUNC} \\ \texttt{,\underline{NOTRUNC}} \end{bmatrix}
\begin{bmatrix} \texttt{,CATALR} \\ \texttt{,\underline{NOCATALR}} \end{bmatrix}
\begin{bmatrix} \texttt{,LIB} \\ \texttt{,\underline{NOLIB}} \end{bmatrix}
\begin{bmatrix} \texttt{,STATE} \\ \texttt{,\underline{NOSTATE}} \end{bmatrix}
\begin{bmatrix} \texttt{,LANGLVL(1)} \\ \texttt{,\underline{LANGLVL(2)}} \end{bmatrix}
\begin{bmatrix} \texttt{,SXREF} \\ \texttt{,\underline{NOSXREF}} \end{bmatrix}
$$

Notes:

1. Defaults are underlined. b represents a blank.
2. Operands cannot extend past position 71. If more operands are necessary, a second CBL statement must be used.
3. The first position of the CBL statement must be blank, and a blank must follow the CBL op code. Operands are separated by commas with no blanks, as in JCL statements.

The options that you should be familiar with are as follows:

1. SEQ   NOSEQ tells the compiler not to sequence check the
    NOSEQ   source statement line numbers.

* Summarized from the IBM *DOS/VS COBOL Programmer's Guide* SC 28-6478, pp. 36–4Ø.

204

2. FLAGW
   FLAGE

FLAGE indicates that warnings (W) will not be listed. Only type C, E, and D are listed.

Code	*EXPLANATION*
W = Warning	An error may have been made, but it is not serious enough to prevent execution of the program.
C = Conditional	An error was made, but the compiler made a corrective assumption. The statement containing the error is compiled using this assumption. Execution will not be attempted.
E = Error	A serious error was made. The statement containing the error is dropped. Execution of the program is not attempted.
D = Disaster	This indicates that compilation will *not* be finished because the error is so serious.

3. SPACEN
   SPACE1

Listings may be single spaced (1), double spaced (2), or triple spaced (3). The default is single spacing.

4. CLIST
   NOCLIST

CLIST gives a condensed listing of addresses for the first generated instruction of each verb in the PROCEDURE DIVISION. This is a shorter method than LISTX for running down the statement where your program aborted. The CLIST option overrides the LISTX option.

5. QUOTE
   APOST

Quote allows " for literals instead of the single apostrophe. If you use ' for literals, you must use the option APOST on a CBL statement.

6. LIB
   NOLIB

LIB indicates that BASIS and/or COPY statements are in the source program. If they are used, this option must be chosen. This will bring in a program from the source statement library. However, POWER users prefer to use the POWER SLI statement to perform this task.

7. STATE
   NOSTATE

STATE provides the programmer with information about the statement being executed at the time of an abnormal job ending (ABEND). It provides the statement number.

8. LANGLVL(1)
   LANGLVL(2)

LANGLVL(1) specifies that the 1968 ANS standards are being used in the compilation. If you are planning to use the JUST RIGHT clause in the DATA DIVISION, you must specify this option. The default, LANGLVL(2), indicates that you are using the 1974 ANS standard.

9. SXREF
   NOSXREF

SXREF causes the compiler to write an alphabetically ordered cross-reference list on the printer. This is helpful in debugging.

Appendix C

Computer Codes

Character	Hollerith Code	EBCDIC Code (Binary)	EBCDIC Code (Hex)
b		0100 0000	40
¢	12-2-8	0100 1010	4A
.	12-3-8	0100 1011	4B
<	12-4-8	0100 1100	4C
(	12-5-8	0100 1101	4D
+	12-6-8	0100 1110	4E
|	12-7-8	0100 1111	4F
&	12	0101 0000	50
!	11-2-8	0101 1010	5A
$	11-3-8	0101 1011	5B
*	11-4-8	0101 1100	5C
)	11-5-8	0101 1101	5D
;	11-6-8	0101 1110	5E
¬	11-7-8	0101 1111	5F
-	11	0110 0000	60
/	0-1	0110 0001	61
, (comma)	0-3-8	0110 1011	6B
%	0-4-8	0110 1100	6C
__ (underline)	0-5-8	0110 1101	6D
>	0-6-8	0110 1110	6E
?	0-7-8	0110 1111	6F
:	2-8	0111 1010	7A
#	3-8	0111 1011	7B
@	4-8	0111 1100	7C
' (apostrophe)	5-8	0111 1101	7D
=	6-8	0111 1110	7E
''	7-8	0111 1111	7F
A	12-1	1100 0001	C1
B	12-2	1100 0010	C2
C	12-3	1100 0011	C3
D	12-4	1100 0100	C4

Character	Hollerith Code	EBCDIC Code (Binary)	EBCDIC Code (Hex)
E	12-5	1100 0101	C5
F	12-6	1100 0110	C6
G	12-7	1100 0111	C7
H	12-8	1100 1000	C8
I	12-9	1100 1001	C9
J	11-1	1101 0001	D1
K	11-2	1101 0010	D2
L	11-3	1101 0011	D3
M	11-4	1101 0100	D4
N	11-5	1101 0101	D5
O	11-6	1101 0110	D6
P	11-7	1101 0111	D7
Q	11-8	1101 1000	D8
R	11-9	1101 1001	D9
S	0-2	1110 0010	E2
T	0-3	1110 0011	E3
U	0-4	1110 0100	E4
V	0-5	1110 0101	E5
W	0-6	1110 0110	E6
X	0-7	1110 0111	E7
Y	0-8	1110 1000	E8
Z	0-9	1110 1001	E9
0	0	1111 0000	F0
1	1	1111 0001	F1
2	2	1111 0010	F2
3	3	1111 0011	F3
4	4	1111 0100	F4
5	5	1111 0101	F5
6	6	1111 0110	F6
7	7	1111 0111	F7
8	8	1111 1000	F8
9	9	1111 1001	F9

Appendix D

Lab Programs and Data

Possible lab programs and data are listed below.

Lab	Chapter Number	Coding Exercise	Topic	Programs To Be Used	Data To Be Used
1	7	5	Card image to printer	GSLIST	1
2	8	12	Card image to tape; tape to printer	CRDTOTP; TPTOPRT	1
3	9	10	Card image to SAM disk; disk to printer	CRDTODSK; DSKTOPRT	2
4	9	11	SAM to ISAM; ISAM to printer	BLDINSEQ; INSEQRET	—
5	10	5	Card image to ESDS disk; disk to printer	CRDTOES; ESDSRET	2
6	10	6	ESDS to KSDS; disk to printer	BLDKSDS; KSDSRET	—
7	11 or 12	10 8	Catalog object and display; execute	Lab 3 or 5 as instructed	2
8	11 or 12	11 9	Catalog source and display	See Lab 1	—
9	11 and 13	9 1	List catalog List VTOC	—	—
10	13 and 13	2, 3, or 4 5 or 6	DITTO as instructed Sort/Merge as instructed	—	—

The student should fill out the chart below according to the lab instructions given by the instructor.

Lab Number To Be Done	Chapter and Exercise	Date Due	Special Instructions

DATA SET 1

```
464362395ADAMS, DANA L.        ACCOUNTING           ASSOCIATE   4000
213202150ASHMORE, ARLENE B.    CHILD CARE           CERTIFICATE 2760
883009901AUSTIN, ROY C.        GENERAL BUSINESS     ASSOCIATE   3255
580356005BECHT, FRED R.        COMPUTER TECHNOLOGY  ASSOCIATE   3000
878044014BROWN, CHRISTENE M.   MUSIC, COMMERCIAL    ASSOCIATE   3250
355777004BUTLER, DAVID M.      REAL ESTATE          CERTIFICATE 3724
910767102CALHOUN, RALPH A.     LAW ENFORCEMENT      ASSOCIATE   3200
230064305CONWAY, TIM C.        BANKING AND FINANCE  ASSOCIATE   3955
395001212COX, WALLY B.         REAL ESTATE          CERTIFICATE 2911
185089608DEMPSEY, KATHY L.     CHILD CARE           ASSOCIATE   3890
407451555DOLENZ, MICKY C.      MUSIC, COMMERCIAL    ASSOCIATE   3066
750065809DVORAK, FRANK E.      ACCOUNTING           ASSOCIATE   2500
577326515ELLIOT, AMANDA W.     SECRETARIAL TRAININGCERTIFICATE 3232
429151382ESTRADA, ERICA E.     COSMETOLOGY          CERTIFICATE 2310
777004400EWING, JOHN R.        GENERAL BUSINESS     ASSOCIATE   3324
903035252FARMER, EDWARD P.     BANKING AND FINANCE  ASSOCIATE   2571
114209333FISHER, LUTHER T.     COMPUTER TECHNOLOGY  ASSOCIATE   3866
778791915FULLER, ROBERT J.     LAW ENFORCEMENT      ASSOCIATE   2071
223223451GAGE, JOHNNY M.       LAW ENFORCEMENT      ASSOCIATE   3330
571329000GIBB, ANDY G.         MUSIC, COMMERCIAL    ASSOCIATE   2033
357890417GONZALEZ, JOSE A.     GENERAL BUSINESS     ASSOCIATE   2333
114087887HARRIS, MARK O.       LAW ENFORCEMENT      ASSOCIATE   3222
907575241HICKMAN, DWAYNE C.    SECRETARIAL TRAININGCERTIFICATE 2574
280899750HUGHES, HOWARD B.     REAL ESTATE          CERTIFICATE 3052
512070118IRWIN, ADRIAN J.      ACCOUNTING           ASSOCIATE   4000
885053223JACKSON, MICHELE J.   COSMETOLOGY          CERTIFICATE 2588
150538267JONES, DAVY L.       MUSIC, COMMERCIAL    ASSOCIATE   3066
924784345JUDD, CHARLES C.      COMPUTER TECHNOLOGY  ASSOCIATE   2445
711207801KELSO, DIANA P.       CHILD CARE           ASSOCIATE   2057
577462355KIRK, JAMES T.        LAW ENFORCEMENT      ASSOCIATE   3850
903409509KNIGHT, ROBERT M.     GENERAL BUSINESS     ASSOCIATE   3000
208104995LEWIS, JERRY M.       REAL ESTATE          CERTIFICATE 2089
732360634LOCKWOOD, GARY R.     SECRETARIAL TRAININGCERTIFICATE 3200
328419964LYNCH, KIRSTEN F.     COSMETOLOGY          CERTIFICATE 3152
423241802MARTIN, CRAIG T.      ACCOUNTING           ASSOCIATE   2000
276705606MOHAN, BARRY C.       GENERAL BUSINESS     ASSOCIATE   3456
```

```
923466511MURPHY, AUDRY A.      CHILD CARE            ASSOCIATE    2950
794050983NESMITH, MICHAEL L.   GENERAL BUSINESS      ASSOCIATE    2300
571581818NOLTE, NICK N.        BANKING AND FINANCE   ASSOCIATE    4000
894005595NYE, CHARLES P.       REAL ESTATE           CERTIFICATE  3055
904600123TAYLOR, MYRA D.       COMPUTER TECHNOLOGY   CERTIFICATE  3500
813300222TORK, PETER M.        MUSIC, COMMERCIAL     ASSOCIATE    2445
617920512UNDERWOOD, BRAD L.    ACCOUNTING            ASSOCIATE    2050
472043611URBANOVSKY, DON D.    REAL ESTATE           CERTIFICATE  3022
691001569VANCE, VINCE T.       GENERAL BUSINESS      ASSOCIATE    3384
343868250WALKER, ROBERTA C.    ACCOUNTING            ASSOCIATE    3554
259057946WEBB, JACK S.         LAW ENFORCEMENT       ASSOCIATE    2743
713453909WORHOL, ERNEST P.     COSMETOLOGY           CERTIFICATE  3210
813147225YARBOROUGH, VICKY N.  GENERAL BUSINESS      ASSOCIATE    2350
696588584YOUNG, LISA M.        CHILD CARE            ASSOCIATE    4000
```

DATA SET 2

```
114087887HARRIS, MARK O.       LAW ENFORCEMENT       ASSOCIATE    3222
114209333FISHER, LUTHER T.     COMPUTER TECHNOLOGY   ASSOCIATE    3866
150538267JONES, DAVY L.        MUSIC, COMMERCIAL     ASSOCIATE    3066
185089608DEMPSEY, KATHY L.     CHILD CARE            ASSOCIATE    3890
208104995LEWIS, JERRY M.       REAL ESTATE           CERTIFICATE  2089
213202150ASHMORE, ARLENE B.    CHILD CARE            CERTIFICATE  2760
223223451GAGE, JOHNNY M.       LAW ENFORCEMENT       ASSOCIATE    3330
230064305CONWAY, TIM C.        BANKING AND FINANCE   ASSOCIATE    3955
259057946WEBB, JACK S.         LAW ENFORCEMENT       ASSOCIATE    2743
276705606MOHAN, BARRY C.       GENERAL BUSINESS      ASSOCIATE    3456
280899750HUGHES, HOWARD B.     REAL ESTATE           CERTIFICATE  3052
328419964LYNCH, KIRSTEN F.     COSMETOLOGY           CERTIFICATE  3152
343868250WALKER, ROBERTA C.    ACCOUNTING            ASSOCIATE    3554
355777004BUTLER, DAVID M.      REAL ESTATE           CERTIFICATE  3724
357890417GONZALEZ, JOSE A.     GENERAL BUSINESS      ASSOCIATE    2333
395001212COX, WALLY B.         REAL ESTATE           CERTIFICATE  2911
407451555DOLENZ, MICKY C.      MUSIC, COMMERCIAL     ASSOCIATE    3066
423241802MARTIN, CRAIG T.      ACCOUNTING            ASSOCIATE    2000
429151382ESTRADA, ERICA E.     COSMETOLOGY           CERTIFICATE  2310
464362395ADAMS, DANA L.        ACCOUNTING            ASSOCIATE    4000
472043611URBANOVSKY, DON D.    REAL ESTATE           CERTIFICATE  3022
512070118IRWIN, ADRIAN J.      ACCOUNTING            ASSOCIATE    4000
571329000GIBB, ANDY G.         MUSIC, COMMERCIAL     ASSOCIATE    2033
571581818NOLTE, NICK N.        BANKING AND FINANCE   ASSOCIATE    4000
577326515ELLIOT, AMANDA W.     SECRETARIAL TRAININGCERTIFICATE   3232
577462355KIRK, JAMES T.        LAW ENFORCEMENT       ASSOCIATE    3850
580356005BECHT, FRED R.        COMPUTER TECHNOLOGY   ASSOCIATE    3000
617920512UNDERWOOD, BRAD L.    ACCOUNTING            ASSOCIATE    2050
691001569VANCE, VINCE T.       GENERAL BUSINESS      ASSOCIATE    3384
696588584YOUNG, LISA M.        CHILD CARE            ASSOCIATE    4000
711207801KELSO, DIANA P.       CHILD CARE            ASSOCIATE    2057
713453909WORHOL, ERNEST P.     COSMETOLOGY           CERTIFICATE  3210
732360634LOCKWOOD, GARY R.     SECRETARIAL TRAININGCERTIFICATE   3200
750065809DVORAK, FRANK E.      ACCOUNTING            ASSOCIATE    2500
777004400EWING, JOHN R.        GENERAL BUSINESS      ASSOCIATE    3324
778791915FULLER, ROBERT J.     LAW ENFORCEMENT       ASSOCIATE    2071
794050983NESMITH, MICHAEL L.   GENERAL BUSINESS      ASSOCIATE    2300
813147225YARBOROUGH, VICKY N.  GENERAL BUSINESS      ASSOCIATE    2350
813300222TORK, PETER M.        MUSIC, COMMERCIAL     ASSOCIATE    2445
878044014BROWN, CHRISTENE M.   MUSIC, COMMERCIAL     ASSOCIATE    3250
883009901AUSTIN, ROY C.        GENERAL BUSINESS      ASSOCIATE    3255
885053223JACKSON, MICHELE J.   COSMETOLOGY           CERTIFICATE  2588
894005595NYE, CHARLES P.       REAL ESTATE           CERTIFICATE  3055
903035252FARMER, EDWARD P.     BANKING AND FINANCE   ASSOCIATE    2571
903409509KNIGHT, ROBERT M.     GENERAL BUSINESS      ASSOCIATE    3000
904600123TAYLOR, MYRA D.       COMPUTER TECHNOLOGY   CERTIFICATE  3500
907575241HICKMAN, DWAYNE C.    SECRETARIAL TRAININGCERTIFICATE   2574
910767102CALHOUN, RALPH A.     LAW ENFORCEMENT       ASSOCIATE    3200
923466511MURPHY, AUDRY A.      CHILD CARE            ASSOCIATE    2950
924784345JUDD, CHARLES C.      COMPUTER TECHNOLOGY   ASSOCIATE    2445
```

PROGRAM GSLIST

```
100100 IDENTIFICATION DIVISION.                                           GSLIST
100200                                                                    GSLIST
100300 PROGRAM-ID.       GSLIST.                                          GSLIST
100400                                                                    GSLIST
100500 AUTHOR.           JOHN DOE.                                        GSLIST
100600 INSTALLATION.     STATE UNIVERSITY.                               GSLIST
100700 DATE-WRITTEN.     08/29/87.                                        GSLIST
100800 DATE-COMPILED.                                                     GSLIST
100900 SECURITY.         NONE.                                            GSLIST
101000 REMARKS.          THIS PROGRAM PRODUCES A LISTING OF GRADUATING    GSLIST
101100                   STUDENTS.                                        GSLIST
101200                                                                    GSLIST
101300 ENVIRONMENT DIVISION.                                             GSLIST
101400                                                                    GSLIST
101500 CONFIGURATION SECTION.                                            GSLIST
101600                                                                    GSLIST
101700 SOURCE-COMPUTER. IBM-4331.                                        GSLIST
101800 OBJECT-COMPUTER. IBM-4331.                                        GSLIST
101900 SPECIAL-NAMES.    C01 IS TO-THE-TOP-OF-THE-PAGE.                  GSLIST
102000                                                                    GSLIST
200100 INPUT-OUTPUT SECTION.                                             GSLIST
200200                                                                    GSLIST
200300 FILE-CONTROL.                                                     GSLIST
200400     SELECT GRADUATE-INPUT-FILE                                    GSLIST
200500         ASSIGN TO SYS006-UR-2540R-S.                             GSLIST
200600     SELECT GRADUATE-OUTPUT-FILE                                   GSLIST
200700         ASSIGN TO SYS009-UR-1403-S.                              GSLIST
200800                                                                    GSLIST
200900 DATA DIVISION.                                                    GSLIST
201000                                                                    GSLIST
201100 FILE SECTION.                                                     GSLIST
201200                                                                    GSLIST
201300 FD  GRADUATE-INPUT-FILE                                           GSLIST
201400     RECORD CONTAINS 80 CHARACTERS                                GSLIST
201600     LABEL RECORDS ARE OMITTED                                    GSLIST
201700     DATA RECORD IS GRADUATE-INPUT-RECORD.                        GSLIST
201800 01  GRADUATE-INPUT-RECORD.                                        GSLIST
201900     05  GRADUATE-ID-IN-1             PIC X(03).                   GSLIST
201920     05  GRADUATE-ID-IN-2             PIC X(02).                   GSLIST
201940     05  GRADUATE-ID-IN-3             PIC X(04).                   GSLIST
202000     05  GRADUATE-NAME-IN             PIC X(20).                   GSLIST
300100     05  GRADUATE-STUDY-IN            PIC X(20).                   GSLIST
300200     05  GRADUATE-DIPLOMA-IN          PIC X(12).                   GSLIST
300300     05  FILLER                       PIC X(19).                   GSLIST
300400                                                                    GSLIST
300500 FD  GRADUATE-OUTPUT-FILE                                          GSLIST
300600     RECORD CONTAINS 133 CHARACTERS                               GSLIST
300800     LABEL RECORDS ARE OMITTED                                    GSLIST
300900     DATA RECORD IS GRADUATE-OUTPUT-RECORD.                       GSLIST
301000 01  GRADUATE-OUTPUT-RECORD.                                       GSLIST
301100     05  CARRIAGE-CONTROL             PIC X(01).                   GSLIST
301200     05  FILLER                       PIC X(27).                   GSLIST
301300     05  GRADUATE-ID-OUT-1            PIC X(03).                   GSLIST
301320     05  DASH-1                       PIC X(01).                   GSLIST
301340     05  GRADUATE-ID-OUT-2            PIC X(02).                   GSLIST
301360     05  DASH-2                       PIC X(01).                   GSLIST
301380     05  GRADUATE-ID-OUT-3            PIC X(04).                   GSLIST
301400     05  FILLER                       PIC X(05).                   GSLIST
301500     05  GRADUATE-NAME-OUT            PIC X(20).                   GSLIST
301600     05  FILLER                       PIC X(05).                   GSLIST
301700     05  GRADUATE-STUDY-OUT           PIC X(20).                   GSLIST
301800     05  FILLER                       PIC X(05).                   GSLIST
301900     05  GRADUATE-DIPLOMA-OUT         PIC X(12).                   GSLIST
302000     05  FILLER                       PIC X(27).                   GSLIST
400100                                                                    GSLIST
400200 WORKING-STORAGE SECTION.                                          GSLIST
400300                                                                    GSLIST
```

```
400400 01   PROGRAM-INDICATORS.                                          GSLIST
400500      05   ARE-THERE-MORE-RECORDS          PIC X(03) VALUE 'YES'.  GSLIST
400600           88   THERE-IS-A-RECORD                    VALUE 'YES'.  GSLIST
400700           88   THERE-ARE-NO-MORE-RECORDS            VALUE 'NO '.  GSLIST
400800                                                                   GSLIST
400900 01   PRINTER-CONTROLS.                                            GSLIST
401000      05   PROPER-SPACING                  PIC 9(01).              GSLIST
401100      05   SPACE-ONE-LINE                  PIC 9(01)  VALUE 1.     GSLIST
401200      05   SPACE-TWO-LINES                 PIC 9(01)  VALUE 2.     GSLIST
401300      05   LINES-PRINTED                   PIC S9(03) VALUE ZERO   GSLIST
401400                                           USAGE IS COMP-3.        GSLIST
401500      05   LINE-MAXIMUM                    PIC S9(03) VALUE +35    GSLIST
401600                                           USAGE IS COMP-3.        GSLIST
401700      05   PAGE-COUNT                      PIC S9(03) VALUE +1     GSLIST
401800                                           USAGE IS COMP-3.        GSLIST
401900           88   FIRST-PAGE                           VALUE +1.     GSLIST
401920                                                                   GSLIST
401940 01   PROGRAM-CONSTANTS.                                           GSLIST
401960      05   DASH                            PIC X(01)  VALUE '-'.   GSLIST
401980                                                                   GSLIST
402000 01   HEADING-LINES.                                               GSLIST
500100      05   MAIN-HEADING-LINE.                                      GSLIST
500200           10   CARRIAGE-CONTROL           PIC X(01) VALUE SPACES. GSLIST
500300           10   FILLER                     PIC X(10) VALUE SPACES. GSLIST
500400           10   DATE-OUT                   PIC X(08).              GSLIST
500500           10   FILLER                     PIC X(40) VALUE SPACES. GSLIST
500600           10   FILLER                     PIC X(16)               GSLIST
500700                                           VALUE 'GRADUATE LISTING'.GSLIST
500800           10   FILLER                     PIC X(36) VALUE SPACES. GSLIST
500900           10   FILLER                     PIC X(05) VALUE 'PAGE '. GSLIST
501000           10   PAGE-OUT                   PIC ZZ9.                GSLIST
501100           10   FILLER                     PIC X(14) VALUE SPACES. GSLIST
501120                                                                   GSLIST
501200      05   FIRST-HEADING-LINE.                                     GSLIST
501300           10   CARRIAGE-CONTROL           PIC X(01) VALUE SPACES. GSLIST
501400           10   FILLER                     PIC X(31) VALUE SPACES. GSLIST
501500           10   FILLER                     PIC X(19) VALUE 'ID'.   GSLIST
501600           10   FILLER                     PIC X(22)               GSLIST
501700                                           VALUE 'STUDENT'.        GSLIST
501800           10   FILLER                     PIC X(23)               GSLIST
501900                                           VALUE 'MAJOR COURSE'.   GSLIST
502000           10   FILLER                     PIC X(37)               GSLIST
600100                                           VALUE 'TYPE OF'.        GSLIST
600200                                                                   GSLIST
600300      05   SECOND-HEADING-LINE.                                    GSLIST
600400           10   CARRIAGE-CONTROL           PIC X(01) VALUE SPACES. GSLIST
600500           10   FILLER                     PIC X(29) VALUE SPACES. GSLIST
600600           10   FILLER                     PIC X(22) VALUE 'NUMBER'.GSLIST
600700           10   FILLER                     PIC X(23) VALUE 'NAME'. GSLIST
600800           10   FILLER                     PIC X(21)               GSLIST
600900                                           VALUE 'OF STUDY'.       GSLIST
601000           10   FILLER                     PIC X(37)               GSLIST
601100                                           VALUE 'DIPLOMA'.        GSLIST
601200                                                                   GSLIST
601300 PROCEDURE DIVISION.                                               GSLIST
601400                                                                   GSLIST
601500 A000-START-MAIN-ROUTINE.                                          GSLIST
601600     OPEN INPUT GRADUATE-INPUT-FILE                                GSLIST
601700          OUTPUT GRADUATE-OUTPUT-FILE.                             GSLIST
601800     READ GRADUATE-INPUT-FILE                                      GSLIST
601900        AT END                                                     GSLIST
602000           MOVE 'NO ' TO ARE-THERE-MORE-RECORDS.                   GSLIST
700100     IF THERE-IS-A-RECORD                                          GSLIST
700200        PERFORM A001-PROCESS-AND-READ                              GSLIST
700300           UNTIL THERE-ARE-NO-MORE-RECORDS.                        GSLIST
700400     CLOSE GRADUATE-INPUT-FILE                                     GSLIST
700500           GRADUATE-OUTPUT-FILE.                                   GSLIST
700600     STOP RUN.                                                     GSLIST
700700                                                                   GSLIST
```

```
700800 A001-PROCESS-AND-READ.                                        GSLIST
700900     PERFORM B000-PROCESS-DETAIL-RECORDS.                      GSLIST
701000     READ GRADUATE-INPUT-FILE                                  GSLIST
701100         AT END                                                GSLIST
701200             MOVE 'NO ' TO ARE-THERE-MORE-RECORDS.             GSLIST
701300                                                               GSLIST
701400 B000-PROCESS-DETAIL-RECORDS.                                  GSLIST
701500     IF LINES-PRINTED IS EQUAL TO LINE-MAXIMUM                 GSLIST
701600         OR IS GREATER THAN LINE-MAXIMUM                       GSLIST
701700         OR FIRST-PAGE                                         GSLIST
701800             PERFORM C000-HEADING-ROUTINE.                     GSLIST
701900     MOVE SPACES TO GRADUATE-OUTPUT-RECORD.                    GSLIST
702000     MOVE DASH TO DASH-1, DASH-2.                              GSLIST
702020     MOVE GRADUATE-ID-IN-1 TO GRADUATE-ID-OUT-1.               GSLIST
702040     MOVE GRADUATE-ID-IN-2 TO GRADUATE-ID-OUT-2.               GSLIST
702060     MOVE GRADUATE-ID-IN-3 TO GRADUATE-ID-OUT-3.               GSLIST
800100     MOVE GRADUATE-NAME-IN TO GRADUATE-NAME-OUT.               GSLIST
800200     MOVE GRADUATE-STUDY-IN TO GRADUATE-STUDY-OUT.             GSLIST
800300     MOVE GRADUATE-DIPLOMA-IN TO GRADUATE-DIPLOMA-OUT.         GSLIST
800400     WRITE GRADUATE-OUTPUT-RECORD                              GSLIST
800500         AFTER PROPER-SPACING.                                 GSLIST
800600     MOVE SPACE-ONE-LINE TO PROPER-SPACING.                    GSLIST
800700     ADD 1 TO LINES-PRINTED.                                   GSLIST
800800                                                               GSLIST
800900 C000-HEADING-ROUTINE.                                         GSLIST
801000     MOVE CURRENT-DATE TO DATE-OUT.                            GSLIST
801100     MOVE PAGE-COUNT TO PAGE-OUT.                              GSLIST
801200     WRITE GRADUATE-OUTPUT-RECORD FROM MAIN-HEADING-LINE       GSLIST
801300         AFTER ADVANCING TO-THE-TOP-OF-THE-PAGE.               GSLIST
801400     WRITE GRADUATE-OUTPUT-RECORD FROM FIRST-HEADING-LINE      GSLIST
801500         AFTER ADVANCING 2 LINES.                              GSLIST
801600     WRITE GRADUATE-OUTPUT-RECORD FROM SECOND-HEADING-LINE     GSLIST
801700         AFTER ADVANCING 1 LINES.                              GSLIST
801800     MOVE SPACE-TWO-LINES TO PROPER-SPACING.                   GSLIST
801900     ADD 1 TO PAGE-COUNT.                                      GSLIST
802000     MOVE ZEROS TO LINES-PRINTED.                              GSLIST
```

PROGRAM CRDTOTP

```
100100 IDENTIFICATION DIVISION.                                      CRDTOTP
100200                                                               CRDTOTP
100300 PROGRAM-ID.       CRDTOTP.                                    CRDTOTP
100400                                                               CRDTOTP
100500 AUTHOR.           JOHN DOE.                                   CRDTOTP
100600 INSTALLATION.     STATE UNIVERSITY.                           CRDTOTP
100700 DATE-WRITTEN.     08/29/87.                                   CRDTOTP
100800 DATE-COMPILED.                                                CRDTOTP
100900 SECURITY.         NONE.                                       CRDTOTP
101100 REMARKS.          THIS PROGRAM PRODUCES A FILE OF GRADUATING  CRDTOTP
101200                   STUDENTS ON TAPE USING CARD INPUT.          CRDTOTP
101300                                                               CRDTOTP
101400 ENVIRONMENT DIVISION.                                         CRDTOTP
101500                                                               CRDTOTP
101600 CONFIGURATION SECTION.                                        CRDTOTP
101700                                                               CRDTOTP
101800 SOURCE-COMPUTER. IBM-4331.                                    CRDTOTP
101900 OBJECT-COMPUTER. IBM-4331.                                    CRDTOTP
102000                                                               CRDTOTP
200100 INPUT-OUTPUT SECTION.                                         CRDTOTP
200200                                                               CRDTOTP
200300 FILE-CONTROL.                                                 CRDTOTP
200400     SELECT GRADUATE-INPUT-FILE                                CRDTOTP
200500         ASSIGN TO SYS004-UR-2540R-S.                          CRDTOTP
200600     SELECT GRADUATE-OUTPUT-FILE                               CRDTOTP
200700         ASSIGN TO SYS006-UT-8809-S-TAPEOUT.                   CRDTOTP
200800                                                               CRDTOTP
200900 DATA DIVISION.                                                CRDTOTP
201000                                                               CRDTOTP
```

```
201100 FILE SECTION.                                              CRDTOTP
201200                                                            CRDTOTP
201300 FD  GRADUATE-INPUT-FILE                                    CRDTOTP
201400     RECORD CONTAINS 80 CHARACTERS                          CRDTOTP
201600     LABEL RECORDS ARE OMITTED                              CRDTOTP
201700     DATA RECORD IS GRADUATE-INPUT-RECORD.                  CRDTOTP
201800 01  GRADUATE-INPUT-RECORD                PIC X(80).        CRDTOTP
201900                                                            CRDTOTP
202000 FD  GRADUATE-OUTPUT-FILE                                   CRDTOTP
300100     RECORD CONTAINS 80 CHARACTERS                          CRDTOTP
300200     BLOCK CONTAINS 5 RECORDS                               CRDTOTP
300400     LABEL RECORDS ARE STANDARD                             CRDTOTP
300500     DATA RECORD IS GRADUATE-OUTPUT-RECORD.                 CRDTOTP
300600 01  GRADUATE-OUTPUT-RECORD               PIC X(80).        CRDTOTP
300700                                                            CRDTOTP
300800 WORKING-STORAGE SECTION.                                   CRDTOTP
300900                                                            CRDTOTP
301000 01  PROGRAM-INDICATORS.                                    CRDTOTP
301100     05  ARE-THERE-MORE-RECORDS        PIC X(03) VALUE 'YES'. CRDTOTP
301200         88  THERE-IS-A-RECORD                   VALUE 'YES'. CRDTOTP
301300         88  THERE-ARE-NO-MORE-RECORDS           VALUE 'NO '. CRDTOTP
400600                                                            CRDTOTP
400700 PROCEDURE DIVISION.                                        CRDTOTP
400800                                                            CRDTOTP
400900 A000-START-MAIN-ROUTINE.                                   CRDTOTP
401000     OPEN INPUT GRADUATE-INPUT-FILE                         CRDTOTP
401100          OUTPUT GRADUATE-OUTPUT-FILE.                      CRDTOTP
401200     READ GRADUATE-INPUT-FILE                               CRDTOTP
401300         AT END                                             CRDTOTP
401400             MOVE 'NO ' TO ARE-THERE-MORE-RECORDS.          CRDTOTP
401500     IF THERE-IS-A-RECORD                                   CRDTOTP
401600         PERFORM A001-PROCESS-AND-READ                      CRDTOTP
401700             UNTIL THERE-ARE-NO-MORE-RECORDS.               CRDTOTP
401800     CLOSE GRADUATE-INPUT-FILE                              CRDTOTP
401900           GRADUATE-OUTPUT-FILE.                            CRDTOTP
402000     STOP RUN.                                              CRDTOTP
500100                                                            CRDTOTP
500200 A001-PROCESS-AND-READ.                                     CRDTOTP
500300     PERFORM B000-PROCESS-DETAIL-RECORDS.                   CRDTOTP
500400     READ GRADUATE-INPUT-FILE                               CRDTOTP
500500         AT END                                             CRDTOTP
500600             MOVE 'NO ' TO ARE-THERE-MORE-RECORDS.          CRDTOTP
500700                                                            CRDTOTP
500800 B000-PROCESS-DETAIL-RECORDS.                               CRDTOTP
500900     MOVE SPACES TO GRADUATE-OUTPUT-RECORD.                 CRDTOTP
501000     MOVE GRADUATE-INPUT-RECORD TO GRADUATE-OUTPUT-RECORD.  CRDTOTP
501100     WRITE GRADUATE-OUTPUT-RECORD.                          CRDTOTP
```

PROGRAM TPTOPRT

```
100100 IDENTIFICATION DIVISION.                                  TPTOPRT
100200                                                           TPTOPRT
100300 PROGRAM-ID.      TPTOPRT.                                 TPTOPRT
100400                                                           TPTOPRT
100500 AUTHOR.          JOHN DOE.                                TPTOPRT
100600 INSTALLATION.    STATE UNIVERSITY.                        TPTOPRT
100700 DATE-WRITTEN.    08/29/87.                                TPTOPRT
100800 DATE-COMPILED.                                            TPTOPRT
100900 SECURITY.        NONE.                                    TPTOPRT
101000 REMARKS.         THIS PROGRAM PRODUCES A LISTING OF GRADUATING TPTOPRT
101100                  STUDENTS USING TAPE INPUT.               TPTOPRT
101200                                                           TPTOPRT
101300 ENVIRONMENT DIVISION.                                     TPTOPRT
101400                                                           TPTOPRT
101500 CONFIGURATION SECTION.                                    TPTOPRT
101600                                                           TPTOPRT
101700 SOURCE-COMPUTER. IBM-4331.                                TPTOPRT
```

```
101800 OBJECT-COMPUTER. IBM-4331.                                          TPTOPRT
101900 SPECIAL-NAMES.    C01 IS TO-THE-TOP-OF-THE-PAGE.                    TPTOPRT
102000                                                                     TPTOPRT
200100 INPUT-OUTPUT SECTION.                                               TPTOPRT
200200                                                                     TPTOPRT
200300 FILE-CONTROL.                                                       TPTOPRT
200400     SELECT GRADUATE-INPUT-FILE                                      TPTOPRT
200500         ASSIGN TO SYS005-UT-8809-S-TAPEIN.                          TPTOPRT
200600     SELECT GRADUATE-OUTPUT-FILE                                     TPTOPRT
200700         ASSIGN TO SYS006-UR-1403-S.                                 TPTOPRT
200800                                                                     TPTOPRT
200900 DATA DIVISION.                                                      TPTOPRT
201000                                                                     TPTOPRT
201100 FILE SECTION.                                                       TPTOPRT
201200                                                                     TPTOPRT
201300 FD  GRADUATE-INPUT-FILE                                            TPTOPRT
201400     RECORD CONTAINS 80 CHARACTERS                                  TPTOPRT
201500     BLOCK CONTAINS 5 RECORDS                                       TPTOPRT
201700     LABEL RECORDS ARE STANDARD                                     TPTOPRT
201800     DATA RECORD IS GRADUATE-INPUT-RECORD.                          TPTOPRT
201900 01  GRADUATE-INPUT-RECORD.                                         TPTOPRT
202000     05  GRADUATE-ID-IN-1              PIC X(03).                    TPTOPRT
202010     05  GRADUATE-ID-IN-2              PIC X(02).                    TPTOPRT
202020     05  GRADUATE-ID-IN-3              PIC X(04).                    TPTOPRT
300100     05  GRADUATE-NAME-IN              PIC X(20).                    TPTOPRT
300200     05  GRADUATE-STUDY-IN             PIC X(20).                    TPTOPRT
300300     05  GRADUATE-DIPLOMA-IN           PIC X(12).                    TPTOPRT
300400     05  GRADUATE-GPA-IN               PIC 9V999.                    TPTOPRT
300500     05  FILLER                        PIC X(15).                    TPTOPRT
300600                                                                     TPTOPRT
300700 FD  GRADUATE-OUTPUT-FILE                                           TPTOPRT
300800     RECORD CONTAINS 133 CHARACTERS                                 TPTOPRT
301000     LABEL RECORDS ARE OMITTED                                      TPTOPRT
301100     DATA RECORD IS GRADUATE-OUTPUT-RECORD.                         TPTOPRT
301200 01  GRADUATE-OUTPUT-RECORD.                                        TPTOPRT
301300     05  CARRIAGE-CONTROL              PIC X(01).                    TPTOPRT
301400     05  FILLER                        PIC X(22).                    TPTOPRT
301500     05  GRADUATE-ID-OUT-1             PIC X(03).                    TPTOPRT
301520     05  DASH-1                        PIC X(01).                    TPTOPRT
301540     05  GRADUATE-ID-OUT-2             PIC X(02).                    TPTOPRT
301560     05  DASH-2                        PIC X(01).                    TPTOPRT
301580     05  GRADUATE-ID-OUT-3             PIC X(04).                    TPTOPRT
301600     05  FILLER                        PIC X(05).                    TPTOPRT
301700     05  GRADUATE-NAME-OUT             PIC X(20).                    TPTOPRT
301800     05  FILLER                        PIC X(05).                    TPTOPRT
301900     05  GRADUATE-STUDY-OUT            PIC X(20).                    TPTOPRT
302000     05  FILLER                        PIC X(05).                    TPTOPRT
400100     05  GRADUATE-DIPLOMA-OUT          PIC X(12).                    TPTOPRT
400200     05  FILLER                        PIC X(05).                    TPTOPRT
400300     05  GRADUATE-GPA-OUT              PIC 9.999.                    TPTOPRT
400400     05  FILLER                        PIC X(22).                    TPTOPRT
400500                                                                     TPTOPRT
400600 WORKING-STORAGE SECTION.                                           TPTOPRT
400700                                                                     TPTOPRT
400800 01  PROGRAM-INDICATORS.                                            TPTOPRT
400900     05  ARE-THERE-MORE-RECORDS        PIC X(03) VALUE 'YES'.       TPTOPRT
401000         88  THERE-IS-A-RECORD                   VALUE 'YES'.       TPTOPRT
401100         88  THERE-ARE-NO-MORE-RECORDS           VALUE 'NO '.       TPTOPRT
401200                                                                     TPTOPRT
401300 01  PRINTER-CONTROLS.                                              TPTOPRT
401400     05  PROPER-SPACING                PIC 9(01).                    TPTOPRT
401500     05  SPACE-ONE-LINE                PIC 9(01)  VALUE 1.           TPTOPRT
401600     05  SPACE-TWO-LINES               PIC 9(01)  VALUE 2.           TPTOPRT
401700     05  LINES-PRINTED                 PIC S9(03) VALUE ZERO         TPTOPRT
401800                                       USAGE IS COMP-3.              TPTOPRT
401900     05  LINE-MAXIMUM                  PIC S9(03) VALUE +35          TPTOPRT
402000                                       USAGE IS COMP-3.              TPTOPRT
500100     05  PAGE-COUNT                    PIC S9(03) VALUE +1           TPTOPRT
500200                                       USAGE IS COMP-3.              TPTOPRT
```

```
500300          88  FIRST-PAGE                                  VALUE +1.      TPTOPRT
500400                                                                         TPTOPRT
500420 01  PROGRAM-CONSTANTS.                                                  TPTOPRT
500440     05  DASH                            PIC X(01)  VALUE '-'.           TPTOPRT
500460                                                                         TPTOPRT
500500 01  HEADING-LINES.                                                      TPTOPRT
500600     05  MAIN-HEADING-LINE.                                              TPTOPRT
500700         10  CARRIAGE-CONTROL            PIC X(01) VALUE SPACES.         TPTOPRT
500800         10  FILLER                      PIC X(10) VALUE SPACES.         TPTOPRT
500900         10  DATE-OUT                    PIC X(08).                      TPTOPRT
501000         10  FILLER                      PIC X(40) VALUE SPACES.         TPTOPRT
501100         10  FILLER                      PIC X(16)                       TPTOPRT
501200                                         VALUE 'GRADUATE LISTING'.TPTOPRT
501300         10  FILLER                      PIC X(36) VALUE SPACES.         TPTOPRT
501400         10  FILLER                      PIC X(05) VALUE 'PAGE '.        TPTOPRT
501500         10  PAGE-OUT                    PIC ZZ9.                        TPTOPRT
501600         10  FILLER                      PIC X(14) VALUE SPACES.         TPTOPRT
501700     05  FIRST-HEADING-LINE.                                            TPTOPRT
501800         10  CARRIAGE-CONTROL            PIC X(01) VALUE SPACES.         TPTOPRT
501900         10  FILLER                      PIC X(26) VALUE SPACES.         TPTOPRT
502000         10  FILLER                      PIC X(19) VALUE 'ID'.           TPTOPRT
600100         10  FILLER                      PIC X(22)                       TPTOPRT
600200                                         VALUE 'STUDENT'.                TPTOPRT
600300         10  FILLER                      PIC X(23)                       TPTOPRT
600400                                         VALUE 'MAJOR COURSE'.           TPTOPRT
600500         10  FILLER                      PIC X(16)                       TPTOPRT
600600                                         VALUE 'TYPE OF'.                TPTOPRT
600700         10  FILLER                      PIC X(26) VALUE 'GPA'.          TPTOPRT
600800                                                                         TPTOPRT
600900     05  SECOND-HEADING-LINE.                                           TPTOPRT
601000         10  CARRIAGE-CONTROL            PIC X(01) VALUE SPACES.         TPTOPRT
601100         10  FILLER                      PIC X(24) VALUE SPACES.         TPTOPRT
601200         10  FILLER                      PIC X(22) VALUE 'NUMBER'.TPTOPRT
601300         10  FILLER                      PIC X(23) VALUE 'NAME'.         TPTOPRT
601400         10  FILLER                      PIC X(21)                       TPTOPRT
601500                                         VALUE 'OF STUDY'.               TPTOPRT
601600         10  FILLER                      PIC X(37)                       TPTOPRT
601700                                         VALUE 'DIPLOMA'.                TPTOPRT
601800                                                                         TPTOPRT
601900 PROCEDURE DIVISION.                                                    TPTOPRT
602000                                                                         TPTOPRT
700100 A000-START-MAIN-ROUTINE.                                               TPTOPRT
700200     OPEN INPUT GRADUATE-INPUT-FILE                                     TPTOPRT
700300          OUTPUT GRADUATE-OUTPUT-FILE.                                  TPTOPRT
700400     READ GRADUATE-INPUT-FILE                                          TPTOPRT
700500         AT END                                                         TPTOPRT
700600             MOVE 'NO ' TO ARE-THERE-MORE-RECORDS.                      TPTOPRT
700700     IF THERE-IS-A-RECORD                                              TPTOPRT
700800         PERFORM A001-PROCESS-AND-READ                                  TPTOPRT
700900             UNTIL THERE-ARE-NO-MORE-RECORDS.                           TPTOPRT
701000     CLOSE GRADUATE-INPUT-FILE                                         TPTOPRT
701100           GRADUATE-OUTPUT-FILE.                                        TPTOPRT
701200     STOP RUN.                                                          TPTOPRT
701300                                                                         TPTOPRT
701400 A001-PROCESS-AND-READ.                                                 TPTOPRT
701500     PERFORM B000-PROCESS-DETAIL-RECORDS.                              TPTOPRT
701600     READ GRADUATE-INPUT-FILE                                          TPTOPRT
701700         AT END                                                         TPTOPRT
701800             MOVE 'NO ' TO ARE-THERE-MORE-RECORDS.                      TPTOPRT
701900                                                                         TPTOPRT
702000 B000-PROCESS-DETAIL-RECORDS.                                           TPTOPRT
800100     IF LINES-PRINTED IS EQUAL TO LINE-MAXIMUM                          TPTOPRT
800200         OR IS GREATER THAN LINE-MAXIMUM                                TPTOPRT
800300         OR FIRST-PAGE                                                  TPTOPRT
800400             PERFORM C000-HEADING-ROUTINE.                              TPTOPRT
800500     MOVE SPACES TO GRADUATE-OUTPUT-RECORD.                            TPTOPRT
800600     MOVE DASH TO DASH-1, DASH-2.                                      TPTOPRT
800620     MOVE GRADUATE-ID-IN-1 TO GRADUATE-ID-OUT-1.                       TPTOPRT
800640     MOVE GRADUATE-ID-IN-2 TO GRADUATE-ID-OUT-2.                       TPTOPRT
```

```
800660         MOVE GRADUATE-ID-IN-3 TO GRADUATE-ID-OUT-3.            TPTOPRT
800700         MOVE GRADUATE-NAME-IN TO GRADUATE-NAME-OUT.            TPTOPRT
800800         MOVE GRADUATE-STUDY-IN TO GRADUATE-STUDY-OUT.          TPTOPRT
800900         MOVE GRADUATE-DIPLOMA-IN TO GRADUATE-DIPLOMA-OUT.      TPTOPRT
801000         MOVE GRADUATE-GPA-IN TO GRADUATE-GPA-OUT.·             TPTOPRT
801100         WRITE GRADUATE-OUTPUT-RECORD                           TPTOPRT
801200             AFTER PROPER-SPACING.                              TPTOPRT
801300         MOVE SPACE-ONE-LINE TO PROPER-SPACING.                 TPTOPRT
801400         ADD 1 TO LINES-PRINTED.                                TPTOPRT
801500                                                                TPTOPRT
801600 C000-HEADING-ROUTINE.                                          TPTOPRT
801700         MOVE CURRENT-DATE TO DATE-OUT.                         TPTOPRT
801800         MOVE PAGE-COUNT TO PAGE-OUT.                           TPTOPRT
801900         WRITE GRADUATE-OUTPUT-RECORD FROM MAIN-HEADING-LINE    TPTOPRT
802000             AFTER ADVANCING TO-THE-TOP-OF-THE-PAGE.            TPTOPRT
900100         WRITE GRADUATE-OUTPUT-RECORD FROM FIRST-HEADING-LINE   TPTOPRT
900200             AFTER ADVANCING 2 LINES.                           TPTOPRT
900300         WRITE GRADUATE-OUTPUT-RECORD FROM SECOND-HEADING-LINE  TPTOPRT
900400             AFTER ADVANCING 1 LINES.                           TPTOPRT
900500         MOVE SPACE-TWO-LINES TO PROPER-SPACING.                TPTOPRT
900600         ADD 1 TO PAGE-COUNT.                                   TPTOPRT
900700         MOVE ZEROS TO LINES-PRINTED.                           TPTOPRT
```

PROGRAM CRDTODSK

```
100100 IDENTIFICATION DIVISION.                                      CRDTODSK
100200                                                               CRDTODSK
100300 PROGRAM-ID.      CRDTODSK.                                    CRDTODSK
100400                                                               CRDTODSK
100500 AUTHOR.          JOHN DOE.                                    CRDTODSK
100600 INSTALLATION.    STATE UNIVERISTY.                            CRDTODSK
100700 DATE-WRITTEN.    08/29/87.                                    CRDTODSK
100800 DATE-COMPILED.                                                CRDTODSK
100900 SECURITY.        NONE.                                        CRDTODSK
101000 REMARKS.         THIS PROGRAM PRODUCES A SEQUENTIAL FILE OF   CRDTODSK
101100                  GRADUATING STUDENTS ON DISK.                 CRDTODSK
101200                                                               CRDTODSK
101300 ENVIRONMENT DIVISION.                                         CRDTODSK
101400                                                               CRDTODSK
101500 CONFIGURATION SECTION.                                        CRDTODSK
101600                                                               CRDTODSK
101700 SOURCE-COMPUTER. IBM-4331.                                    CRDTODSK
101800 OBJECT-COMPUTER. IBM-4331.                                    CRDTODSK
101900                                                               CRDTODSK
102000 INPUT-OUTPUT SECTION.                                         CRDTODSK
200100                                                               CRDTODSK
200200 FILE-CONTROL.                                                 CRDTODSK
200300     SELECT GRADUATE-INPUT-FILE                                CRDTODSK
200400         ASSIGN TO SYS004-UR-2540R-S.                          CRDTQDSK
200500     SELECT GRADUATE-OUTPUT-FILE                               CRDTODSK
200600         ASSIGN TO SYS009-DA-FBA1-S-DISKOUT.                   CRDTODSK
200700                                                               CRDTODSK
200800 DATA DIVISION.                                                CRDTODSK
200900                                                               CRDTODSK
201000 FILE SECTION.                                                 CRDTODSK
201100                                                               CRDTODSK
201200 FD  GRADUATE-INPUT-FILE                                       CRDTODSK
201300     RECORD CONTAINS 80 CHARACTERS                             CRDTODSK
201500     LABEL RECORDS ARE OMITTED                                 CRDTODSK
201600     DATA RECORD IS GRADUATE-INPUT-RECORD.                     CRDTODSK
201700 01  GRADUATE-INPUT-RECORD            PIC X(80).               CRDTODSK
201800                                                               CRDTODSK
201900 FD  GRADUATE-OUTPUT-FILE                                      CRDTODSK
202000     RECORD CONTAINS 80 CHARACTERS                             CRDTODSK
300100     BLOCK CONTAINS 10 RECORDS                                 CRDTODSK
300300     LABEL RECORDS ARE STANDARD                                CRDTODSK
300400     DATA RECORD IS GRADUATE-OUTPUT-RECORD.                    CRDTODSK
```

```
300500 01   GRADUATE-OUTPUT-RECORD              PIC X(80).              CRDTODSK
300600                                                                  CRDTODSK
300700 WORKING-STORAGE SECTION.                                         CRDTODSK
300800                                                                  CRDTODSK
300900 01   PROGRAM-INDICATORS.                                         CRDTODSK
301000      05   ARE-THERE-MORE-RECORDS         PIC X(03) VALUE 'YES'.  CRDTODSK
301100           88   THERE-IS-A-RECORD                   VALUE 'YES'.  CRDTODSK
301200           88   THERE-ARE-NO-MORE-RECORDS           VALUE 'NO '.  CRDTODSK
400500                                                                  CRDTODSK
400600 PROCEDURE DIVISION.                                              CRDTODSK
400700                                                                  CRDTODSK
400800 A000-START-MAIN-ROUTINE.                                         CRDTODSK
400900     OPEN INPUT GRADUATE-INPUT-FILE                               CRDTODSK
401000          OUTPUT GRADUATE-OUTPUT-FILE.                            CRDTODSK
401100     READ GRADUATE-INPUT-FILE                                     CRDTODSK
401200        AT END                                                    CRDTODSK
401300           MOVE 'NO ' TO ARE-THERE-MORE-RECORDS.                  CRDTODSK
401400     IF THERE-IS-A-RECORD                                         CRDTODSK
401500        PERFORM A001-PROCESS-AND-READ                             CRDTODSK
401600           UNTIL THERE-ARE-NO-MORE-RECORDS.                       CRDTODSK
401700     CLOSE GRADUATE-INPUT-FILE                                    CRDTODSK
401800           GRADUATE-OUTPUT-FILE.                                  CRDTODSK
401900     STOP RUN.                                                    CRDTODSK
402000                                                                  CRDTODSK
500100 A001-PROCESS-AND-READ.                                           CRDTODSK
500200     PERFORM B000-PROCESS-DETAIL-RECORDS.                         CRDTODSK
500300     READ GRADUATE-INPUT-FILE                                     CRDTODSK
500400        AT END                                                    CRDTODSK
500500           MOVE 'NO ' TO ARE-THERE-MORE-RECORDS.                  CRDTODSK
500600                                                                  CRDTODSK
500700 B000-PROCESS-DETAIL-RECORDS.                                     CRDTODSK
500800     MOVE SPACES TO GRADUATE-OUTPUT-RECORD.                       CRDTODSK
500900     MOVE GRADUATE-INPUT-RECORD TO GRADUATE-OUTPUT-RECORD.        CRDTODSK
501000     WRITE GRADUATE-OUTPUT-RECORD.                                CRDTODSK
```

PROGRAM DSKTOPRT

```
100100 IDENTIFICATION DIVISION.                                         DSKTOPRT
100200                                                                  DSKTOPRT
100300 PROGRAM-ID.      DSKTOPRT.                                       DSKTOPRT
100400                                                                  DSKTOPRT
100500 AUTHOR.          JOHN DOE.                                       DSKTOPRT
100600 INSTALLATION.    STATE UNIVERSITY.                               DSKTOPRT
100700 DATE-WRITTEN.    08/29/87.                                       DSKTOPRT
100800 DATE-COMPILED.                                                   DSKTOPRT
100900 SECURITY.        NONE.                                           DSKTOPRT
101000 REMARKS.         THIS PROGRAM PRODUCES A LISTING OF GRADUATING   DSKTOPRT
101100                  STUDENTS USING DISK INPUT.                      DSKTOPRT
101200                                                                  DSKTOPRT
101300 ENVIRONMENT DIVISION.                                            DSKTOPRT
101400                                                                  DSKTOPRT
101500 CONFIGURATION SECTION.                                           DSKTOPRT
101600                                                                  DSKTOPRT
101700 SOURCE-COMPUTER. IBM-4331.                                       DSKTOPRT
101800 OBJECT-COMPUTER. IBM-4331.                                       DSKTOPRT
101900 SPECIAL-NAMES.   C01 IS TO-THE-TOP-OF-THE-PAGE.                  DSKTOPRT
102000                                                                  DSKTOPRT
200100 INPUT-OUTPUT SECTION.                                            DSKTOPRT
200200                                                                  DSKTOPRT
200300 FILE-CONTROL.                                                    DSKTOPRT
200400     SELECT GRADUATE-INPUT-FILE                                   DSKTOPRT
200500         ASSIGN TO SYS006-DA-FBA1-S-DISKIN.                       DSKTOPRT
200600     SELECT GRADUATE-OUTPUT-FILE                                  DSKTOPRT
200700         ASSIGN TO SYS004-UR-1403-S.                              DSKTOPRT
200800                                                                  DSKTOPRT
200900 DATA DIVISION.                                                   DSKTOPRT
201000                                                                  DSKTOPRT
```

```
201100 FILE SECTION.                                                  DSKTOPRT
201200                                                                DSKTOPRT
201300 FD   GRADUATE-INPUT-FILE                                       DSKTOPRT
201400      RECORD CONTAINS 80 CHARACTERS                             DSKTOPRT
201500      BLOCK CONTAINS 10 RECORDS                                 DSKTOPRT
201700      LABEL RECORDS ARE STANDARD                                DSKTOPRT
201800      DATA RECORD IS GRADUATE-INPUT-RECORD.                     DSKTOPRT
201900 01   GRADUATE-INPUT-RECORD.                                    DSKTOPRT
202000      05   GRADUATE-ID-IN-1          PIC X(03).                 DSKTOPRT
202020      05   GRADUATE-ID-IN-2          PIC X(02).                 DSKTOPRT
202040      05   GRADUATE-ID-IN-3          PIC X(04).                 DSKTOPRT
300100      05   GRADUATE-NAME-IN          PIC X(20).                 DSKTOPRT
300200      05   GRADUATE-STUDY-IN         PIC X(20).                 DSKTOPRT
300300      05   GRADUATE-DIPLOMA-IN       PIC X(12).                 DSKTOPRT
300400      05   GRADUATE-GPA-IN           PIC 9V999.                 DSKTOPRT
300500      05   FILLER                    PIC X(15).                 DSKTOPRT
300600                                                                DSKTOPRT
300700 FD   GRADUATE-OUTPUT-FILE                                      DSKTOPRT
300800      RECORD CONTAINS 133 CHARACTERS                            DSKTOPRT
301000      LABEL RECORDS ARE OMITTED                                 DSKTOPRT
301100      DATA RECORD IS GRADUATE-OUTPUT-RECORD.                    DSKTOPRT
301200 01   GRADUATE-OUTPUT-RECORD.                                   DSKTOPRT
301300      05   CARRIAGE-CONTROL          PIC X(01).                 DSKTOPRT
301400      05   FILLER                    PIC X(22).                 DSKTOPRT
301500      05   GRADUATE-ID-OUT-1         PIC X(03).                 DSKTOPRT
301520      05   DASH-1                    PIC X(01).                 DSKTOPRT
301540      05   GRADUATE-ID-OUT-2         PIC X(02).                 DSKTOPRT
301560      05   DASH-2                    PIC X(01).                 DSKTOPRT
301580      05   GRADUATE-ID-OUT-3         PIC X(04).                 DSKTOPRT
301600      05   FILLER                    PIC X(05).                 DSKTOPRT
301700      05   GRADUATE-NAME-OUT         PIC X(20).                 DSKTOPRT
301800      05   FILLER                    PIC X(05).                 DSKTOPRT
301900      05   GRADUATE-STUDY-OUT        PIC X(20).                 DSKTOPRT
302000      05   FILLER                    PIC X(05).                 DSKTOPRT
400100      05   GRADUATE-DIPLOMA-OUT      PIC X(12).                 DSKTOPRT
400200      05   FILLER                    PIC X(05).                 DSKTOPRT
400300      05   GRADUATE-GPA-OUT          PIC 9.999.                 DSKTOPRT
400400      05   FILLER                    PIC X(22).                 DSKTOPRT
400500                                                                DSKTOPRT
400600 WORKING-STORAGE SECTION.                                       DSKTOPRT
400700                                                                DSKTOPRT
400800 01   PROGRAM-INDICATORS.                                       DSKTOPRT
400900      05   ARE-THERE-MORE-RECORDS    PIC X(03) VALUE 'YES'.     DSKTOPRT
401000          88   THERE-IS-A-RECORD                VALUE 'YES'.    DSKTOPRT
401100          88   THERE-ARE-NO-MORE-RECORDS        VALUE 'NO '.    DSKTOPRT
401200                                                                DSKTOPRT
401300 01   PRINTER-CONTROLS.                                         DSKTOPRT
401400      05   PROPER-SPACING            PIC 9(01).                 DSKTOPRT
401500      05   SPACE-ONE-LINE            PIC 9(01)  VALUE 1.        DSKTOPRT
401600      05   SPACE-TWO-LINES           PIC 9(01)  VALUE 2.        DSKTOPRT
401700      05   LINES-PRINTED             PIC S9(03) VALUE ZERO      DSKTOPRT
401800                                     USAGE IS COMP-3.           DSKTOPRT
401900      05   LINE-MAXIMUM              PIC S9(03) VALUE +35       DSKTOPRT
402000                                     USAGE IS COMP-3.           DSKTOPRT
500100      05   PAGE-COUNT                PIC S9(03) VALUE +1        DSKTOPRT
500200                                     USAGE IS COMP-3.           DSKTOPRT
500300          88   FIRST-PAGE                       VALUE +1.       DSKTOPRT
500400                                                                DSKTOPRT
500420 01   PROGRAM-CONSTANTS.                                        DSKTOPRT
500440      05   DASH                      PIC X(01) VALUE '-'.       DSKTOPRT
500460                                                                DSKTOPRT
500500 01   HEADING-LINES.                                            DSKTOPRT
500600      05   MAIN-HEADING-LINE.                                   DSKTOPRT
500700          10   CARRIAGE-CONTROL      PIC X(01) VALUE SPACES.    DSKTOPRT
500800          10   FILLER                PIC X(10) VALUE SPACES.    DSKTOPRT
500900          10   DATE-OUT              PIC X(08)                  DSKTOPRT
501000          10   FILLER                PIC X(40) VALUE SPACES.    DSKTOPRT
501100          10   FILLER                PIC X(16)                  DSKTOPRT
501200                                     VALUE 'GRADUATE LISTING'.  DSKTOPRT
```

```
501300          10   FILLER                    PIC X(36) VALUE SPACES.   DSKTOPRT
501400          10   FILLER                    PIC X(05) VALUE 'PAGE '.  DSKTOPRT
501500          10   PAGE-OUT                  PIC ZZ9.                  DSKTOPRT
501600          10   FILLER                    PIC X(14) VALUE SPACES.   DSKTOPRT
501700      05  FIRST-HEADING-LINE.                                     DSKTOPRT
501800          10   CARRIAGE-CONTROL          PIC X(01) VALUE SPACES.   DSKTOPRT
501900          10   FILLER                    PIC X(26) VALUE SPACES.   DSKTOPRT
502000          10   FILLER                    PIC X(19) VALUE 'ID'.     DSKTOPRT
600100          10   FILLER                    PIC X(22)                 DSKTOPRT
600200                                         VALUE 'STUDENT'.          DSKTOPRT
600300          10   FILLER                    PIC X(23)                 DSKTOPRT
600400                                         VALUE 'MAJOR COURSE'.     DSKTOPRT
600500          10   FILLER                    PIC X(16)                 DSKTOPRT
600600                                         VALUE 'TYPE OF'.          DSKTOPRT
600700          10   FILLER                    PIC X(26) VALUE 'GPA'.    DSKTOPRT
600800                                                                   DSKTOPRT
600900      05  SECOND-HEADING-LINE.                                    DSKTOPRT
601000          10   CARRIAGE-CONTROL          PIC X(01) VALUE SPACES.   DSKTOPRT
601100          10   FILLER                    PIC X(24) VALUE SPACES.   DSKTOPRT
601200          10   FILLER                    PIC X(22) VALUE 'NUMBER'. DSKTOPRT
601300          10   FILLER                    PIC X(23) VALUE 'NAME'.   DSKTOPRT
601400          10   FILLER                    PIC X(21)                 DSKTOPRT
601500                                         VALUE 'OF STUDY'.         DSKTOPRT
601600          10   FILLER                    PIC X(37)                 DSKTOPRT
601700                                         VALUE 'DIPLOMA'.          DSKTOPRT
601800                                                                   DSKTOPRT
601900 PROCEDURE DIVISION.                                              DSKTOPRT
602000                                                                   DSKTOPRT
700100 A000-START-MAIN-ROUTINE.                                         DSKTOPRT
700200      OPEN INPUT GRADUATE-INPUT-FILE                              DSKTOPRT
700300          OUTPUT GRADUATE-OUTPUT-FILE.                            DSKTOPRT
700400      READ GRADUATE-INPUT-FILE                                    DSKTOPRT
700500          AT END                                                  DSKTOPRT
700600              MOVE 'NO ' TO ARE-THERE-MORE-RECORDS.               DSKTOPRT
700700      IF THERE-IS-A-RECORD                                        DSKTOPRT
700800          PERFORM A001-PROCESS-AND-READ                           DSKTOPRT
700900              UNTIL THERE-ARE-NO-MORE-RECORDS.                    DSKTOPRT
701000      CLOSE GRADUATE-INPUT-FILE                                   DSKTOPRT
701100          GRADUATE-OUTPUT-FILE.                                   DSKTOPRT
701200      STOP RUN.                                                   DSKTOPRT
701300                                                                   DSKTOPRT
701400 A001-PROCESS-AND-READ.                                           DSKTOPRT
701500      PERFORM B000-PROCESS-DETAIL-RECORDS.                        DSKTOPRT
701600      READ GRADUATE-INPUT-FILE                                    DSKTOPRT
701700          AT END                                                  DSKTOPRT
701800              MOVE 'NO ' TO ARE-THERE-MORE-RECORDS.               DSKTOPRT
701900                                                                   DSKTOPRT
702000 B000-PROCESS-DETAIL-RECORDS.                                     DSKTOPRT
800100      IF LINES-PRINTED IS EQUAL TO LINE-MAXIMUM                   DSKTOPRT
800200          OR IS GREATER THAN LINE-MAXIMUM                         DSKTOPRT
800300          OR FIRST-PAGE                                           DSKTOPRT
800400              PERFORM C000-HEADING-ROUTINE.                       DSKTOPRT
800500      MOVE SPACES TO GRADUATE-OUTPUT-RECORD.                      DSKTOPRT
800600      MOVE DASH TO DASH-1, DASH-2.                                DSKTOPRT
800620      MOVE GRADUATE-ID-IN-1 TO GRADUATE-ID-OUT-1.                 DSKTOPRT
800640      MOVE GRADUATE-ID-IN-2 TO GRADUATE-ID-OUT-2.                 DSKTOPRT
800660      MOVE GRADUATE-ID-IN-3 TO GRADUATE-ID-OUT-3.                 DSKTOPRT
800700      MOVE GRADUATE-NAME-IN TO GRADUATE-NAME-OUT.                 DSKTOPRT
800800      MOVE GRADUATE-STUDY-IN TO GRADUATE-STUDY-OUT.               DSKTOPRT
800900      MOVE GRADUATE-DIPLOMA-IN TO GRADUATE-DIPLOMA-OUT.           DSKTOPRT
801000      MOVE GRADUATE-GPA-IN TO GRADUATE-GPA-OUT.                   DSKTOPRT
801100      WRITE GRADUATE-OUTPUT-RECORD                                DSKTOPRT
801200          AFTER PROPER-SPACING.                                   DSKTOPRT
801300      MOVE SPACE-ONE-LINE TO PROPER-SPACING.                      DSKTOPRT
801400      ADD 1 TO LINES-PRINTED.                                     DSKTOPRT
801500                                                                   DSKTOPRT
801600 C000-HEADING-ROUTINE.                                            DSKTOPRT
801700      MOVE CURRENT-DATE TO DATE-OUT.                              DSKTOPRT
801800      MOVE PAGE-COUNT TO PAGE-OUT.                                DSKTOPRT
```

```
801900        WRITE GRADUATE-OUTPUT-RECORD FROM MAIN-HEADING-LINE          DSKTOPRT
802000             AFTER ADVANCING TO-THE-TOP-OF-THE-PAGE.                 DSKTOPRT
900100        WRITE GRADUATE-OUTPUT-RECORD FROM FIRST-HEADING-LINE         DSKTOPRT
900200             AFTER ADVANCING 2 LINES.                                DSKTOPRT
900300        WRITE GRADUATE-OUTPUT-RECORD FROM SECOND-HEADING-LINE        DSKTOPRT
900400             AFTER ADVANCING 1 LINES.                                DSKTOPRT
900500        MOVE SPACE-TWO-LINES TO PROPER-SPACING.                      DSKTOPRT
900600        ADD 1 TO PAGE-COUNT.                                         DSKTOPRT
900700        MOVE ZEROS TO LINES-PRINTED.                                 DSKTOPRT
```

PROGRAM BLDINSEQ

```
100100 IDENTIFICATION DIVISION.                                           BLDINSEQ
100200                                                                    BLDINSEQ
100300 PROGRAM-ID.       BLDINSEQ.                                        BLDINSEQ
100400                                                                    BLDINSEQ
100500 AUTHOR.           JOHN DOE.                                        BLDINSEQ
100600 INSTALLATION.     STATE UNIVERSITY.                               BLDINSEQ
100700 DATE-WRITTEN.     08/29/87.                                       BLDINSEQ
100800 DATE-COMPILED.                                                     BLDINSEQ
100900 SECURITY.         NONE.                                           BLDINSEQ
101000 REMARKS.          THIS PROGRAM PRODUCES AN INDEXED SEQUENTIAL FILE BLDINSEQ
101100                   OF GRADUATING STUDENTS.                         BLDINSEQ
101200                                                                    BLDINSEQ
101300 ENVIRONMENT DIVISION.                                             BLDINSEQ
101400                                                                    BLDINSEQ
101500 CONFIGURATION SECTION.                                            BLDINSEQ
101600                                                                    BLDINSEQ
101700 SOURCE-COMPUTER. IBM-4331.                                        BLDINSEQ
101800 OBJECT-COMPUTER. IBM-4331.                                        BLDINSEQ
101900                                                                    BLDINSEQ
102000 INPUT-OUTPUT SECTION.                                             BLDINSEQ
200100                                                                    BLDINSEQ
200200 FILE-CONTROL.                                                     BLDINSEQ
200300     SELECT GRADUATE-INPUT-FILE                                    BLDINSEQ
200400         ASSIGN TO SYS006-UT-3340-S-SEQDISK.                       BLDINSEQ
200500     SELECT GRADUATE-OUTPUT-FILE                                   BLDINSEQ
200600         ASSIGN TO SYS008-DA-3340-I-ISFILE                         BLDINSEQ
200700         ACCESS IS SEQUENTIAL                                      BLDINSEQ
200800         RECORD KEY IS GRADUATE-ID-NUMBER.                         BLDINSEQ
200900                                                                    BLDINSEQ
201000 DATA DIVISION.                                                    BLDINSEQ
201100                                                                    BLDINSEQ
201200 FILE SECTION.                                                     BLDINSEQ
201300                                                                    BLDINSEQ
201400 FD  GRADUATE-INPUT-FILE                                           BLDINSEQ
201500     RECORD CONTAINS 80 CHARACTERS                                 BLDINSEQ
201600     BLOCK CONTAINS 10 RECORDS                                     BLDINSEQ
201800     LABEL RECORDS ARE STANDARD                                    BLDINSEQ
201900     DATA RECORD IS GRADUATE-INPUT-RECORD.                         BLDINSEQ
202000 01  GRADUATE-INPUT-RECORD               PIC X(80).               BLDINSEQ
300100                                                                    BLDINSEQ
300200 FD  GRADUATE-OUTPUT-FILE                                          BLDINSEQ
300300     RECORD CONTAINS 80 CHARACTERS                                 BLDINSEQ
300400     BLOCK CONTAINS 10 RECORDS                                     BLDINSEQ
300600     LABEL RECORDS ARE STANDARD                                    BLDINSEQ
300700     DATA RECORD IS GRADUATE-OUTPUT-RECORD.                        BLDINSEQ
300800 01  GRADUATE-OUTPUT-RECORD.                                       BLDINSEQ
300900     05  GRADUATE-ID-NUMBER              PIC X(09).               BLDINSEQ
301000     05  FILLER                          PIC X(71).               BLDINSEQ
301100                                                                    BLDINSEQ
301200 WORKING-STORAGE SECTION.                                         BLDINSEQ
301300                                                                    BLDINSEQ
301400 01  PROGRAM-INDICATORS.                                          BLDINSEQ
301500     05  ARE-THERE-MORE-RECORDS     PIC X(03) VALUE 'YES'.        BLDINSEQ
301600         88  THERE-IS-A-RECORD                 VALUE 'YES'.       BLDINSEQ
301700         88  THERE-ARE-NO-MORE-RECORDS         VALUE 'NO '.       BLDINSEQ
401000                                                                    BLDINSEQ
```

```
401100 PROCEDURE DIVISION.                                              BLDINSEQ
401200                                                                  BLDINSEQ
401300 A000-START-MAIN-ROUTINE.                                         BLDINSEQ
401400     OPEN INPUT GRADUATE-INPUT-FILE                               BLDINSEQ
401500         OUTPUT GRADUATE-OUTPUT-FILE.                             BLDINSEQ
401600     READ GRADUATE-INPUT-FILE                                     BLDINSEQ
401700         AT END                                                   BLDINSEQ
401800             MOVE 'NO ' TO ARE-THERE-MORE-RECORDS.                BLDINSEQ
401900     IF THERE-IS-A-RECORD                                         BLDINSEQ
402000         PERFORM A001-PROCESS-AND-READ                            BLDINSEQ
500100             UNTIL THERE-ARE-NO-MORE-RECORDS.                     BLDINSEQ
500200     CLOSE GRADUATE-INPUT-FILE                                    BLDINSEQ
500300           GRADUATE-OUTPUT-FILE.                                  BLDINSEQ
500400     STOP RUN.                                                    BLDINSEQ
500500                                                                  BLDINSEQ
500600 A001-PROCESS-AND-READ.                                           BLDINSEQ
500700     PERFORM B000-PROCESS-DETAIL-RECORDS.                         BLDINSEQ
500800     READ GRADUATE-INPUT-FILE                                     BLDINSEQ
500900         AT END                                                   BLDINSEQ
501000             MOVE 'NO ' TO ARE-THERE-MORE-RECORDS.                BLDINSEQ
501100                                                                  BLDINSEQ
501200 B000-PROCESS-DETAIL-RECORDS.                                     BLDINSEQ
501300     MOVE SPACES TO GRADUATE-OUTPUT-RECORD.                       BLDINSEQ
501400     MOVE GRADUATE-INPUT-RECORD TO GRADUATE-OUTPUT-RECORD.        BLDINSEQ
501500     WRITE GRADUATE-OUTPUT-RECORD                                 BLDINSEQ
501600         INVALID KEY                                              BLDINSEQ
501700             DISPLAY '** INVALID KEY **  ', GRADUATE-ID-NUMBER.   BLDINSEQ
```

PROGRAM INSEQRET

```
100100 IDENTIFICATION DIVISION.                                        INSEQRET
100200                                                                 INSEQRET
100300 PROGRAM-ID.      INSEQRET.                                      INSEQRET
100400                                                                 INSEQRET
100500 AUTHOR.          JOHN DOE.                                      INSEQRET
100600 INSTALLATION.    STATE UNIVERSITY.                             INSEQRET
100700 DATE-WRITTEN.    08/29/87.                                      INSEQRET
100800 DATE-COMPILED.                                                  INSEQRET
100900 SECURITY.        NONE.                                          INSEQRET
101000 REMARKS.         THIS PROGRAM PRODUCES A LISTING OF GRADUATING  INSEQRET
101100                  STUDENTS FROM AN INDEXED SEQUENTIAL FILE.      INSEQRET
101200                                                                 INSEQRET
101300 ENVIRONMENT DIVISION.                                           INSEQRET
101400                                                                 INSEQRET
101500 CONFIGURATION SECTION.                                          INSEQRET
101600                                                                 INSEQRET
101700 SOURCE-COMPUTER. IBM-4331.                                      INSEQRET
101800 OBJECT-COMPUTER. IBM-4331.                                      INSEQRET
101900 SPECIAL-NAMES.   C01 IS TO-THE-TOP-OF-THE-PAGE.                INSEQRET
102000                                                                 INSEQRET
200100 INPUT-OUTPUT SECTION.                                           INSEQRET
200200                                                                 INSEQRET
200300 FILE-CONTROL.                                                   INSEQRET
200400     SELECT GRADUATE-INPUT-FILE                                  INSEQRET
200500         ASSIGN TO SYS010-DA-3340-I-ISFILE                       INSEQRET
200600         ACCESS IS SEQUENTIAL                                    INSEQRET
200700         RECORD KEY IS GRADUATE-ID-IN.                           INSEQRET
200800     SELECT GRADUATE-OUTPUT-FILE                                 INSEQRET
200900         ASSIGN TO SYS006-UR-1403-S.                             INSEQRET
201000                                                                 INSEQRET
201100 DATA DIVISION.                                                  INSEQRET
201200                                                                 INSEQRET
201300 FILE SECTION.                                                   INSEQRET
201400                                                                 INSEQRET
201500 FD  GRADUATE-INPUT-FILE                                         INSEQRET
201600     RECORD CONTAINS 80 CHARACTERS                              INSEQRET
201700     BLOCK CONTAINS 10 RECORDS                                  INSEQRET
```

```
201900          LABEL RECORDS ARE STANDARD                                          INSEQRET
202000          DATA RECORD IS GRADUATE-INPUT-RECORD.                               INSEQRET
300100 01  GRADUATE-INPUT-RECORD.                                                   INSEQRET
300105     05   GRADUATE-ID-IN.                                                     INSEQRET
300200          10   GRADUATE-ID-IN-1               PIC X(03).                      INSEQRET
300220          10   GRADUATE-ID-IN-2               PIC X(02).                      INSEQRET
300240          10   GRADUATE-ID-IN-3               PIC X(04).                      INSEQRET
300300     05   GRADUATE-NAME-IN                    PIC X(20).                      INSEQRET
300400     05   GRADUATE-STUDY-IN                   PIC X(20).                      INSEQRET
300500     05   GRADUATE-DIPLOMA-IN                 PIC X(12).                      INSEQRET
300600     05   GRADUATE-GPA-IN                     PIC 9V999.                      INSEQRET
300700     05   FILLER                              PIC X(15).                      INSEQRET
300800                                                                              INSEQRET
300900 FD  GRADUATE-OUTPUT-FILE                                                     INSEQRET
301000          RECORD CONTAINS 133 CHARACTERS                                      INSEQRET
301200          LABEL RECORDS ARE OMITTED                                           INSEQRET
301300          DATA RECORD IS GRADUATE-OUTPUT-RECORD.                              INSEQRET
301400 01  GRADUATE-OUTPUT-RECORD.                                                  INSEQRET
301500     05   CARRIAGE-CONTROL                    PIC X(01).                      INSEQRET
301600     05   FILLER                              PIC X(22).                      INSEQRET
301700     05   GRADUATE-ID-OUT-1                   PIC X(03).                      INSEQRET
301720     05   DASH-1                              PIC X(01).                      INSEQRET
301740     05   GRADUATE-ID-OUT-2                   PIC X(02).                      INSEQRET
301760     05   DASH-2                              PIC X(01).                      INSEQRET
301780     05   GRADUATE-ID-OUT-3                   PIC X(04).                      INSEQRET
301800     05   FILLER                              PIC X(05).                      INSEQRET
301900     05   GRADUATE-NAME-OUT                   PIC X(20).                      INSEQRET
302000     05   FILLER                              PIC X(05).                      INSEQRET
400100     05   GRADUATE-STUDY-OUT                  PIC X(20).                      INSEQRET
400200     05   FILLER                              PIC X(05).                      INSEQRET
400300     05   GRADUATE-DIPLOMA-OUT                PIC X(12).                      INSEQRET
400400     05   FILLER                              PIC X(05).                      INSEQRET
400500     05   GRADUATE-GPA-OUT                    PIC 9.999.                      INSEQRET
400600     05   FILLER                              PIC X(22).                      INSEQRET
400700                                                                              INSEQRET
400800 WORKING-STORAGE SECTION.                                                     INSEQRET
400900                                                                              INSEQRET
401000 01  PROGRAM-INDICATORS.                                                      INSEQRET
401100     05   ARE-THERE-MORE-RECORDS             PIC X(03) VALUE 'YES'.           INSEQRET
401200          88   THERE-IS-A-RECORD                       VALUE 'YES'.           INSEQRET
401300          88   THERE-ARE-NO-MORE-RECORDS               VALUE 'NO '.           INSEQRET
401400                                                                              INSEQRET
401500 01  PRINTER-CONTROLS.                                                        INSEQRET
401600     05   PROPER-SPACING                     PIC 9(01).                       INSEQRET
401700     05   SPACE-ONE-LINE                     PIC 9(01)   VALUE 1.             INSEQRET
401800     05   SPACE-TWO-LINES                    PIC 9(01)   VALUE 2.             INSEQRET
401900     05   LINES-PRINTED                      PIC S9(03) VALUE ZERO            INSEQRET
402000                                             USAGE IS COMP-3.                 INSEQRET
500100     05   LINE-MAXIMUM                       PIC S9(03) VALUE +35             INSEQRET
500200                                             USAGE IS COMP-3.                 INSEQRET
500300     05   PAGE-COUNT                         PIC S9(03) VALUE +1              INSEQRET
500400                                             USAGE IS COMP-3.                 INSEQRET
500500          88   FIRST-PAGE                              VALUE +1.              INSEQRET
500520                                                                              INSEQRET
500540 01  PROGRAM-CONSTANTS.                                                       INSEQRET
500560     05   DASH                               PIC X(01)   VALUE '-'.           INSEQRET
500580                                                                              INSEQRET
500600 01  HEADING-LINES.                                                           INSEQRET
500700     05   MAIN-HEADING-LINE.                                                  INSEQRET
500800          10   CARRIAGE-CONTROL              PIC X(01) VALUE SPACES.          INSEQRET
500900          10   FILLER                        PIC X(10) VALUE SPACES.          INSEQRET
501000          10   DATE-OUT                      PIC X(08).                       INSEQRET
501100          10   FILLER                        PIC X(40) VALUE SPACES.          INSEQRET
501200          10   FILLER                        PIC X(16)                        INSEQRET
501300                                             VALUE 'GRADUATE LISTING'.INSEQRET
501400          10   FILLER                        PIC X(36) VALUE SPACES.          INSEQRET
501500          10   FILLER                        PIC X(05) VALUE 'PAGE '. INSEQRET
501600          10   PAGE-OUT                      PIC ZZ9.                         INSEQRET
501700          10   FILLER                        PIC X(14) VALUE SPACES.          INSEQRET
```

```
501720                                                                   INSEQRET
501800        05   FIRST-HEADING-LINE.                                   INSEQRET
501900             10   CARRIAGE-CONTROL        PIC X(01) VALUE SPACES.  INSEQRET
502000             10   FILLER                  PIC X(26) VALUE SPACES.  INSEQRET
600100             10   FILLER                  PIC X(19) VALUE 'ID'.    INSEQRET
600200             10   FILLER                  PIC X(22)               INSEQRET
600300                                          VALUE 'STUDENT'.         INSEQRET
600400             10   FILLER                  PIC X(23)               INSEQRET
600500                                          VALUE 'MAJOR COURSE'.    INSEQRET
600600             10   FILLER                  PIC X(16)               INSEQRET
600700                                          VALUE 'TYPE OF'.         INSEQRET
600800             10   FILLER                  PIC X(26) VALUE 'GPA'.   INSEQRET
600900                                                                   INSEQRET
601000        05   SECOND-HEADING-LINE.                                  INSEQRET
601100             10   CARRIAGE-CONTROL        PIC X(01) VALUE SPACES.  INSEQRET
601200             10   FILLER                  PIC X(24) VALUE SPACES.  INSEQRET
601300             10   FILLER                  PIC X(22) VALUE 'NUMBER'.INSEQRET
601400             10   FILLER                  PIC X(23) VALUE 'NAME'.  INSEQRET
601500             10   FILLER                  PIC X(21)               INSEQRET
601600                                          VALUE 'OF STUDY'.        INSEQRET
601700             10   FILLER                  PIC X(37)               INSEQRET
601800                                          VALUE 'DIPLOMA'.         INSEQRET
601900                                                                   INSEQRET
602000 PROCEDURE DIVISION.                                               INSEQRET
700100                                                                   INSEQRET
700200 A000-START-MAIN-ROUTINE.                                          INSEQRET
700300     OPEN INPUT GRADUATE-INPUT-FILE                                INSEQRET
700400         OUTPUT GRADUATE-OUTPUT-FILE.                              INSEQRET
700500     READ GRADUATE-INPUT-FILE                                      INSEQRET
700600         AT END                                                    INSEQRET
700700             MOVE 'NO ' TO ARE-THERE-MORE-RECORDS.                 INSEQRET
700800     IF THERE-IS-A-RECORD                                          INSEQRET
700900         PERFORM A001-PROCESS-AND-READ                             INSEQRET
701000             UNTIL THERE-ARE-NO-MORE-RECORDS.                      INSEQRET
701100     CLOSE GRADUATE-INPUT-FILE                                     INSEQRET
701200           GRADUATE-OUTPUT-FILE.                                   INSEQRET
701300     STOP RUN.                                                     INSEQRET
701400                                                                   INSEQRET
701500 A001-PROCESS-AND-READ.                                            INSEQRET
701600     PERFORM B000-PROCESS-DETAIL-RECORDS.                          INSEQRET
701700     READ GRADUATE-INPUT-FILE                                      INSEQRET
701800         AT END                                                    INSEQRET
701900             MOVE 'NO ' TO ARE-THERE-MORE-RECORDS.                 INSEQRET
702000                                                                   INSEQRET
800100 B000-PROCESS-DETAIL-RECORDS.                                      INSEQRET
800200     IF LINES-PRINTED IS EQUAL TO LINE-MAXIMUM                     INSEQRET
800300         OR IS GREATER THAN LINE-MAXIMUM                           INSEQRET
800400         OR FIRST-PAGE                                             INSEQRET
800500             PERFORM C000-HEADING-ROUTINE.                         INSEQRET
800600     MOVE SPACES TO GRADUATE-OUTPUT-RECORD.                        INSEQRET
800700     MOVE DASH TO DASH-1, DASH-2.                                  INSEQRET
800720     MOVE GRADUATE-ID-IN-1 TO GRADUATE-ID-OUT-1.                   INSEQRET
800740     MOVE GRADUATE-ID-IN-2 TO GRADUATE-ID-OUT-2.                   INSEQRET
800760     MOVE GRADUATE-ID-IN-3 TO GRADUATE-ID-OUT-3.                   INSEQRET
800800     MOVE GRADUATE-NAME-IN TO GRADUATE-NAME-OUT.                   INSEQRET
800900     MOVE GRADUATE-STUDY-IN TO GRADUATE-STUDY-OUT.                 INSEQRET
801000     MOVE GRADUATE-DIPLOMA-IN TO GRADUATE-DIPLOMA-OUT.             INSEQRET
801100     MOVE GRADUATE-GPA-IN TO GRADUATE-GPA-OUT.                     INSEQRET
801200     WRITE GRADUATE-OUTPUT-RECORD                                  INSEQRET
801300         AFTER PROPER-SPACING.                                     INSEQRET
801400     MOVE SPACE-ONE-LINE TO PROPER-SPACING.                        INSEQRET
801500     ADD 1 TO LINES-PRINTED.                                       INSEQRET
801600                                                                   INSEQRET
801700 C000-HEADING-ROUTINE.                                             INSEQRET
801800     MOVE CURRENT-DATE TO DATE-OUT.                                INSEQRET
801900     MOVE PAGE-COUNT TO PAGE-OUT.                                  INSEQRET
802000     WRITE GRADUATE-OUTPUT-RECORD FROM MAIN-HEADING-LINE           INSEQRET
900100         AFTER ADVANCING TO-THE-TOP-OF-THE-PAGE.                   INSEQRET
900200     WRITE GRADUATE-OUTPUT-RECORD FROM FIRST-HEADING-LINE          INSEQRET
```

```
900300          AFTER ADVANCING 2 LINES.                           INSEQRET
900400      WRITE GRADUATE-OUTPUT-RECORD FROM SECOND-HEADING-LINE   INSEQRET
900500          AFTER ADVANCING 1 LINES.                           INSEQRET
900600      MOVE SPACE-TWO-LINES TO PROPER-SPACING.                INSEQRET
900700      ADD 1 TO PAGE-COUNT.                                   INSEQRET
900800      MOVE ZEROS TO LINES-PRINTED.                           INSEQRET
```

PROGRAM CRDTOES

```
100100 IDENTIFICATION DIVISION.                                    CRDTOES
100200                                                             CRDTOES
100300 PROGRAM-ID.      CRDTOES.                                   CRDTOES
100400                                                             CRDTOES
100500 AUTHOR.          JOHN DOE.                                  CRDTOES
100600 INSTALLATION.    STATE UNIVERISTY.                          CRDTOES
100700 DATE-WRITTEN.    08/29/87.                                  CRDTOES
100800 DATE-COMPILED.                                              CRDTOES
100900 SECURITY.        NONE.                                      CRDTOES
101000 REMARKS.         THIS PROGRAM PRODUCES AN ESDS (FILE) OF    CRDTOES
101100                  GRADUATING STUDENTS ON DISK.               CRDTOES
101200                                                             CRDTOES
101300 ENVIRONMENT DIVISION.                                       CRDTOES
101400                                                             CRDTOES
101500 CONFIGURATION SECTION.                                      CRDTOES
101600                                                             CRDTOES
101700 SOURCE-COMPUTER. IBM-4331.                                  CRDTOES
101800 OBJECT-COMPUTER. IBM-4331.                                  CRDTOES
101900                                                             CRDTOES
102000 INPUT-OUTPUT SECTION.                                       CRDTOES
200100                                                             CRDTOES
200200 FILE-CONTROL.                                               CRDTOES
200300     SELECT GRADUATE-INPUT-FILE                              CRDTOES
200400         ASSIGN TO SYS004-UR-2540R-S.                        CRDTOES
200500     SELECT GRADUATE-OUTPUT-FILE                             CRDTOES
200600         ASSIGN TO SYS009-AS-ESFILE                          CRDTOES
200605         ORGANIZATION IS SEQUENTIAL                          CRDTOES
200610         ACCESS IS SEQUENTIAL                                CRDTOES
200615         FILE STATUS IS ESFILE-STAT.                         CRDTOES
200700                                                             CRDTOES
200800 DATA DIVISION.                                              CRDTOES
200900                                                             CRDTOES
201000 FILE SECTION.                                               CRDTOES
201100                                                             CRDTOES
201200 FD  GRADUATE-INPUT-FILE                                     CRDTOES
201300     RECORD CONTAINS 80 CHARACTERS                           CRDTOES
201500     LABEL RECORDS ARE OMITTED                               CRDTOES
201600     DATA RECORD IS GRADUATE-INPUT-RECORD.                   CRDTOES
201700 01  GRADUATE-INPUT-RECORD           PIC X(80).              CRDTOES
201800                                                             CRDTOES
201900 FD  GRADUATE-OUTPUT-FILE                                    CRDTOES
202000     RECORD CONTAINS 80 CHARACTERS                           CRDTOES
202010     LABEL RECORDS ARE OMITTED                               CRDTOES
300400     DATA RECORD IS GRADUATE-OUTPUT-RECORD.                  CRDTOES
300500 01  GRADUATE-OUTPUT-RECORD          PIC X(80).              CRDTOES
300600                                                             CRDTOES
300700 WORKING-STORAGE SECTION.                                    CRDTOES
300800                                                             CRDTOES
300900 01  PROGRAM-INDICATORS.                                     CRDTOES
301000     05  ARE-THERE-MORE-RECORDS      PIC X(03) VALUE 'YES'.  CRDTOES
301100         88  THERE-IS-A-RECORD                 VALUE 'YES'.  CRDTOES
301200         88  THERE-ARE-NO-MORE-RECORDS         VALUE 'NO '.  CRDTOES
400500                                                             CRDTOES
400505 01  STATUS-RETURN-CODES.                                    CRDTOES
400510     05  ESFILE-STAT                 PIC 99.                 CRDTOES
400515                                                             CRDTOES
400600 PROCEDURE DIVISION.                                         CRDTOES
400700                                                             CRDTOES
```

```
400800 A000-START-MAIN-ROUTINE.                                         CRDTOES
400900     OPEN INPUT GRADUATE-INPUT-FILE                               CRDTOES
401000          OUTPUT GRADUATE-OUTPUT-FILE.                            CRDTOES
401100     READ GRADUATE-INPUT-FILE                                     CRDTOES
401200        AT END                                                    CRDTOES
401300            MOVE 'NO ' TO ARE-THERE-MORE-RECORDS.                 CRDTOES
401400     IF THERE-IS-A-RECORD                                         CRDTOES
401500         PERFORM A001-PROCESS-AND-READ                            CRDTOES
401600             UNTIL THERE-ARE-NO-MORE-RECORDS.                     CRDTOES
401700     CLOSE GRADUATE-INPUT-FILE                                    CRDTOES
401800           GRADUATE-OUTPUT-FILE.                                  CRDTOES
401900     STOP RUN.                                                    CRDTOES
402000                                                                  CRDTOES
500100 A001-PROCESS-AND-READ.                                           CRDTOES
500200     PERFORM B000-PROCESS-DETAIL-RECORDS.                         CRDTOES
500300     READ GRADUATE-INPUT-FILE                                     CRDTOES
500400        AT END                                                    CRDTOES
500500            MOVE 'NO ' TO ARE-THERE-MORE-RECORDS.                 CRDTOES
500600                                                                  CRDTOES
500700 B000-PROCESS-DETAIL-RECORDS.                                     CRDTOES
500800     MOVE SPACES TO GRADUATE-OUTPUT-RECORD.                       CRDTOES
500900     MOVE GRADUATE-INPUT-RECORD TO GRADUATE-OUTPUT-RECORD.        CRDTOES
501000     WRITE GRADUATE-OUTPUT-RECORD.                                CRDTOES
```

PROGRAM ESDSRET

```
100100 IDENTIFICATION DIVISION.                                         ESDSRET
100200                                                                  ESDSRET
100300 PROGRAM-ID.       ESDSRET.                                       ESDSRET
100400                                                                  ESDSRET
100500 AUTHOR.           JOHN DOE.                                      ESDSRET
100600 INSTALLATION.     STATE UNIVERSITY.                              ESDSRET
100700 DATE-WRITTEN.     08/29/87.                                      ESDSRET
100800 DATE-COMPILED.                                                   ESDSRET
100900 SECURITY.         NONE.                                          ESDSRET
101000 REMARKS.          THIS PROGRAM PRODUCES A LISTING OF GRADUATING  ESDSRET
101100                   STUDENTS FROM AN ESDS FILE.                    ESDSRET
101200                                                                  ESDSRET
101300 ENVIRONMENT DIVISION.                                            ESDSRET
101400                                                                  ESDSRET
101500 CONFIGURATION SECTION.                                           ESDSRET
101600                                                                  ESDSRET
101700 SOURCE-COMPUTER. IBM-4331.                                       ESDSRET
101800 OBJECT-COMPUTER. IBM-4331.                                       ESDSRET
101900 SPECIAL-NAMES.   C01 IS TO-THE-TOP-OF-THE-PAGE.                  ESDSRET
102000                                                                  ESDSRET
200100 INPUT-OUTPUT SECTION.                                            ESDSRET
200200                                                                  ESDSRET
200300 FILE-CONTROL.                                                    ESDSRET
200400     SELECT GRADUATE-INPUT-FILE                                   ESDSRET
200500         ASSIGN TO SYS010-AS-ESFILE                               ESDSRET
200605         ORGANIZATION IS SEQUENTIAL                               ESDSRET
200610         FILE STATUS IS ESFILE-STAT.                              ESDSRET
200800     SELECT GRADUATE-OUTPUT-FILE                                  ESDSRET
200900         ASSIGN TO SYS006-UR-1403-S.                              ESDSRET
201000                                                                  ESDSRET
201100 DATA DIVISION.                                                   ESDSRET
201200                                                                  ESDSRET
201300 FILE SECTION.                                                    ESDSRET
201400                                                                  ESDSRET
201500 FD  GRADUATE-INPUT-FILE                                          ESDSRET
201600     RECORD CONTAINS 80 CHARACTERS                                ESDSRET
201700     LABEL RECORDS ARE OMITTED                                    ESDSRET
202000     DATA RECORD IS GRADUATE-INPUT-RECORD.                        ESDSRET
300100 01  GRADUATE-INPUT-RECORD.                                       ESDSRET
300200     05  GRADUATE-ID-IN-1              PIC X(03).                  ESDSRET
300220     05  GRADUATE-ID-IN-2              PIC X(02).                  ESDSRET
300240     05  GRADUATE-ID-IN-3              PIC X(04).                  ESDSRET
300300     05  GRADUATE-NAME-IN              PIC X(20).                  ESDSRET
```

```
300400        05   GRADUATE-STUDY-IN              PIC X(20).              ESDSRET
300500        05   GRADUATE-DIPLOMA-IN            PIC X(12).              ESDSRET
300600        05   GRADUATE-GPA-IN                PIC 9V999.              ESDSRET
300700        05   FILLER                         PIC X(15).              ESDSRET
300800                                                                    ESDSRET
300900 FD  GRADUATE-OUTPUT-FILE                                           ESDSRET
301000     RECORD CONTAINS 133 CHARACTERS                                 ESDSRET
301200     LABEL RECORDS ARE OMITTED                                      ESDSRET
301300     DATA RECORD IS GRADUATE-OUTPUT-RECORD.                         ESDSRET
301400 01  GRADUATE-OUTPUT-RECORD.                                        ESDSRET
301500        05   CARRIAGE-CONTROL               PIC X(01).              ESDSRET
301600        05   FILLER                         PIC X(22).              ESDSRET
301700        05   GRADUATE-ID-OUT-1              PIC X(03).              ESDSRET
301720        05   DASH-1                         PIC X(01).              ESDSRET
301740        05   GRADUATE-ID-OUT-2              PIC X(02).              ESDSRET
301760        05   DASH-2                         PIC X(01).              ESDSRET
301780        05   GRADUATE-ID-OUT-3              PIC X(04).              ESDSRET
301800        05   FILLER                         PIC X(05).              ESDSRET
301900        05   GRADUATE-NAME-OUT              PIC X(20).              ESDSRET
302000        05   FILLER                         PIC X(05).              ESDSRET
400100        05   GRADUATE-STUDY-OUT             PIC X(20).              ESDSRET
400200        05   FILLER                         PIC X(05).              ESDSRET
400300        05   GRADUATE-DIPLOMA-OUT           PIC X(12).              ESDSRET
400400        05   FILLER                         PIC X(05).              ESDSRET
400500        05   GRADUATE-GPA-OUT               PIC 9.999.              ESDSRET
400600        05   FILLER                         PIC X(22).              ESDSRET
400700                                                                    ESDSRET
400800 WORKING-STORAGE SECTION.                                           ESDSRET
400900                                                                    ESDSRET
401000 01  PROGRAM-INDICATORS.                                           ESDSRET
401100        05   ARE-THERE-MORE-RECORDS         PIC X(03) VALUE 'YES'.  ESDSRET
401200             88   THERE-IS-A-RECORD                   VALUE 'YES'.  ESDSRET
401300             88   THERE-ARE-NO-MORE-RECORDS           VALUE 'NO '.  ESDSRET
401400                                                                    ESDSRET
401405 01  STATUS-RETURN-CODES.                                          ESDSRET
401410        05   ESFILE-STAT                    PIC 99.                 ESDSRET
401415                                                                    ESDSRET
401500 01  PRINTER-CONTROLS.                                             ESDSRET
401600        05   PROPER-SPACING                 PIC 9(01).              ESDSRET
401700        05   SPACE-ONE-LINE                 PIC 9(01)  VALUE 1.     ESDSRET
401800        05   SPACE-TWO-LINES                PIC 9(01)  VALUE 2.     ESDSRET
401900        05   LINES-PRINTED                  PIC S9(03) VALUE ZERO   ESDSRET
402000                                            USAGE IS COMP-3.        ESDSRET
500100        05   LINE-MAXIMUM                   PIC S9(03) VALUE +35    ESDSRET
500200                                            USAGE IS COMP-3.        ESDSRET
500300        05   PAGE-COUNT                     PIC S9(03) VALUE +1     ESDSRET
500400                                            USAGE IS COMP-3.        ESDSRET
500500             88   FIRST-PAGE                          VALUE +1.     ESDSRET
500520                                                                    ESDSRET
500540 01  PROGRAM-CONSTANTS.                                            ESDSRET
500560        05   DASH                           PIC X(01)  VALUE '-'.   ESDSRET
500580                                                                    ESDSRET
500600 01  HEADING-LINES.                                                ESDSRET
500700        05   MAIN-HEADING-LINE.                                     ESDSRET
500800             10   CARRIAGE-CONTROL          PIC X(01) VALUE SPACES. ESDSRET
500900             10   FILLER                    PIC X(10) VALUE SPACES. ESDSRET
501000             10   DATE-OUT                  PIC X(08).              ESDSRET
501100             10   FILLER                    PIC X(40) VALUE SPACES. ESDSRET
501200             10   FILLER                    PIC X(16)               ESDSRET
501300                                            VALUE 'GRADUATE LISTING'.ESDSRET
501400             10   FILLER                    PIC X(36) VALUE SPACES. ESDSRET
501500             10   FILLER                    PIC X(05) VALUE 'PAGE '. ESDSRET
501600             10   PAGE-OUT                  PIC ZZ9.                ESDSRET
501700             10   FILLER                    PIC X(14) VALUE SPACES. ESDSRET
501720                                                                    ESDSRET
501800        05   FIRST-HEADING-LINE.                                    ESDSRET
501900             10   CARRIAGE-CONTROL          PIC X(01) VALUE SPACES. ESDSRET
502000             10   FILLER                    PIC X(26) VALUE SPACES. ESDSRET
600100             10   FILLER                    PIC X(19) VALUE 'ID'.   ESDSRET
```

```
600200          10   FILLER                  PIC X(22)                ESDSRET
600300                                       VALUE 'STUDENT'.         ESDSRET
600400          10   FILLER                  PIC X(23)                ESDSRET
600500                                       VALUE 'MAJOR COURSE'.    ESDSRET
600600          10   FILLER                  PIC X(16)                ESDSRET
600700                                       VALUE 'TYPE OF'.         ESDSRET
600800          10   FILLER                  PIC X(26) VALUE 'GPA'.   ESDSRET
600900                                                                ESDSRET
601000      05   SECOND-HEADING-LINE.                                 ESDSRET
601100          10   CARRIAGE-CONTROL        PIC X(01) VALUE SPACES.  ESDSRET
601200          10   FILLER                  PIC X(24) VALUE SPACES.  ESDSRET
601300          10   FILLER                  PIC X(22) VALUE 'NUMBER'.ESDSRET
601400          10   FILLER                  PIC X(23) VALUE 'NAME'.  ESDSRET
601500          10   FILLER                  PIC X(21)                ESDSRET
601600                                       VALUE 'OF STUDY'.        ESDSRET
601700          10   FILLER                  PIC X(37)                ESDSRET
601800                                       VALUE 'DIPLOMA'.         ESDSRET
601900                                                                ESDSRET
602000 PROCEDURE DIVISION.                                            ESDSRET
700100                                                                ESDSRET
700200 A000-START-MAIN-ROUTINE.                                       ESDSRET
700300      OPEN INPUT GRADUATE-INPUT-FILE                            ESDSRET
700400           OUTPUT GRADUATE-OUTPUT-FILE.                         ESDSRET
700500      READ GRADUATE-INPUT-FILE                                  ESDSRET
700600         AT END                                                 ESDSRET
700700             MOVE 'NO ' TO ARE-THERE-MORE-RECORDS.              ESDSRET
700800      IF THERE-IS-A-RECORD                                      ESDSRET
700900         PERFORM A001-PROCESS-AND-READ                          ESDSRET
701000             UNTIL THERE-ARE-NO-MORE-RECORDS.                   ESDSRET
701100      CLOSE GRADUATE-INPUT-FILE                                 ESDSRET
701200            GRADUATE-OUTPUT-FILE.                               ESDSRET
701300      STOP RUN.                                                 ESDSRET
701400                                                                ESDSRET
701500 A001-PROCESS-AND-READ.                                         ESDSRET
701600      PERFORM B000-PROCESS-DETAIL-RECORDS.                      ESDSRET
701700      READ GRADUATE-INPUT-FILE                                  ESDSRET
701800         AT END                                                 ESDSRET
701900             MOVE 'NO ' TO ARE-THERE-MORE-RECORDS.              ESDSRET
702000                                                                ESDSRET
800100 B000-PROCESS-DETAIL-RECORDS.                                   ESDSRET
800200      IF LINES-PRINTED IS EQUAL TO LINE-MAXIMUM                 ESDSRET
800300          OR IS GREATER THAN LINE-MAXIMUM                       ESDSRET
800400          OR FIRST-PAGE                                         ESDSRET
800500              PERFORM C000-HEADING-ROUTINE.                     ESDSRET
800600      MOVE SPACES TO GRADUATE-OUTPUT-RECORD.                    ESDSRET
800700      MOVE DASH TO DASH-1, DASH-2.                              ESDSRET
800720      MOVE GRADUATE-ID-IN-1 TO GRADUATE-ID-OUT-1.               ESDSRET
800740      MOVE GRADUATE-ID-IN-2 TO GRADUATE-ID-OUT-2.               ESDSRET
800760      MOVE GRADUATE-ID-IN-3 TO GRADUATE-ID-OUT-3.               ESDSRET
800800      MOVE GRADUATE-NAME-IN TO GRADUATE-NAME-OUT.               ESDSRET
800900      MOVE GRADUATE-STUDY-IN TO GRADUATE-STUDY-OUT.             ESDSRET
801000      MOVE GRADUATE-DIPLOMA-IN TO GRADUATE-DIPLOMA-OUT.         ESDSRET
801100      MOVE GRADUATE-GPA-IN TO GRADUATE-GPA-OUT.                 ESDSRET
801200      WRITE GRADUATE-OUTPUT-RECORD                              ESDSRET
801300            AFTER PROPER-SPACING.                               ESDSRET
801400      MOVE SPACE-ONE-LINE TO PROPER-SPACING.                    ESDSRET
801500      ADD 1 TO LINES-PRINTED.                                   ESDSRET
801600                                                                ESDSRET
801700 C000-HEADING-ROUTINE.                                          ESDSRET
801800      MOVE CURRENT-DATE TO DATE-OUT.                            ESDSRET
801900      MOVE PAGE-COUNT TO PAGE-OUT.                              ESDSRET
802000      WRITE GRADUATE-OUTPUT-RECORD FROM MAIN-HEADING-LINE       ESDSRET
900100            AFTER ADVANCING TO-THE-TOP-OF-THE-PAGE.             ESDSRET
900200      WRITE GRADUATE-OUTPUT-RECORD FROM FIRST-HEADING-LINE      ESDSRET
900300            AFTER ADVANCING 2 LINES.                            ESDSRET
900400      WRITE GRADUATE-OUTPUT-RECORD FROM SECOND-HEADING-LINE     ESDSRET
900500            AFTER ADVANCING 1 LINES.                            ESDSRET
900600      MOVE SPACE-TWO-LINES TO PROPER-SPACING.                   ESDSRET
900700      ADD 1 TO PAGE-COUNT.                                      ESDSRET
900800      MOVE ZEROS TO LINES-PRINTED.                             ESDSRET
```

PROGRAM BLDKSDS

```
100100 IDENTIFICATION DIVISION.                                          BLDKSDS
100200                                                                   BLDKSDS
100300 PROGRAM-ID.        BLDKSDS.                                       BLDKSDS
100400                                                                   BLDKSDS
100500 AUTHOR.            JOHN DOE.                                      BLDKSDS
100600 INSTALLATION.      STATE UNIVERSITY.                             BLDKSDS
100700 DATE-WRITTEN.      08/29/87.                                     BLDKSDS
100800 DATE-COMPILED.                                                    BLDKSDS
100900 SECURITY.          NONE.                                         BLDKSDS
101000 REMARKS.           THIS PROGRAM PRODUCES A KEY SEQUENCED DS OR FILE BLDKSDS
101100                    OF GRADUATING STUDENTS.                       BLDKSDS
101200                                                                   BLDKSDS
101300 ENVIRONMENT DIVISION.                                            BLDKSDS
101400                                                                   BLDKSDS
101500 CONFIGURATION SECTION.                                           BLDKSDS
101600                                                                   BLDKSDS
101700 SOURCE-COMPUTER. IBM-4331.                                       BLDKSDS
101800 OBJECT-COMPUTER. IBM-4331.                                       BLDKSDS
101900                                                                   BLDKSDS
102000 INPUT-OUTPUT SECTION.                                            BLDKSDS
200100                                                                   BLDKSDS
200200 FILE-CONTROL.                                                    BLDKSDS
200300     SELECT GRADUATE-INPUT-FILE                                   BLDKSDS
200400         ASSIGN TO SYS006-AS-ESFILE                               BLDKSDS
200410         ORGANIZATION IS SEQUENTIAL                               BLDKSDS
200420         ACCESS MODE IS SEQUENTIAL                                BLDKSDS
200430         FILE STATUS IS ESFILE-STAT.                              BLDKSDS
200500     SELECT GRADUATE-OUTPUT-FILE                                  BLDKSDS
200600         ASSIGN TO SYS008-KSFILE                                  BLDKSDS
200605         ORGANIZATION IS INDEXED                                  BLDKSDS
200610         FILE STATUS IS KSFILE-STAT                               BLDKSDS
200700         ACCESS MODE IS SEQUENTIAL                                BLDKSDS
200800         RECORD KEY IS GRADUATE-ID-NUMBER.                        BLDKSDS
200900                                                                   BLDKSDS
201000 DATA DIVISION.                                                   BLDKSDS
201100                                                                   BLDKSDS
201200 FILE SECTION.                                                    BLDKSDS
201300                                                                   BLDKSDS
201400 FD  GRADUATE-INPUT-FILE                                          BLDKSDS
201500     RECORD CONTAINS 80 CHARACTERS                                BLDKSDS
201800     LABEL RECORDS ARE OMITTED                                    BLDKSDS
201900     DATA RECORD IS GRADUATE-INPUT-RECORD.                        BLDKSDS
202000 01  GRADUATE-INPUT-RECORD               PIC X(80).               BLDKSDS
300100                                                                   BLDKSDS
300200 FD  GRADUATE-OUTPUT-FILE                                         BLDKSDS
300300     RECORD CONTAINS 80 CHARACTERS                                BLDKSDS
300600     LABEL RECORDS ARE OMITTED                                    BLDKSDS
300700     DATA RECORD IS GRADUATE-OUTPUT-RECORD.                       BLDKSDS
300800 01  GRADUATE-OUTPUT-RECORD.                                      BLDKSDS
300900     05  GRADUATE-ID-NUMBER              PIC X(09).               BLDKSDS
301000     05  FILLER                          PIC X(71).               BLDKSDS
301100                                                                   BLDKSDS
301200 WORKING-STORAGE SECTION.                                         BLDKSDS
301300                                                                   BLDKSDS
301400 01  PROGRAM-INDICATORS.                                          BLDKSDS
301500     05  ARE-THERE-MORE-RECORDS     PIC X(03) VALUE 'YES'.        BLDKSDS
301600         88  THERE-IS-A-RECORD                 VALUE 'YES'.       BLDKSDS
301700         88  THERE-ARE-NO-MORE-RECORDS         VALUE 'NO '.       BLDKSDS
401000                                                                   BLDKSDS
401005 01  STATUS-RETURN-CODES.                                         BLDKSDS
401010     05  KSFILE-STAT                    PIC 99.                   BLDKSDS
401020     05  ESFILE-STAT                    PIC 99.                   BLDKSDS
401030                                                                   BLDKSDS
401100 PROCEDURE DIVISION.                                              BLDKSDS
401200                                                                   BLDKSDS
401300 A000-START-MAIN-ROUTINE.                                         BLDKSDS
401400     OPEN INPUT GRADUATE-INPUT-FILE                               BLDKSDS
401500          OUTPUT GRADUATE-OUTPUT-FILE.                            BLDKSDS
```

```
401600        READ GRADUATE-INPUT-FILE                                 BLDKSDS
401700           AT END                                                BLDKSDS
401800              MOVE 'NO ' TO ARE-THERE-MORE-RECORDS.              BLDKSDS
401900        IF THERE-IS-A-RECORD                                     BLDKSDS
402000           PERFORM A001-PROCESS-AND-READ                         BLDKSDS
500100              UNTIL THERE-ARE-NO-MORE-RECORDS.                   BLDKSDS
500200        CLOSE GRADUATE-INPUT-FILE                                BLDKSDS
500300              GRADUATE-OUTPUT-FILE.                              BLDKSDS
500400        STOP RUN.                                                BLDKSDS
500500                                                                 BLDKSDS
500600 A001-PROCESS-AND-READ.                                          BLDKSDS
500700        PERFORM B000-PROCESS-DETAIL-RECORDS.                     BLDKSDS
500800        READ GRADUATE-INPUT-FILE                                 BLDKSDS
500900           AT END                                                BLDKSDS
501000              MOVE 'NO ' TO ARE-THERE-MORE-RECORDS.              BLDKSDS
501100                                                                 BLDKSDS
501200 B000-PROCESS-DETAIL-RECORDS.                                    BLDKSDS
501300        MOVE SPACES TO GRADUATE-OUTPUT-RECORD.                   BLDKSDS
501400        MOVE GRADUATE-INPUT-RECORD TO GRADUATE-OUTPUT-RECORD.    BLDKSDS
501500        WRITE GRADUATE-OUTPUT-RECORD                             BLDKSDS
501600           INVALID KEY                                           BLDKSDS
501700              DISPLAY '** INVALID KEY ** ', GRADUATE-ID-NUMBER.  BLDKSDS
```

PROGRAM KSDSRET

```
100100 IDENTIFICATION DIVISION.                                        KSDSRET
100200                                                                 KSDSRET
100300 PROGRAM-ID.      KSDSRET.                                       KSDSRET
100400                                                                 KSDSRET
100500 AUTHOR.          JOHN DOE.                                      KSDSRET
100600 INSTALLATION.    STATE UNIVERSITY.                              KSDSRET
100700 DATE-WRITTEN.    08/29/87.                                      KSDSRET
100800 DATE-COMPILED.                                                  KSDSRET
100900 SECURITY.        NONE.                                          KSDSRET
101000 REMARKS.         THIS PROGRAM PRODUCES A LISTING OF GRADUATING  KSDSRET
101100                  STUDENTS FROM A KSDS.                          KSDSRET
101200                                                                 KSDSRET
101300 ENVIRONMENT DIVISION.                                           KSDSRET
101400                                                                 KSDSRET
101500 CONFIGURATION SECTION.                                          KSDSRET
101600                                                                 KSDSRET
101700 SOURCE-COMPUTER. IBM-4331.                                      KSDSRET
101800 OBJECT-COMPUTER. IBM-4331.                                      KSDSRET
101900 SPECIAL-NAMES.   C01 IS TO-THE-TOP-OF-THE-PAGE.                 KSDSRET
102000                                                                 KSDSRET
200100 INPUT-OUTPUT SECTION.                                           KSDSRET
200200                                                                 KSDSRET
200300 FILE-CONTROL.                                                   KSDSRET
200400     SELECT GRADUATE-INPUT-FILE                                  KSDSRET
200500         ASSIGN TO SYS010-KSFILE                                 KSDSRET
200600         ACCESS MODE IS SEQUENTIAL                               KSDSRET
200605         ORGANIZATION IS INDEXED                                 KSDSRET
200610         FILE STATUS IS KSFILE-STAT                              KSDSRET
200700         RECORD KEY IS GRADUATE-ID-IN.                           KSDSRET
200800     SELECT GRADUATE-OUTPUT-FILE                                 KSDSRET
200900         ASSIGN TO SYS006-UR-1403-S.                             KSDSRET
201000                                                                 KSDSRET
201100 DATA DIVISION.                                                  KSDSRET
201200                                                                 KSDSRET
201300 FILE SECTION.                                                   KSDSRET
201400                                                                 KSDSRET
201500 FD  GRADUATE-INPUT-FILE                                         KSDSRET
201600     RECORD CONTAINS 80 CHARACTERS                              KSDSRET
201900     LABEL RECORDS ARE OMITTED                                   KSDSRET
202000     DATA RECORD IS GRADUATE-INPUT-RECORD.                       KSDSRET
300100 01  GRADUATE-INPUT-RECORD.                                      KSDSRET
300150     05  GRADUATE-ID-IN.                                         KSDSRET
300200         10  GRADUATE-ID-IN-1          PIC X(03).                KSDSRET
300220         10  GRADUATE-ID-IN-2          PIC X(02).                KSDSRET
```

```
300240              10  GRADUATE-ID-IN-3        PIC X(04).                KSDSRET
300300         05  GRADUATE-NAME-IN             PIC X(20).                KSDSRET
300400         05  GRADUATE-STUDY-IN            PIC X(20).                KSDSRET
300500         05  GRADUATE-DIPLOMA-IN          PIC X(12).                KSDSRET
300600         05  GRADUATE-GPA-IN              PIC 9V999.                KSDSRET
300700         05  FILLER                       PIC X(15).                KSDSRET
300800                                                                    KSDSRET
300900 FD  GRADUATE-OUTPUT-FILE                                           KSDSRET
301000     RECORD CONTAINS 133 CHARACTERS                                 KSDSRET
301200     LABEL RECORDS ARE OMITTED                                      KSDSRET
301300     DATA RECORD IS GRADUATE-OUTPUT-RECORD.                         KSDSRET
301400 01  GRADUATE-OUTPUT-RECORD.                                        KSDSRET
301500         05  CARRIAGE-CONTROL             PIC X(01).                KSDSRET
301600         05  FILLER                       PIC X(22).                KSDSRET
301700         05  GRADUATE-ID-OUT-1            PIC X(03).                KSDSRET
301720         05  DASH-1                       PIC X(01).                KSDSRET
301740         05  GRADUATE-ID-OUT-2            PIC X(02).                KSDSRET
301760         05  DASH-2                       PIC X(01).                KSDSRET
301780         05  GRADUATE-ID-OUT-3            PIC X(04).                KSDSRET
301800         05  FILLER                       PIC X(05).                KSDSRET
301900         05  GRADUATE-NAME-OUT            PIC X(20).                KSDSRET
302000         05  FILLER                       PIC X(05).                KSDSRET
400100         05  GRADUATE-STUDY-OUT           PIC X(20).                KSDSRET
400200         05  FILLER                       PIC X(05).                KSDSRET
400300         05  GRADUATE-DIPLOMA-OUT         PIC X(12).                KSDSRET
400400         05  FILLER                       PIC X(05).                KSDSRET
400500         05  GRADUATE-GPA-OUT             PIC 9.999.                KSDSRET
400600         05  FILLER                       PIC X(22).                KSDSRET
400700                                                                    KSDSRET
400800 WORKING-STORAGE SECTION.                                           KSDSRET
400900                                                                    KSDSRET
401000 01   PROGRAM-INDICATORS.                                          KSDSRET
401100         05  ARE-THERE-MORE-RECORDS       PIC X(03) VALUE 'YES'.    KSDSRET
401200             88  THERE-IS-A-RECORD                  VALUE 'YES'.    KSDSRET
401300             88  THERE-ARE-NO-MORE-RECORDS          VALUE 'NO '.    KSDSRET
401400                                                                    KSDSRET
401405 01   STATUS-RETURN-CODES.                                         KSDSRET
401410         05  KSFILE-STAT                  PIC 99.                   KSDSRET
401500 01   PRINTER-CONTROLS.                                            KSDSRET
401600         05  PROPER-SPACING               PIC 9(01).                KSDSRET
401700         05  SPACE-ONE-LINE               PIC 9(01)   VALUE 1.      KSDSRET
401800         05  SPACE-TWO-LINES              PIC 9(01)   VALUE 2.      KSDSRET
401900         05  LINES-PRINTED                PIC S9(03) VALUE ZERO     KSDSRET
402000                                          USAGE IS COMP-3.          KSDSRET
500100         05  LINE-MAXIMUM                 PIC S9(03) VALUE +35      KSDSRET
500200                                          USAGE IS COMP-3.          KSDSRET
500300         05  PAGE-COUNT                   PIC S9(03) VALUE +1       KSDSRET
500400                                          USAGE IS COMP-3.          KSDSRET
500500             88  FIRST-PAGE                          VALUE +1.      KSDSRET
500520                                                                    KSDSRET
500540 01   PROGRAM-CONSTANTS.                                           KSDSRET
500560         05  DASH                         PIC X(01)   VALUE '-'.    KSDSRET
500580                                                                    KSDSRET
500600 01   HEADING-LINES.                                               KSDSRET
500700         05  MAIN-HEADING-LINE.                                     KSDSRET
500800             10  CARRIAGE-CONTROL         PIC X(01) VALUE SPACES.   KSDSRET
500900             10  FILLER                   PIC X(10) VALUE SPACES.   KSDSRET
501000             10  DATE-OUT                 PIC X(08).                KSDSRET
501100             10  FILLER                   PIC X(40) VALUE SPACES.   KSDSRET
501200             10  FILLER                   PIC X(16)                 KSDSRET
501300                                          VALUE 'GRADUATE LISTING'. KSDSRET
501400             10  FILLER                   PIC X(36) VALUE SPACES.   KSDSRET
501500             10  FILLER                   PIC X(05) VALUE 'PAGE '.  KSDSRET
501600             10  PAGE-OUT                 PIC ZZ9.                  KSDSRET
501700             10  FILLER                   PIC X(14) VALUE SPACES.   KSDSRET
501720                                                                    KSDSRET
501800         05  FIRST-HEADING-LINE.                                    KSDSRET
501900             10  CARRIAGE-CONTROL         PIC X(01) VALUE SPACES.   KSDSRET
502000             10  FILLER                   PIC X(26) VALUE SPACES.   KSDSRET
600100             10  FILLER                   PIC X(19) VALUE 'ID'.     KSDSRET
```

```
600200          10  FILLER              PIC X(22)               KSDSRET
600300                                  VALUE 'STUDENT'.        KSDSRET
600400          10  FILLER              PIC X(23)               KSDSRET
600500                                  VALUE 'MAJOR COURSE'.   KSDSRET
600600          10  FILLER              PIC X(16)               KSDSRET
600700                                  VALUE 'TYPE OF'.        KSDSRET
600800          10  FILLER              PIC X(26) VALUE 'GPA'.  KSDSRET
600900                                                          KSDSRET
601000      05  SECOND-HEADING-LINE.                            KSDSRET
601100          10  CARRIAGE-CONTROL    PIC X(01) VALUE SPACES. KSDSRET
601200          10  FILLER              PIC X(24) VALUE SPACES. KSDSRET
601300          10  FILLER              PIC X(22) VALUE 'NUMBER'.KSDSRET
601400          10  FILLER              PIC X(23) VALUE 'NAME'. KSDSRET
601500          10  FILLER              PIC X(21)               KSDSRET
601600                                  VALUE 'OF STUDY'.       KSDSRET
601700          10  FILLER              PIC X(37)               KSDSRET
601800                                  VALUE 'DIPLOMA'.        KSDSRET
601900                                                          KSDSRET
602000  PROCEDURE DIVISION.                                     KSDSRET
700100                                                          KSDSRET
700200  A000-START-MAIN-ROUTINE.                                KSDSRET
700300      OPEN INPUT GRADUATE-INPUT-FILE                      KSDSRET
700400          OUTPUT GRADUATE-OUTPUT-FILE.                    KSDSRET
700500      READ GRADUATE-INPUT-FILE                            KSDSRET
700600          AT END                                          KSDSRET
700700              MOVE 'NO ' TO ARE-THERE-MORE-RECORDS.       KSDSRET
700800      IF THERE-IS-A-RECORD                                KSDSRET
700900          PERFORM A001-PROCESS-AND-READ                   KSDSRET
701000              UNTIL THERE-ARE-NO-MORE-RECORDS.            KSDSRET
701100      CLOSE GRADUATE-INPUT-FILE                           KSDSRET
701200              GRADUATE-OUTPUT-FILE.                       KSDSRET
701300      STOP RUN.                                           KSDSRET
701400                                                          KSDSRET
701500  A001-PROCESS-AND-READ.                                  KSDSRET
701600      PERFORM B000-PROCESS-DETAIL-RECORDS.                KSDSRET
701700      READ GRADUATE-INPUT-FILE                            KSDSRET
701800          AT END                                          KSDSRET
701900              MOVE 'NO ' TO ARE-THERE-MORE-RECORDS.       KSDSRET
702000                                                          KSDSRET
800100  B000-PROCESS-DETAIL-RECORDS.                            KSDSRET
800200      IF LINES-PRINTED IS EQUAL TO LINE-MAXIMUM           KSDSRET
800300          OR IS GREATER THAN LINE-MAXIMUM                 KSDSRET
800400          OR FIRST-PAGE                                   KSDSRET
800500              PERFORM C000-HEADING-ROUTINE.               KSDSRET
800600      MOVE SPACES TO GRADUATE-OUTPUT-RECORD.              KSDSRET
800700      MOVE DASH TO DASH-1, DASH-2.                        KSDSRET
800720      MOVE GRADUATE-ID-IN-1 TO GRADUATE-ID-OUT-1.         KSDSRET
800740      MOVE GRADUATE-ID-IN-2 TO GRADUATE-ID-OUT-2.         KSDSRET
800760      MOVE GRADUATE-ID-IN-3 TO GRADUATE-ID-OUT-3.         KSDSRET
800800      MOVE GRADUATE-NAME-IN TO GRADUATE-NAME-OUT.         KSDSRET
800900      MOVE GRADUATE-STUDY-IN TO GRADUATE-STUDY-OUT.       KSDSRET
801000      MOVE GRADUATE-DIPLOMA-IN TO GRADUATE-DIPLOMA-OUT.   KSDSRET
801100      MOVE GRADUATE-GPA-IN TO GRADUATE-GPA-OUT.           KSDSRET
801200      WRITE GRADUATE-OUTPUT-RECORD                        KSDSRET
801300          AFTER PROPER-SPACING.                           KSDSRET
801400      MOVE SPACE-ONE-LINE TO PROPER-SPACING.              KSDSRET
801500      ADD 1 TO LINES-PRINTED.                             KSDSRET
801600                                                          KSDSRET
801700  C000-HEADING-ROUTINE.                                   KSDSRET
801800      MOVE CURRENT-DATE TO DATE-OUT.                      KSDSRET
801900      MOVE PAGE-COUNT TO PAGE-OUT.                        KSDSRET
802000      WRITE GRADUATE-OUTPUT-RECORD FROM MAIN-HEADING-LINE KSDSRET
900100          AFTER ADVANCING TO-THE-TOP-OF-THE-PAGE.         KSDSRET
900200      WRITE GRADUATE-OUTPUT-RECORD FROM FIRST-HEADING-LINE KSDSRET
900300          AFTER ADVANCING 2 LINES.                        KSDSRET
900400      WRITE GRADUATE-OUTPUT-RECORD FROM SECOND-HEADING-LINE KSDSRET
900500          AFTER ADVANCING 1 LINES.                        KSDSRET
900600      MOVE SPACE-TWO-LINES TO PROPER-SPACING.             KSDSRET
900700      ADD 1 TO PAGE-COUNT.                                KSDSRET
900800      MOVE ZEROS TO LINES-PRINTED.                        KSDSRET
```

Glossary

ABEND   An acronym for *ab*normal *end*ing. This word is used to describe a process in which a program ends abnormally.

Access method   The technique used for moving data from an I/O device to storage.

Access method services (AMS)   A service program that is used to create and maintain VSAM files.

Adapter   *See* I/O adapter.

Address-list assignment   A combination of the specific and generic assignments allowing up to seven hex addresses to be listed.

AMS   An abbreviation for *a*ccess *m*ethod *s*ervices.

Application program   A program that applies to the user's work (e.g., an accounts receivable program or a payroll register program).

AR   An abbreviation for "*a*ttention *r*outine."

Assembler   A translator that converts assembly language source programs to machine language.

Attention routine   Commands that may be issued at any time through the console.

Attribute   Characteristic.

Backup and restore   A method used by the computer operator to reformat the system or private libraries.

Backup copy   A copy of data or programs that is kept in case the current copy is destroyed. These copies are usually kept on disk or tape.

BCD code   *B*inary-*c*oded *d*ecimal. A six-bit code.

Block   A physical record.

Blocking factor   The number of logical records per block.

Block multiplexor   A channel that has fast I/O devices attached to it (tape or disk).

Book   A group of source statements or data statements in a library.

BPI   An abbreviation for bytes per inch.

Byte   Eight data bits. A check or parity bit is added on tape or disk.

Byte multiplexor   A channel that usually has slow-speed I/O devices attached to it (printers, card readers, etc.)

Catalog   To place an entry or a member in a system or private library.

Channel   A device that connects the CPU and I/O devices. It transmits data and acts as a small computer.

Checkpoint   A place in a computer program at which a check is made, or at which a recording of data is made for restart purposes.

CICS   An abbreviation for *c*ustomer *i*nformation *c*ontrol *s*ystem. CICS is an IBM program product that enables transactions to be entered and processed at remote terminals.

CIL   An abbreviation for *c*ore *i*mage *l*ibrary.

CKD   An abbreviation for *c*ount *key* *d*ata.

Class   A means of grouping jobs that require the same set of resources for their execution. The JOB command class specifies the partition a job will execute in. The LST command class specifies the output device to be used for printing.

Class priority   A value that determines which job of several waiting will run in a particular partition.

Cluster   A VSAM logical structure that contains all the physical components of a VSAM file. A KSDS cluster has indices as well as the data.

Comment field   A field in a command that is used for informational purposes only. It is not translated by the translator or job control program.

Common library (ICCF)   A library available to all users on a read-only basis.

Compiler   A translator that translates higher-level language or source language into machine language.

Concatenate   To link together in a series or chain.

Condense   A method of physically deleting unused space in libraries.

Conditional job control statement   A job control statement that allows the system to execute or bypass parts of the job control stream conditionally, depending on the result of previously executed steps within the same job.

Continuation field   In job control, column 72 of a command. If nonblank, it indicates a command will be continued. It is seldom used.

Control area   A grouping of control intervals forming a data set. A VSAM control area is similar to a file.

Control area split   A process in which there is no more room to add a record to a VSAM DSDS control area. The control intervals are split and a new control area is formed.

Control interval   An area where VSAM records are stored. It is similar to a physical record.

Control interval split   A process in which there is no more room to add a record to a VSAM KSDS control interval. The records are split in half and a new control interval is formed.

Control program   A program that controls the execution of IBM and user-supplied programs.

COPY program   A DOS/VSE version 1 service program that is part of the LIBRARIAN program. It copies systems packs, creates private libraries, and merges entries in libraries.

Core image library   A library containing programs in executable form. (The programs have been link edited.)

Count key data device A disk device for which data is accessed by a cylinder and track number.

Cross-reference dictionary A listing of symbolic names in a program and the statement numbers in the program where the name is used. It is obtained by using the XREF or SXREF options in the OPTION job control statement.

CSERV (program) A DOS/VSE version 1 service program that prints or punches a core image library member.

Cylinder That portion of a disk pack accessible by one movement of the read/write arm.

Cylinder index An index of an indexed sequential file. It contains the highest key in each cylinder and the track index address for that cylinder.

Cylinder overflow An area at the end of a cylinder that is used for track overflow.

DAM An acronym for *d*irect-*a*ccess *m*ethod.

Data division map A list of all symbolic names used in a program and their offset location in the program. It is obtained by using the SYM operand in the OPTION job control statement.

Data management program A program that assists in organizing, storing, and retrieving data.

Data set A VSAM file.

Data space An area on a DASD that is set up for a VSAM file. It is similar to an extent.

Default The value assumed if none is specified.

Delimiter statement A statement that marks the end of data or a job.

Density The number of bytes per inch.

Device address A three-digit number that identifies a particular I/O device.

Diagnostics Error messages provided by compilers. These messages indicate a violation of the rules of the language.

Disposition A JECL operand that specifies how POWER is to route and schedule the associated entry in a queue.

DITTO An acronym for *d*ata *i*nterfile *t*ransfer, *t*esting, and *o*perations. A utility program that provides a set of functions needed in day-to-day computer activities.

DOS/VSE An abbreviation for *D*isk *O*perating *S*ystem/*V*irtual *S*torage *E*xtended. The name of an IBM operating system.

DSERV (program) A DOS/VSE VERSION 1 service program that prints the entries in a library directory.

Dump A listing of the contents of memory or main storage.

Dynamic memory Memory for which information disappears or is erased when the power is turned off.

Dynamic storage allocation A technique in which storage is assigned to computer programs and data at the moment of need (i.e., when executing).

EBCDIC An acronym for *e*xtended *b*inary-*c*oded *d*ecimal *i*nterchange *c*ode, an eight bit code.

Ellipsis Three dots (. . .) indicating that a variable number of items may be chosen. Used in job control format descriptions.

Entry sequenced data set A VSAM (nonnative) file similar to the native SAM file.

EOD An abbreviation for *e*nd *o*f *d*ata.

EOJ An abbreviation for *e*nd *o*f *j*ob.

EOR marker An abbreviation for *e*nd *o*f *r*eel marker. *See also* EOT marker.

EOT marker   A small silver marker 12 feet from the end of a tape. It indicates the end of the recording area.

ESDS   An abbreviation for *entry-sequenced data set.*

ESERV   A DOS/VSE version 1 service program that prints, punches, de-edits, verifies, or updates an edited assembly language macro from a source library.

Extent   A continuous portion of disk defined by some upper and lower limit.

FBA   An abbreviation for *fixed block architecture.*

FBA device   A disk device for which data is accessed by a block number.

File label (tape)   A header, trailer, or end-of-volume label.

File organization   The method used for arranging data records on a storage device when the file is originally built or loaded.

File processing   The act of retrieving, updating, and adding records to a file.

File reorganization   A process where all undeleted records is an indexed sequential file are retrieved sequentially and rewritten as a new indexed file in another area. Usually, but not always, the extents are enlarged for the reorganized file.

Fixed block architecture device   *See* FBA device.

Fixed-length record   A record in which all fields and the record itself are of unchanging length.

Free space   An overflow area for a KSDS. It is similar to the ISAM overflow area.

Functional command (AMS)   A command that is used to request that actual work be done.

Gap   *See* Interrecord gap.

Generic   Of a particular class or type but *not* a specific kind.

Generic assignment   A device assignment that is *not* made to a particular device number.

GETVIS area   An area in memory allowed for programs that need additional memory as they execute.

Global condition   A condition existing for *several* job steps.

Hard copy   A printed copy of machine output in a visually readable form (e.g., a printed report).

HASP   An acronym for *Houston automatic spooling program.* A spooling program written by NASA and IBM which is often used instead of POWER.

Header (HDR1) label   An IBM 80-byte fixed-format (standard) file label at the beginning of each file of data. Its first field has HDR; and it contains among other things a file identifier, volume serial number, and creation and expiration dates.

High activity (file)   A file for which there is a large number of records processed out of the entire file (i.e., 60 percent or more).

ICCF   An abbreviation for *interactive computing and control facility.* ICCF is an IBM program product that allows users to use a terminal on an interactive basis as well as a batch basis.

ICCF administrator   A person, usually a systems programmer, who controls access to ICCF and ensures that it is working at a maximum level.

ICCF library file   An area on a DASD reserved for ICCF.

IDCAMS   A program in AMS.

Identification field   The first field in a command.

Incore sort   A sort in which the intermediate storage used for the sort is in main storage rather than on a secondary storage device.

Independent overflow An area on disk in an ISAM file that contains overflow records from a cylinder.

Indexed sequential file A file for which records are loaded sequentially by a unique key. An index is built for the file.

Index set A VSAM index. It is similar to an ISAM cylinder index.

Initialize The process of writing a volume label on a magnetic tape or disk.

Interblock gap *See* Interrecord gap.

Interpreter A translator that translates one instruction and then attempts to execute it. An example is a BASIC interpreter. This is in contrast to compilers which translate *all* instructions with execution occurring later.

Interrecord gap A space between physical records or blocks.

IPL (program) An abbreviation for *i*nitial *p*rogram *l*oad. This is a program used when the computer is powered up. It loads the nucleus of the supervisor into main storage. It is sometimes referred to by computer operators as the bootstrap program.

I/O adapter A device that can be used instead of a channel to connect I/O devices to the CPU.

IPL routine The initial program load time or powering up the computer.

ISAM An acronym for *i*ndexed *s*equential *a*ccess *m*ethod.

JCC An abbreviation for *j*ob *c*ontrol *c*ommand.

JCL An abbreviation for *j*ob *c*ontrol *l*anguage. These are DOS/VSE commands. Often loosely used to mean any batch commands, including POWER commands.

JCP An abbreviation for *j*ob *c*ontrol *p*rogram.

JCS An abbreviation for *j*ob *c*ontrol *s*tatement.

JECL An abbreviation for *j*ob *e*ntry *c*ontrol *l*anguage. These are batch POWER commands.

JECL commands POWER commands that allow the *programmer* to specify how a particular POWER job will be handled.

Job catalog A user catalog that has been declared *the* catalog for all files in a *current* job.

Job control command (DOS/VSE) Commands that are issued between jobs.

Job control program (DOS/VSE) A program that read and interprets DOS/VSE job control statements.

Job control statement (DOS/VSE) Job control language statements that are written by the programmer and are part of the input stream.

Job (DOS/VSE) A specified group of job tasks. It begins with a // JOB statement and ends with a /* statement.

Job entry control language POWER commands.

Job entry statement (ICCF) These commands, similar in format to ICCF system commands, do not take effect until a job is run.

Job step (DOS/VSE) The execution of a single processing program. The job step begins with a DOS // EXEC statement.

Job task *See* Job step.

Julian date A date in the form YYDDD, where YY is the last two digits of the year and DDD is the day number in the year. Examples: 87/Ø31 = Jan. 31, 1987; 87/Ø35 = Feb. 4, 1987.

Key (primary) A field or data item that uniquely identifies a logical record. Examples: a social security number; a part number.

Key-sequenced data set A VSAM (nonnative) file similar to the native ISAM file.

Keyword format   A type of command for which operands are written with keywords and may be written in any order.

KSDS   An abbreviation for *key-sequenced data set.*

Label information area (LIA)   An area, normally on the system residence pack, that has label information read from job control statements or commands.

LIBRARIAN   The name of a set of programs used to maintain, service, and organize the system and private libraries.

Library   A collection of files or programs that are related by some common characteristic.

Library member   A unit in a library.

Linkage editor program   A program that prepares the output from language translators for execution. It links or combines the object program with any subroutines or I/O routines needed for execution.

Link edit   To combine routines in the relocatable library with a user program and produce an executable program.

LISTLOG   A utility program that will cause all console communications regarding that job to be printed along with the job output.

List queue   A queue on disk of jobs waiting to be printed.

Load point marker   A small silver marker 12 feet from the beginning of a tape. It indicates the beginning of the recording area.

Local condition   A condition that applies for that job step only.

Log   A record of transactions made on the console display unit.

Logical record   A collection of related fields of data.

Logical unit   A name used in a program to represent an I/O device address. The name usually begins with the letters SYS, although in FORTRAN it is a number.

LST queue   *See* List queue.

Macro command (ICCF)   A command that invokes a sequence of ICCF statements that perform a frequently used function. It can be used in edit mode and is always preceded by an @ sign.

Main storage   Interval storage in a computer from which information can be retrieved faster than from secondary storage.

MAINT program   A service maintenance program that catalogs, renames, deletes, and condenses programs in a library.

Master catalog   A catalog that contains extensive file and volume information that assists in locating files. If user catalogs exist, the master catalog has entries that point to the user catalogs.

Master index   An optional index for an indexed sequential file. It contains the address for each track in the cylinder index.

Modal command (AMS)   A command that specifies options and allows the conditional execution of functional commands.

Module   A library program unit that has been compiled but not link edited.

Multifile volume   A tape or disk pack that contains more than one data file.

Multiplexor channel   A channel that can have more than one I/O device connected to it.

Multiprocessing   Using more than one processor or CPU in a computer system.

Multiprogramming   A process in which more than one program is executed at the same time or concurrently in one CPU.

Multitasking   A process in which more than one program is executed at the same time or concurrently in one partition.

Multivolume file   A data file that requires more than one tape reel or disk pack.

Native file organization   Those types of file organization that were original to the first DOS release (i.e., sequential, indexed sequential, and direct file organization).

Nested procedure   A procedure within a procedure.

Nine-track tape   A tape written in the EBCDIC code (eight data bits plus one check bit = nine tracks).

Node   Any terminal, station, or communications computer in a network.

Nucleus   *See* Supervisor.

Object program   A machine language program in number form. The output from a translator.

Op code   Slang for "operation code."

Operand field   Fields following the operation code in a statement or command. The fields are usually separated by commas.

Operating system   A group of programs (software) that control the activities and resources of a computer system.

Operation code   An word or abbreviation in a statement or command that specifies the type of operation to be performed.

Operation field   An area in an instruction in which the operation code is coded.

Page   1. A fixed-length block of instructions and/or data that can be transferred between real and virtual storage. In DOS/VSE a page is 4K or 2K bytes.

    2. The act of transferring 4K or 2K bytes or a page between real and virtual storage.

Page data set   An extent on a DASD where pages are stored.

Page in   The process of transferring a page from virtual storage to real or main storage.

Page out   The process of transferring a page from main or real storage to virtual storage.

Parameter   A variable that is given a constant value for a specified purpose or process.

Parameterized procedure   A sequence of job control statements in which a means exists for altering the sequence of execution and/or the values of operands at the time of execution.

Parity (odd or even)   All characters represented on a storage medium are composed of either an even or an odd number of bits.

Partition   A subdivision of memory.

Partition priority   A rank determining that partition's precedence in receiving processing time.

Permanent assignment   A device assignment which is in effect for *all* jobs until unassigned.

Phase   (1) An executable program in a library. (2) A part of the Sort/Merge program.

Physical record   One or more logical records or a block.

Physical unit   A hex device number or address in the form cuu, where c = channel number and uu = unit number.

PL   An abbreviation for "procedure library."

Pointer   An address or other indication of the location of information on disk.

Positional format   A type of command for which operands must be written in a definite prescribed order.

POWER   An IBM program product designed to improve the throughput of the computer system.

Primary library (ICCF)   An area assigned to a user for storing job control, programs, and data.

Prime data   Data that is in sequential order by a key.

Prime data area   An area on disk containing the track index, prime data, and the cylinder overflow area for an ISAM file.

Priority   A rank assigned to each job within its class that determines its precedence in receiving system resources.

Private library (DOS/VSE)   A library that is not on SYSRES. It may have core image library members, relocatable library members, source statement library members, and procedure library members.

Private library (ICCF)   An area that can be owned by one or more users.

Procedural command (ICCF)   A command that invokes a sequence of ICCF statements that perform a frequently used function. It must be entered in command mode.

Procedure   A group of job control language statements in a library.

PROCEDURE DIVISION map   An assembly language listing of a higher-level language source program. It is obtained by using the LISTX operand in the OPTION job control statement.

Procedure library   Library with entries consisting of job control statements.

Processing programs   Programs whose execution is begun or initiated by the job control program.

PSERV (program)   A DOS/VSE version 1 service program that prints or punches a procedure library member.

PSTART command   The PSTART command is a POWER central operator command that starts a partition or task. It specifies, among other things, the default class for specific devices.

Public library (ICCF)   A library accessible to all users on a read/write basis.

Punch queue   A queue on disk of jobs waiting to be punched into cards.

PUN queue   *See* Punch queue.

Queue   A line of tasks on disk waiting to be processed.

Random processing   User specifies key by which a specified record is retrieved.

RDR queue   *See* Reader queue.

Reader queue   A queue on disk of jobs waiting to be executed.

Real storage   Storage in the CPU where instructions and data can be directly obtained.

Record addition   The addition of a new record to an already established file.

Record deletion   The removal of a record from a file either by a physical removal or a deletion code.

Record update   A change in all or some of the information in a record in a file.

Relative record data set   A VSAM (non-native) file similar to the native DAM file.

Relative record number   A number that indicates the location of a logical record, expressed as a difference with respect to a base address.

Relocatable library   A DOS/VSE version 1 library that contains subroutines and I/O macros in object form. The entries may be used by main programs.

Relocation dictionary (RLD)   This list describes the contents of the RLD records passed to the linkage editor in the object module.

Return code   A value ($\emptyset$–4$\emptyset$95) set and returned in general register 15 by a program that has been executed. The code can be used by a conditional job control statement to bypass a sequence of statements.

Reusable file   A file that can be used as a work file.

RJE   An abbreviation for *remote job entry*. The submission of jobs through terminals to the host computer.

RL   An abbreviation for *relocatable library*.

RRDS   An abbreviation for *relative record data set*.

RRN   An abbreviation for *relative record number*.

RSERV (program)   A DOS/VSE version 1 program that prints or punches a relocatable library member.

SAM   An acronym for *sequential access method*.

Secondary storage   Storage other than main storage in which data, information, and programs may be kept when the computer is not in operation. Examples of secondary storage are disk, tapes, diskettes, magnetic drums, and mass storage systems.

Selector channel   A channel that can have only one I/O device connected to it.

Sequence field   In job control, columns 72–8$\emptyset$, which is seldom used. It can be used for sequence numbers.

Sequence set   A VSAM index. It is similar to the ISAM track index.

Sequential file   A file for which records are arranged on a storage media in the physical sequence that they will be processed.

Sequential processing   Each record is examined and processed in the order in which it was loaded.

Service program   A program that assists in the successful execution of problem programs without directly controlling the system or production results. An example is the linkage editor program.

Seven-track tape   A tape written in the BCD code (six bits plus one check or parity bit = seven tracks).

SL   An abbreviation for *source library*.

SLI   An abbreviation for *source library input*.

Soft copy   A display on a terminal screen which is in a visually readable form.

Sort/merge program   A utility program that is used to sequence and/or merge records in one or more files.

Source library   A DOS/VSE version 1 library containing source programs or data records.

Source program   A higher-level language or assembly-level language that has not been processed into machine language.

Specific assignment   A device assignment where a system logical unit is assigned to a specific physical unit.

Split cylinder   A condition where a cylinder has more than one file.

SSERV (program)   A DOS/VSE version 1 service program that prints or punches a source library member.

Standard labels   IBM tape or disk labels that are fixed in length and format. *See also* Volume label, Header label and Trailer label.

Static memory   Memory for which information does not disappear when the power is cut off.

Storage (instruction) control unit   Receives and interprets instructions.

String   A group of sequenced records, usually on an intermediate storage device.

Sublibrary   A subdivision of a library where library members are stored.

Sublibrary member   A unit in a sublibrary that is identified by a member name and member type.

Supervisor   The part of the operating system that remains in lower memory at all times during operation.

Symbolic parameter   A name which, when preceded with an & and used in job control, can have values assigned to it through other job control statements in the job stream.

SYSCAT   The logical disk device for the VSE/VSAM master catalog.

SYSCLB   The logical device for an area on disk used for a private core image library in DOS/VSE version 1.

SYSDUMP or SYSDMP   The logical disk device that is used for the dump files.

SYSGEN   An acronym for *system generation*.

SYSIN   A symbolic name that can be used to assign SYSRDR and SYSIPT to the same card reader or tape.

SYSIPT   The logical unit used as the input unit for programs and data. It can be assigned to the card reader, tape, disk, or diskette.

SYSLNK   The logical disk device for an area on disk used as input to the linkage editor.

SYSLOG   The operator console used for communication between the system and the operator and for logging job control statements.

SYSLST   The logical unit used for printed output. It can be assigned to a printer, tape, disk, or diskette.

SYSOUT   A symbolic name that can be used to assign SYSPCH and SYSLST to the same tape unit.

SYSPCH   The logical device used for punched output. It can be assigned to the card punch, tape, disk, or diskette.

SYSRDR   The logical unit used as the input unit for job control statements or commands. It can be assigned to the card reader, tape, disk, or diskette.

SYSREC   The logical disk device where the system recorder file is stored.

SYSRES   The logical disk unit that contains the system residence file (the system libraries).

SYSRLB   The logical unit that contains an area on disk used for a private relocatable library in DOS/VSE version 1.

SYSSLB   The logical unit that contains an area on disk used for a private source statement library in DOS/VSE version 1.

System command (ICCF)   An ICCF command that begins with one slash and must be entered in command mode.

System dump file   A disk area where dumps may be stored. The use of this feature is optional.

System generation   A process of tailoring an operating system for the specific needs of a particular computer center.

System history file   A disk area that contains information about any software updates that are made. Its logical unit is SYSREC.

System library   A library on the SYSRES drive.

System recorder file   An area on disk where information is stored about CPU and I/O errors for later use by the IBM customer engineer.

System residence file   A disk area that contains the system libraries and other work areas.

Tape mark   A special character written on tape to indicate the beginning or end of an associated group of records. These records may be data records or label records.

Thrashing   A condition in which the system is so busy paging in and out that it cannot do useful work.

Track   That portion of a storage medium accessible to one read/write head.

Track index   An area at the beginning of an ISAM cylinder. It gives the highest key in each track and the disk address of that track.

Trailer label (tape)   An IBM 80-byte fixed-format (standard) label at the end of each file. It follows the data records. It is similar to the header label except that it begins with a field that contains EOF.

Transient routine   A program in the operating system that remains on disk until it is needed. It is then called into main storage by the supervisor.

Translator   A program provided by DOS/VSE which translates higher-level or source programs into machine language programs. Examples are the COBOL, RPG, and FORTRAN compilers.

Type I commands (ICCF)   Commands that relate to controlling the edit session. An example would be locating specific lines. These commands are unique to the full screen editor and must be entered in the command I and II area.

Type II commands (ICCF)   Commands that are similar to type I commands except that they may be used with the context editor or the full screen editor.

Type III commands (ICCF)   Commands that carry out editing functions for one or more lines on the screen. They do not necessarily alter the current line pointer. They must be entered in the command III area of the screen.

Unique   One of a kind (e.g., a social security number is a unique key field).

User catalog   An optional VSAM which is pointed to by the master catalog. It lessens the required search time when many file entries exist and can serve as backup for the master catalog.

User profile   A record that contains, among other things, a user ID, a password, security level, and the library numbers that the user is allowed to access.

Utility program   A program that performs day-to-day jobs such as copying data from one I/O device to another or sorting data.

Variable-length record   A record that contains one or more variable-length fields and/or contains a variable number of fixed-length fields.

Verified file   The data in the file has been rekeyed to detect any keying errors. This process is sometimes used for punched card and diskette data files.

Virtual storage   Addressable storage on a DASD that appears as real storage.

Virtual storage access method   An access method for direct or sequential processing in a virtual storage environment.

Volatile file   A file for which there is a high rate of additions and deletions.

Volume   That portion of a storage medium accessible to one read/write arm: for example, a tape reel or a disk pack.

Volume label   An IBM 80-byte fixed-format (standard) label at the beginning of a magnetic tape or disk volume. Its first fields begin with VOL1 and a six-byte serial number.

Volume serial number   A unique six-byte number that is assigned to a tape or disk volume.

Volume table of contents (VTOC)   1. A directory containing all the standard file labels on a disk pack or volume. 2. To do a VTOC: to list all the standard file labels on a disk pack.

VSAM   An acronym for *v*irtual *s*torage *a*ccess *m*ethod.

VSAM catalog   A file containing extensive file and volume information that VSAM requires to locate and process files.

VSE/VSAM space management   A program that allows you to define and process SAM files within a VSAM data space.

VTOC   An acronym for *v*olume *t*able *o*f *c*ontents.

Work area   An area of main storage or intermediate storage used for temporary storage.

Work file   An intermediate file used for temporary storage of data between sort phases.

Index